J. Francis Angier

DONATED BY
CAROL JERKOVICH

READY OR NOT
Into the Wild Blue
The aviation career of a B-17 Bomber Pilot,
457th Bomb Group 8th AAF

J. Francis Angier

Major (RET.)

FAIT ACCOMPLI

Published by
Success Networks International
2048 Win-Win Way
South Burlington, Vermont 05407-2048
www.SuccessNet.org
802.862.0812

Written by
J. Francis Angier
7 Chelsea Place
Williston Vermont 05495-9479
802.879.7215
JFrancisAngier.com
Francis@AngierMail.net

Edited by Michael & Dawn Angier

Published in the United States by
Success Networks International, Inc.
2048 Win-Win Way
South Burlington, Vermont 05407-2048
www.SuccessNet.org

Library of Congress Control Number: 2003094091
ISBN 0-9704175-1-9
Fifth Printing, September 2004

Printed in the United States of America

Cover and book design by Michael Angier

Cover photographs by Philip Makanna of GHOSTS
www.ghosts.com

Acclaim

"You've written a great book. I stayed awake until midnight reading it cover to cover. Your story reminds me of a line from Shakespeare: "With this story shall the good man teach his son."

—Ken Blakebrough

"Seldom in the course of human history are we privileged enough to know the personalities we read about. With J. Francis Angier, his sacrifices and endeavors brings realism to the vast uncertainty of war. This book was hard to put down—a fascinating read."

—Thomas Van Bramer

"A poignant piece of history beautifully narrated by a man for whom I have much respect and affection."

—Karen Shulin

"Thank you for writing such a wonderful and inspiring book; what a tremendously moving testimony of a very good man, dedicated to fight for and protect our precious country."

—Eleanor Richardson-Isleib

"When the book arrived, I started reading immediately and could hardly put it down."

—Ruth Cheney Ryan

"I have enjoyed your book. It's excellent! It opened my eyes more to what you all endured for the sake of freedom. I believe God spared you from death and brought you home for a reason—perhaps to write this book."

—Florence Vincent

"A wonderful anthology of experiences from a real Vermonter that should be shared with the generations. Thank God for men like J. Francis Angier who were willing to do so much to protect the freedoms we enjoy today. In my mind a hero, but then I would have expected nothing less of a fellow "Green Mountain Boy."
—Jeffery P. Lyon, Brigadier General (RET.)
Vermont Air National Guard

"Vermont produces great milk, sweet maple syrup and rock solid individuals. J. Francis Angier is one of those people and his book Ready or Not should be mandatory reading for all Vermont schoolchildren.

It is the story of a hard working young man whose early dreams of flight carried him from the hay fields of Vermont to the great air war that would liberate all of Europe. After being shot down over Germany it was his determination and strength of character that enabled him to survive as a POW.

As a fellow Green Mountain Boy and Vermonter I highly recommend this colorful and inspiring narrative. J. Francis Angier's story of "service over self" shines like a beacon in today's uncertain world, to guide future generations on the importance of fortitude, family, faith and freedom."

—Lt. Governor Brian Dubie, State of Vermont
Colonel, Vermont Air National Guard

READY OR NOT
Into the Wild Blue
The Aviation Career of a B-17 Bomber Pilot

Some gave a little. Some gave more. Some gave all.
These three crewmen gave all on October 25th, 1944:
2nd Lt Samuel A. Plestine
T/Sgt Howard H. Lang
S/Sgt Maynard E. Judson

Remember Them

Somewhere a starry runway glimmers
Out of space, out of time
Where the ghosts of a host of airmen gather
Lost to loved ones before their time.

—J. Francis Angier

Dedication

This book is dedicated to the families and loved ones of those who gave their lives. They are mourned by all who knew them—family, friends and acquaintances.

The MIA and POW status caused great agony and anxiety for those at home who waited sometimes many months for word of their fate. As the survivors came home to happy reunions, those who had lost sons and daughters, brothers and sisters had mixed emotions. They were happy for those coming home but were saddened by the contrast of the lives of the survivors and the awareness of their loved ones whom they would never see again. The anguish suffered by those at home may well have been the more difficult—and long-lasting—sacrifice.

Acknowledgements

My sons John and Pierre extracted nine hours of taped memories from me in June 1987. Karen Shulin, unfamiliar with aviation and military jargon, transcribed the tapes with difficulty and surprising perception. While some of her interpretations were quite humorous, she overcame my hesitant and sometimes reluctant recollections generated by questions from John and Pierre.

Second son Michael and his wife Dawn supplied me with a more practical computer and invaluable advice. My wife, Madeleine gave me correct spelling faster and more accurately than my machine and kept me supplied with nutrients and good companionship. She has driven me to doctors, hospitals and emergency rooms dozens of times over a ten-year period while I struggled with mini-strokes and other ailments. She has always been supportive and concerned for my health and any projects or endeavors in which I've been involved.

Donna Cunningham corrected my gross errors in punctuation and sentence structure and provided valuable advice and input. Michael and Dawn did final corrections, formatting, cover design and production to put the material in condition for printing. They all had the professionalism I lacked.

To refresh my memory, I referred to portions of my Aunt Emma Clark's diaries. And for dates of missions, newspaper clippings, Roger Freeman's "Mighty Eighth War Diary" and Ron Byers' books, "Flak Dodger" and "Black Puff Polly".

Foreword
by Michael Angier

When I was four years old, I remember sitting at the dining room table with my mother and brothers when we heard a loud—and to me—unfamiliar noise. We ran outside just in time to see the fighter jet make another low pass over the house as it streaked across the sky—afterburners aglow. I'd seen planes before, but this was different—this was my dad.

Coincidentally, my father's first recollection of an airplane begins when he was about the same age. In 1927 Vermont, such a sighting was a rare occurrence. Lindbergh had yet to make his famous solo across the Atlantic. Jet planes weren't to be seen for another 20 years.

Ever since he saw his first flying machine, my father has had a passionate obsession with planes and aviation. His aeronautical career spanned three decades, stretching from open-cockpit biplanes to supersonic jets. His love of flying is exceeded only by his love of family and country.

My father has always been a hero to me. My dad's war stories of valor and courage in the face of seemingly overwhelming odds have always been fascinating and inspiring.

Of all of his accomplishments, I think those months as a pilot and crew leader were the pinnacle of his life. To paraphrase Churchill, "It was his finest hour."

During the last year of World War II, the Eighth Air Force pounded the German manufacturing plants, railroads and atomic labs, which brought an end to the evil Nazi war machine that so threatened the world's freedom.

We owe the "Mighty Eighth" an eternal debt of gratitude. Few people know how close we came to the annihilation of freedom and democracy. Had Germany successfully completed the atomic bomb before we did, it would have been all over. The world would not be the same.

Dad has never fully recovered from his war injuries. He's suffered from chronic back, neck and shoulder pain ever since. As recently as five years ago, he dug a piece of shrapnel from his skin after it had spent more almost sixty years traveling through his body. In spite of his many ailments, he married, farmed for over forty years, raised five boys and flew in the Air and Army National Guard.

My father instilled in me and my brothers a sense of responsibility and a commitment to what's right that hasn't always been easy to live up to. I think everyone, deep down, wants to make a lasting difference in the world. My father did that in many ways and continues to be an inspiration for me to do something good with my life.

Once, during a discussion about epitaphs on tombstones, I asked my father what he would want on his. He said he would like it to be very simple. He wanted it to read, "Farmer and Patriot."

It's been a pleasure and an honor for me to produce and publish this book. As many times as I've heard my father relate his experiences, they've always been enthralling to me. I know they will be for you, too.

This book is the story of his career in aviation. In it, you'll learn of the people and experiences that shaped his life. You'll come to understand his passion for flying. You'll feel the pain of his struggle and survival. You'll see how the events of the war impacted his life and others.

You will get to know the man I call "Dad".

—Michael Angier,
second son of five

High Flight

Oh! I have slipped the surly bonds of Earth
And danced the skies on laughter-silvered wings;
Sunward I've climbed, and joined the tumbling mirth
Of sun-split clouds—and done a hundred things
You have not dreamed of—wheeled and soared and swung
High in the sunlit silence. Hov'ring there,
I've chased the shouting wind along, and flung
My eager craft through footless halls of air. . . .
Up, up the long, delirious burning blue
I've topped the wind-swept heights with easy grace
Where never lark, or even eagle flew—
And, while with silent, lifting mind I've trod
The high untresspassed sanctity of space,
Put out my hand, and touched the face of God.

—John Gillespie Magee, Jr.

Contents

Introduction

It has been my good fortune to survive years of flying and the dangers aviation presents. Fighting a war in the air over hostile territory and enduring deprivations and uncertainties as a prisoner of war has often caused me to wonder how any of us were able to live through it.

A powerful desire to come home to our great country and our families was certainly a factor. My conclusions are that it took faith, dedication, skills and luck—in that order.

So, how did young men from diverse backgrounds come together and sacrifice so much?

Some individuals are born with that rare inherent ability to deal with the expected and the unexpected, while others have to develop the trait as circumstances arise to challenge their reactions. Sometimes it comes to the "fight or flight" decision, but all too often these choices are simply not options.

The brave young men deposited wave after wave on the beaches of Iwo Jima, Tarawa and Normandy did not have a chance at flight. Those of us in the air had no place to run, no fox hole to dig, no tree to take refuge behind and no escape from the massive anti-aircraft barrages or the determined and desperate fighter attacks. Each combatant had to develop his own way of dealing with the likely consequences of every engagement.

There are those who direct all feelings, energy and skills to the crisis at hand. They put the fear and apprehension aside hoping to survive by successfully carrying out the mission or to hold on until relieved. Some turn to prayer. Others curse, while the fatalists just carry on with the day's assignment—hoping for the best.

Unfortunately, there are those who are daredevils, to whom life is cheap, who take unacceptable chances. They drive recklessly, fly planes with abandon, often endangering others as well as jeopardizing the outcome of operations. All too often, their "macho" deportment is actually a façade to mask fear and inadequacy and sadly, some of their companions adopt similar attitudes to give the appearance of being brave and fearless.

My own experiences in aviation and aerial combat left me baffled and astonished to have survived. My attitude after a few missions was to do my best at flying the airplane, calling on the skills developed in training and attempting to train my crew members to be prepared with contingences for every possible event we could envision. Beyond that, we would have to accept whatever was beyond our control.

We worked on procedures for ditching in the sea, crash landing under control, dealing with the ever-present danger of fire and explosion that is inherent—whether an aircraft is flying or sitting on the ground. If all attempts to save our damaged plane were exhausted, we had to be prepared to exit safely. We had observed people jumping out of crippled planes without their parachute harness being properly adjusted. Unfastening the leg straps of the harness was more comfortable in the plane but opening the chute in this conformation meant sliding out of the harness, resulting in certain death.

The use and care of parachutes, Mae West floatation devices, the all-important oxygen mask, proper clothing and complete understanding of all equipment provided, as well as familiarization of the aircraft, were duties that could contribute to survival. The failure of equipment, the accuracy of the enemy anti-aircraft fire and the encounters with enemy fighters were beyond our control. Constant vigilance and continual preparedness was always critical.

This book is only concerned with my small part of the air war over Europe and an attempt to describe how my up-bringing turned out to help greatly in dealing with the challenges.

Fortunately, I grew up with an ingrained sense of responsibility as well as an ability to tolerate loneliness, austerity, strict discipline, hard work and adversity. Looking back to the dark days of the Great Depression, I am grateful to have had enough to eat, a warm house to live in and extraordinary role models who set valuable examples for me. These role models without a doubt contributed the most to my survival during the war years, as well as any successes later on.

My life was not a sheltered one, no one spoiled me by making things easier, and I knew the meaning of heartache.

In wartime, one must be available to go at any time. A headache, a hangover, emotional problems, fear of what the day might bring or a lack of motivation were not acceptable excuses. We had to go—ready or not.

Missions failed, lives were lost because some people were not prepared physically or emotionally to carry out orders.

There were perhaps less than 300,000 young men in that particular age bracket who participated in the great armadas of 3,000 to 4,000 aircraft and 30,000 to 50,000 men assaulting the enemy. Never before had the world seen such massive attacks through the air. Our formations stretched from horizon to horizon, often taking over 90 minutes to pass a given point.

Many times the contrails from so many aircraft formed solid cloud layers that remained for many hours while the sound of the thousands of engines could be heard for a hundred miles on each side. From our prison camp in Poland, the vibration of the bombs was strongly felt when Berlin was under attack ninety miles away. I was bombed by the Germans and later by the British and Americans. It was a frightening experience no matter who was dropping the bombs.

The purpose of this book is to tell my family and any others about my experiences and how my early interest in aviation led to the role I played. It is written without elegant style to be, hopefully, better understood—especially by young people. For all others interested in this era of history and how it has affected me, I've tried to touch on the most interesting and significant events to hold the reader's interest.

All that happened during the first twenty-two years of my life left me with perhaps a different set of standards and may explain why I sometimes think in a different dimension from my peers.

Throughout the sequence of events I have tried to emphasize how the fortunate circumstances of my developing years, my role models and passion for aviation influenced my flying career and helped me survive the rigors of air combat and incarceration.

Let me state that my imprisonment in Poland and Germany was not only of shorter duration than hundreds of thousands of others, but the treatment I received from my captors was almost inconsequential compared to the suffering endured by Russian prisoners or those captured by the Japanese.

Although captured American airmen were sentenced to death three times by Hitler and some of us were burdened by the knowledge that Germany might develop a nuclear weapon to change the outcome of the war, Americans were treated far better than other nationalities.

However, prisons were not country clubs and were far from being fun places. Many years passed before it occurred to me that the deprivation, poor nutrition and several months of enduring painful injuries caused more than lingering discomfort following my return to civilian life.

Post Traumatic Stress Disorder hadn't been invented by the medical or psychiatric experts at that time. Writing this book entailed recalling events that were long ago pushed out of mind. It has been emotionally wrenching at times. But for the persistence of relatives and friends I might never have been motivated enough to put this together.

The most graphic happenings have been omitted with the thought they might not be appropriate for young readers. My intent has not been to seek sympathy or hero status but rather to portray some of the humbleness many airmen were left with after facing substantial dangers and hardships.

Realizing that many innocent people who never really supported Hitler died from our bombing was humbling. We begrudged every bomb that missed its mark in spite of our attempts to carry out a surgical, precision-type of strategic bombing campaign against the Nazis.

I happened to be one of many who had to go into the wild blue, READY OR NOT.

1927 May, When it All Started

The sound came from everywhere. It echoed between the groves of pine trees that surrounded the pasture south of our house. It was a strange, roaring, very loud sound that startled me and seemed to vibrate through my body. There was a strong north wind that day—cold for the season—cold enough for me to cover up with a blanket in the yard on the sunny south side of the house.

My mother, Mamie Odette Angier, was trimming a lilac bush nearby and ran to me just as we saw the airplane coming at us at a very low altitude.

It seemed like a gigantic grasshopper or dragonfly and was a terrifying sight for a boy not quite four years old. It was flying into the wind, very low, just over the treetops, and as it passed over us, we could see the pilot inside the cabin, as well as the details of the craft. It had an exposed radial engine (no cowlings in those days) and a wide landing gear with high narrow wheels enclosed by canvas coverings. We could see the stitching on the fabric along the fuselage, a dark stain on the underside and the large, very clean windows allowed us to see some of the interior as it passed slowly just above us.

The pilot must have been following the Rutland Railroad on his left and Route 7 on his right where, no doubt, the cars were passing him in his struggle against the wind. We watched until the plane was just a speck in the distance. My mother tolerated my questions about something she knew very little about for the rest of the day until my sisters and brother came home from school. They had heard the plane and had seen one or two in the distance earlier.

I learned to read two years later and my memory served me well: The plane we saw was, without a doubt, either a high-wing Ryan or Fairchild, as they were very similar. In the 1920s, Fairchild had developed a monoplane for aerial photography, with large windows such as the ones my mother and I had observed. The *National Geographic Magazine* made considerable use of this model plane in remote corners of the world.

Within days of our sighting, my father Frank Xavier Angier, came home from work and said a man was attempting to fly alone across the ocean. The next evening, we went to the neighbors and listened to the radio, supposedly a broadcast from France. The primitive radio had earphones that could be separated to allow two people to listen at once, but my turn was very short and I heard mostly static. Having only a vague idea of what the ocean was like, "the sound of the waves" fascinated me, but Lindbergh and his voyage dominated conversation for days.

It was my destiny to follow a considerable portion of his flight path across the Atlantic 17 years later.

This day, without a doubt, was the start of my genuine interest in aviation, the yearning to soar through the sky, between the big, white, fluffy clouds and see the beauty of the world down below. Most people, at that time, looked on flying as a dangerous and daring pastime—but to me, from the beginning—it inspired the most fascinating and compelling urge and these feelings never left me.

Eleven years after seeing that first airplane, I finally experienced the thrill of actually taking the controls of a flying machine.

The environment I grew up in had a tremendous impact on all my later years, not only in aviation but in all the enterprises it was my privilege to be a part of.

A sequence of events removed me from a life of poverty, a life without newspapers, radio, books or exposure to world happenings, to a home filled with the tools for knowledge. It was a tragic, emotionally wrenching separation from my parents and siblings. But in the end, it turned out to be a most fortunate life change for me. For my parents, it was a heartbreaking disruption of their lives.

1927 October

They came for us during the day, while my father was at work. Unknown to me, people were busy attempting to alleviate a situation in our family that had become a crisis. My parents were desperately poor. My mother had health problems that were beyond my father's ability as a laborer to meet. It was an overwhelming challenge for him to keep food on the table and wood in the shed.

My father worked long days, on the job from six in the morning until six at night, often traveling four or five miles each way with only his old blind horse and a buggy for transportation. There was no electricity in the house, an inadequate water supply, a garden with tough clay soil and an old barn at the edge of the road to shelter the horse, chickens and two hogs. Wood had to be available in the kitchen year around for heating and cooking.

The "road" past our house had not been worked on for many years, and from 1917 until 1945—the period during which my father lived there—the town of New Haven spent nothing on its upkeep. The third-of-a-mile section from the main road, Route 7, was badly eroded and bisected halfway to our house by a rounded ledge of blue limestone. This was a formidable barrier and few automobiles were able to negotiate it. For my father's blind horse it was a slippery obstacle shaped like the back of a whale and especially treacherous in winter. The deep mud in spring was almost impassable for any vehicle, but strangely the road became quite stable just beyond our house and was a beautiful lane for a couple of miles to the next road at Huntington Falls.

My father often took this route in good weather to go to Middlebury and one of my fondest memories is riding in his "road cart," a light two-wheeled rig with a curved canvas area in front of the seat, where I preferred to ride. Crossing the railroad tracks just below the house was an event for me: just seeing the shiny rails stretching to infinity and hoping to see a train right up close.

My mother, who was born in 1888, had had a series of operations for mastoid infections and, as a consequence, suffered almost constant earaches and headaches. Her balance was also affected due to damage to the inner ear, and this eventually led to a serious fall down the cellar stairs, injuring her back. The fall occurred shortly after seeing the airplane, so during that summer she was able to do only a part of her work, with a great deal of pain.

She was also pregnant. My sisters Rena 11 and Viola 13 did most of the housework, while my father, in his spare time from work, struggled with the garden, getting up wood for the winter and getting hay for his horse. To put in his 12 hours a day meant driving for more than an hour before and after work six days a week.

There was not much in the way of welfare in those years, but an organization called the Vermont Children's Aid Society was doing its best. The Society's decision regarding my family may not have been the best one, but perhaps it was the only one. It decided to separate the children—a heart-rending episode for all of us. Two cars drove down the barely passable road to our house to transport us. Viola would accompany me to my new home and return that evening to care for our mother; Rena went to a foster home—to work for her board as was the custom at that time. My brother Carl was taken temporarily to an orphanage while my youngest sister Marcelline, only 15 months old, was taken to another foster home.

They dropped me off at my father's sister's place. She and her husband were called "Aunt Emma and Uncle Byron Clark" by everyone who knew them. They had a farm with a large house and were hard-working and generous people. My father worked there at times, as well, so we saw each other often. The plan was for me to stay a few weeks and then return home. My mother never regained her health, so my temporary stay stretched out to 14 years.

The connected buildings on the farm in New Haven, Vermont where I was brought up. Fire destroyed this complex during a severe storm in 1938. (I am sitting on the portion of the porch across the end of the house wearing a white shirt and overalls).

The trauma of separation was easier for me than for the others due to many factors. My age made it easier, and my new home was so interesting it occupied most of my attention. There were people with varied interests and backgrounds living at the house. My grandmother made her home with her daughter Emma. My cousin Irene boarded with them while attending high school and "Uncle" Sam Goodman (no relation) was an old gentleman who had boarded with the family for years. He had emigrated from England in 1864 at age 16, had worked in west Texas herding sheep and was an ardent sportsman. He shared many experiences with me. A maiden sister of my Uncle Byron Clark, Bertha, was living there at the time as well and spent considerable time with me reading books, teaching me words and how to draw. The house was very large—some 80 feet long, connected to a three-story building that, in turn, connected to the large barn. A lot of exploring to do.

A Professor Weld had owned the farm and had been a frequent traveler, collecting curios from around the world. He was interested in all the sciences and had a library of many thousands of books. Exploring the complex—an ongoing adventure that lasted 11 years—I found a laboratory with everything as he had left it: chemicals, telescopes, huge lenses, even a movie camera and projector he had constructed in 1900.

The laboratory was a well-finished room, with wainscoting along the walls, plenty of windows, a sink, two stoves, cupboards filled with containers of unknown ingredients and a large tool chest. It was located in the three-story building that connected the house to the barn. This building contained a well-equipped workshop, fuel storage space, a garage and a huge gasoline engine that could be belted for several uses.

The engine had a winch to lift the hay from wagons on the second floor of the barn to the haymow above and, with a movement of a lever, pulled the ropes connected to the hayfork back to the wagon for another forkful. By switching the drive belt, the operator could use the engine to turn a shaft that ran through the building to run saws and other equipment in the various rooms as well as a saw located on the ground floor for cutting firewood. My uncle never used this interesting contraption because of the fire hazard in the barn, but my playmates from neighboring farms spent many hours with me, attempting to start it up.

Among the projects I built over the ensuing years were a sail for skating, an ice boat that proved unmanageable because of its excessive speed on the pond and winding creek where I tried it out and, finally, my most ambitious endeavor, something we would call a hang glider today.

In a thick book published by *Popular Mechanics Magazine* were plans and a list of materials to construct two gliders of 1910 vintage. They would be called hang gliders today. One was a tandem-wing affair while the other was a single-wing model that was much more complex to assemble. As a 14-year-old aspiring pilot, I found the simpler one appealing. Because there was a supply of straight, sturdy bamboo and miles of very fine wire about the shop, materials were not a problem. Both of the gliders were to be controlled by the pilot shifting his weight, according to the instructions in the book.

Mine was about 90 percent complete when our buildings were destroyed by fire and, perhaps by good fortune, the flying machine also burned, probably saving my life.

My plan was to launch it from the top of the high barn by sliding down the slate roof, hoping to gain enough flying speed to soar away like a bird. If not killed outright, I would probably have been crippled for life. A friend of mine, who helped me at times with the construction, thought perhaps we could get his sister to make the initial flight—if we could catch her.

The books on astronomy were my favorites, but those on geology, history and travel were fascinating as well. All of these interesting subjects took my mind off the separation from my family, and although there were infrequent visits to the old home, seeing my father at work and following him about took the edge off. There was a minimum of contact among siblings, although the day I started first grade (in 1929), my sister Viola started high school. Rena started high school two years later, and as all 12 grades were housed in the same building, I saw my sisters frequently.

Although the sadness of having my family disrupted persisted for some time, I gradually began to accept my new environment as the best thing that could have happened to me.

1929 December

My grandmother Elmira Cadieux Angier died in December 1929.

This was my first encounter with death, and for a few weeks after her demise I felt a great sense of remorse and a little guilt for not having spent more time with her. She was quite strict in her last years and seemed somewhat domineering toward me but very docile and submissive toward my aunt and uncle. I suppose this was a concession on her part to convey her gratitude for having a comfortable home during her last years. She worked until her final weeks, sewing, knitting and assisting my aunt—often taking her work out into the yard under her favorite tree. She loved to hear the birds and enjoyed my aunt's flowers as she worked, sitting in a large chair on the lawn.

It was here she talked to me the most. She had raised a family of eight children but lost three of them in their teens to typhoid fever. Industrious, assertive and independent—she was ahead of her time in many ways.

I believe it was one of her sons, Uncle George, who told me humorous stories about her widowhood after she turned the little farm over to her son Joe. My favorite tale was about one of the various transactions she enjoyed conducting more for pleasure than for profit.

Apparently, she always wanted a business deal, however inconsequential, to be an enjoyable affair and to look back on it with a good feeling. There was a widowed neighbor Fred, who also pretended to make a real occasion out of any little business they could conclude together, whether it was agreeing to repair her roof, fix a fence or perform some needed chore. They would haggle over the details, such as the cost, how it would be accomplished, materials to use and many other fine points of the project. They both made more of the arrangements than necessary just for the pleasure they derived from making a deal.

My great-grandmother Julia Cadieux lived with her daughter, Elmira, as a widow of many years after her husband died in a soldier's home, a veteran of the Civil War. He enlisted at age 52 and was incapacitated in 1863.

He was never well enough to return home. The two women worked at their spinning wheels, turning out wool and linen garments as well as down comforters, using down plucked from the numerous geese on the farm. Great-grandmother raised, processed and administered herbs until she was past 100 years old.

Coming from Connecticut, she grew tobacco and made up cigars and pipe tobacco as gifts to relatives and friends. Elmira and

Julia bought a two-horse carriage in the 1880s and used it until my father, their favorite driver, moved away. After my grandfather died, Elmira stored the carriage in her neighbor Fred's barn.

One day, as the two friends visited, Elmira said she was going to sell the carriage if she could get $30 for it. After lengthy bargaining, Fred paid her price and they parted, probably each feeling satisfied with the bargaining, if not the bargain as well. Fred's daughter—a sharp-tongued, domineering, extremely frugal and frustrated woman—lived with him. When Fred got home for lunch, she interrogated him until he told her about the carriage. She nearly went berserk in her tirade. "You gave 'that woman' $30! You are crazy! Get over there and get some of that money back—in fact, get it all back! You're 80 years old, and you don't have a horse, say nothing of two horses. Get back over there before she spends it all." Fred went back after lunch and returned later in the afternoon with a smug, satisfied look on his face. "How much money did she give you?" his daughter screamed. "No money," said Fred, "but she extended the warranty for another 15 years."

1931, Exploring and Learning

Events that were to shape my life and prepare me for my part in world affairs began to come together after I learned to read and the contents of my uncle's house were a fertile field for knowledge.

There were books covering almost every subject. A hall library on the first floor held some very valuable books including a large, illustrated history of Napoleon, a book measuring about 14 x 20 inches. There was a colorful and detailed painting on each page with space for a lengthy narrative of the scene at the bottom. This book covered the life of Napoleon from his birth on Corsica to his death in exile on the lonely island of St. Helena in the South Atlantic. Although I had an intense interest in history, Napoleon was not one of my heroes. Too many of his campaigns were ego trips that cost millions of lives.

Large dictionaries, encyclopedias and illustrated history books were kept here as well, along with first-edition copies of <u>The Sinking of the Titanic</u>, <u>The Great Chicago Fire</u>, <u>The Death of Floyd Collins</u> and several accounts of <u>The Great War</u>. Several other factual accounts of happenings of great interest filled a special bookcase in this room. Fictional books held no interest for me unless they were based on historical fact. On the second floor was a bedroom converted to a library, lined with bookshelves from floor to ceiling. The two very large rooms in the attic had shelves along the walls as well as books piled shoulder high down the main floor. The partitions of the 16-room house had been reinforced from the basement up to carry the weight. Interspersed among the books were swords, bayonets, a printing press and gadgets of unknown purposes. A large closet on the second floor held an assortment of guns, perhaps a dozen or so, including my uncle's and Sam Goodman's hunting guns.

An astronomy book dated 1849 described the technology for escaping Earth's gravity. Calculations indicated it would require a speed of 25,000 miles per hour to break free but offered no solution for re-entry or how to attain the required speed. This was the very best environment for me, and as time went on I realized that being removed from my parent's primitive home turned out to be the most valuable event of my early years. It proved to have the greatest impact on my preparation for the future.

Along with the books, three magazines were sent to me monthly by Larry Goodman from Rhode Island, a nephew of Uncle Sam Goodman. *Popular Science*, *Popular Mechanics* and *Popular Aviation* opened new worlds to me, and soon the nomenclature and performance of all the famous planes were quite familiar to me. Each of the early flights was plotted on a large world map in our kitchen, and the news of each flight in progress was followed on the radio. These were the days of "Atlantic fever," when many pilots were preparing to emulate Lindbergh as well as planning long-distance flights to all parts of the world. *National Geographic Magazines* from the 1880s were piled about the place, broadening my knowledge of the world.

The wall map was a gift from the local librarian Mabel Clark and had routes of discovery dating from medieval times up to 1931. The great voyages by land, sea and air were drawn, with the dates and durations. Trips by Marco Polo, Columbus, Captain Cooke, Admiral Byrd and the early flights of aeronautical pioneers gave me much to study about history and geography. I followed Wiley Post's first flight around the world (in 1931) in his beautiful "Winnie Mae" for the eight days of his journey. His solo flight around the world in 1933 was an epic journey and an example of human endurance. After completing the circumnavigation of the world in seven days, 18 hours and 15 minutes, he announced he could do it in two days. He envisioned flying alone with a modernized auto pilot through the stratosphere.

Post became one of my idols. Although he had lost an eye working in the oil fields, he continued to fly. He was offered $4,500 compensation from the oil company, in installments, but settled instead for $3,000 cash and bought his first plane. It turned out to be a honeymoon plane, as he and his wife eloped in it. He soon talked his boss, H.C. Hall into buying one of the first "business" planes to keep in touch with his numerous oil businesses. His famous "Winnie Mae," a Lockheed Vega, was designed in 1927, carried four to six passengers and had a cruising speed of 140 miles an hour. Post improved the plane, won a transcontinental air race, and flew it around the world twice. In 1935 he started high-altitude flying. His eight-year-old revamped craft reached a speed of 340 miles per hour and an altitude of 50,000 feet. I followed his flights into the stratosphere with great interest.

I knew the dimensions, the fuel and oil capacities of the "Winnie Mae," as well as its performance and capabilities. It can be seen in a special room at the Air and Space Museum in Washington, D.C.

1933, Role Models

By the time I was 10 years old, the role models who would most influence my life were selected. It was natural that my father would come first because of his influence on my earliest formative years. He was a quiet, gentle man with very little formal education, but he remembered everything he read and heard. A very powerful man, he had great strength and endurance. In his twenties, he drove stagecoaches over the mountain pass from Bristol to Warren, Vermont, as well as the difficult route from Rochester to Bethel over very primitive roads. Around 1900, he carried passengers from the railway stations to the hotels in Bristol and Middlebury. He was born in 1871, married at 35 and was 52 years old when I was born.

He loved his children and was devoted to my mother who was an invalid for her last 25 years and required almost constant care. The misfortunes of his life never made him bitter but did cause him great heartache. Even so, he maintained a sly humor, never swore or used foul language and had great kindness for people as well as animals. For example, he kept his blind horse for 35 years and guided her with his gentle voice, never with a whip. She seemed to reward his kindness with total trust and loyalty.

My father had tremendous endurance, often working out in the cold all day without adequate clothing or footgear. He might have needed boots for working in the woods in winter but went without so his children could have some. He saw a doctor only once in his life for a nearly severed toe and was never sick in bed until his terminal illness, which lasted two weeks. He taught me to endure without complaining and to never give in without a struggle.

My Uncle Byron Clark was really my foster father, as I spent more of my life with him than with any other man. He was a strict but fair disciplinarian, and he was self-disciplined as well. He paid for his farm in 10 years and never had another mortgage. When he needed a car or a machine or livestock, he waited until he had the money to pay for it.

The routine on his farm was a study in punctuality: breakfast at seven, dinner at precisely noon and supper at six. We never had to wait for a meal, and scarcely anyone was ever late for a meal. The meals were *that* good. He started his milking machine at 4:20, night and morning. The cows had to be in their stalls and everything else ready. When I was told to do something at a certain time—get the cows, for instance, at four o'clock—that was *forever*. It was not something to be reminded of every day.

An interesting example of his insistence on punctuality and following instructions was when he took in a very poor and hungry boy of 15. The boy begged for a place to stay and something to eat. My uncle didn't need any more help but made an agreement with the boy, Harold Smith.

Harold would be required to stay for a year, follow the rules and do as he was told. In return, he would have school clothes, work clothes and necessities. After a few months, Harold said he wanted to leave—the regimen was too strict. My uncle said he couldn't force him to stay, but if left he could take only what he came with. His old clothes were too small, and after standing out by the road getting cold, he returned and asked if he could take his new things if he stayed for the year. Of course, my Uncle agreed because that was the contract they had made. There was method in his plans for Harold: to teach him some lessons, including following through whenever he started something.

Before he was 30 years old, Harold Smith was a multi-millionaire. He founded Harold's Club in Reno, Nevada. Thirty years later, his mother lived next door to my Aunt Emma in a hotel in Vergennes. He came periodically to visit and take the two widows to dinner.

It was natural for "Uncle Sam" Goodman to become a role model as well. He was a grandfather type (although he never had children of his own), very quiet, well spoken and helpful around the house. He had boarded with my aunt and uncle for many years. He taught me to shoot, hunt and trap. During the Depression, skunk pelts sold for about 4 dollars and fox hides brought 25 to 30 dollars. My little trap line brought in money enough for the whole year, to buy shoes, haircuts and movies and to have extra spending money.

Uncle Sam was born in Brighton, England in 1848 and migrated to Canada, arriving at Quebec City on his sixteenth birthday. He soon made his way to southwest Texas, where he herded sheep along the Pecos River, alone with his dog, horse and wagon for months at a time. He passed the time sketching and keeping notes on the wildlife.

It was there that he developed an interest in guns and hunting. Everyone in the West carried guns in the 1870s and 80s. He acquired an interesting 38.55-caliber buffalo gun, two shotguns and a very accurate pistol that I admired. I was allowed to keep this pistol after he died, but all the other guns went to a nephew. Sam was an avid reader and interested in many things, so we had valuable conversations that helped me to understand the world.

Sam became a cabinet maker, settled in Rhode Island in the 1880s and was married for a short time. Tragically, his wife died soon after they were married, and although he never spoke of it, I learned from his nephew that he closed his shop and moved to the hills of Lincoln, Vermont because of his loss. He fished and hunted for many years and worked as a night watchman at a factory. During the six years I knew him, he devoted a lot of time to me, and I learned a great deal. His extreme patience never rubbed off on me, but some other traits did, and I grieved for him after he passed on. He died in 1933, when I was 10 and he was 85. He had a modest estate, for those times, of perhaps $11,000, most of which he sent to England to his sisters. His trunk and most personal items were left to me.

In my spare time from the farm, I started working for Frank Shackett, who had a place just down the street. I was nine years old. He was a remarkable gentleman of "the old school," born in 1867, raised by his mother in a house he later bought for himself and where he lived the last 50 years of his life. His grandfather was a chaplain at the Battle of Plattsburg. His grandmother stayed on the farm in Addison, where she heard the sound of the battle 50 miles away. Before Mr. Shackett died, I took him to that farm in Addison, which I owned at the time. There was a small cemetery in one field, where he showed me his grandparents' graves.

He had large lawns, gardens, fruit trees, a wonderful barn and eight acres of land. He wanted me to take care of his grounds and his car and work in the cemetery for which he was the superintendent.

He'd gone West at age 15 with a trainload of sheep to west Texas—coincidentally to the same Pecos River area where Sam Goodman worked—although they never met out there. His job was to feed and water the sheep on the long journey from Vermont. He didn't stay long at the ranch on the Pecos River, as he was offered work at a hotel in Austin. This led to managing hotels in Dallas, Wichita and finally, St. Paul, Minnesota, where he prospered before retiring to Vermont in 1900 at the age of 33.

He was frugal and made sound investments when he retired that provided him with sufficient income to enable him to winter in Florida for more than 50 years. His wife was a quite beautiful woman who taught music.

They had been married only 11 years when she was crippled and deformed by polio. For the rest of their married life, he was devoted to her, helping her in and out of cars and hotels and around their house. He did the housework and cooking, and he canned produce from his extensive gardens. They carried most of the canned goods to Florida each year.

He was very particular and insisted that everything be done in a precise manner. He taught me how to live and work in a way that led to my enjoying the respect of people in the little hamlet of New Haven, Vermont. Because I drove his car for him whenever I could find time, we went for my driver's license on my sixteenth birthday, and he allowed me to take his expensive car for my own purposes without asking me where I was going or where I had been.

This built my self-esteem. In return for his interest in me, I used to go to his place every evening to get in his wood and water and feed his sheep for the princely sum of 10 cents an hour.

His interest in me, a boy from a very poor family, manifested itself in many ways. The fact that he never had children of his own may have been a factor.

In the fall of 1937, he bought a car made to his specifications—a 1938 Oldsmobile with spare wheels and tires in the front fenders, allowing for a much larger trunk and a swivel seat on the passenger side to facilitate getting his crippled wife in and out. It was the epitome of style and luxury.

Frank Shackett was a frugal man, but he was very picky—almost extravagant—when it came to cars. He kept his vehicles in a darkened barn that was clean, orderly and always locked. After driving into the barn he immediately dusted the car off and then covered it with a flannel cover, over which he placed a heavier cloth cover. The car seats had two layers of fine material with his initials F.L.S. embroidered front and back as well as on the pillows.

I spent many hours polishing his car and enjoyed working in the cool garage part of the barn. The first car I saw him driving was a 1922 Chalmers, a long, black touring car.

Then he purchased a beautiful light blue, oversized 1930 Buick sedan that was in like-new condition when he traded it for the Oldsmobile.

The new automobile arrived in the boxcar of a train, and he would not allow the people from the garage, who would be servicing it, to drive it out of the boxcar, down a ramp and to the garage. That great privilege fell to me, along with the responsibility not to damage it getting out of the rail car and across town under the skeptical gaze of the mechanics. He refused to have it road tested after servicing unless he and I were in the car. This was very embarrassing to me, but the event inspired me and gave me great confidence and self assurance. He was, without a doubt, an ideal role model for me.

It seemed that fate had placed me under the influence of four exemplary gentlemen through most of my formative years. All of them had good traits—frugality, good manners, no swearing or foul language, no smoking—and they helped me prepare for life in a manner for which I have always been grateful. There were other men and women who encouraged me and set good examples, and I have never forgotten them. I can't say all the good advice and examples were followed to the letter, and as with all growing boys, (and grown-up boys) there had to be a little mischief.

1935 May, First Flight

It was time for me to take my first airplane ride when the town of Bristol, just five miles from home, had a dedication of its new airport. For three days, the airspace around Bristol and New Haven was filled with several types of planes performing astounding aerobatics and taking hundreds of people for rides at $1.50 for about 15 minutes. It was, for many of us, the first time we could look down on familiar farms and roads and rise up alongside the nearby mountains.

After waiting in line a long time with my dollar and a half clutched tightly, I was beckoned to an available seat in a four-place Stinson cabin plane. I watched the right landing wheel so I could tell the moment we left the ground, then I looked out at a scene of great beauty. There was a lake I'd never seen (Lake Winona), and directly below was the source of a brook that had been my goal to find by following the stream from my fishing hole in New Haven. There were more cows than I had ever seen at one time grazing in the pastures, teams of horses working the fields and cars zipping along the roads. We flew over my uncle's farm, where he was planting corn, and from our low altitude of about 500 feet I saw how extensive our buildings were and how the fields were laid out.

There were three cabin planes at the field, a Waco five-place biplane, two four-place Stinsons, and three Waco open-cockpit bi-planes that were doing a great business giving thrill rides to the braver members of the crowd. The stunt planes had propeller-driven sirens on the underside that gave a frightening sound as the pilots climbed and dove, rolled and did tail spins. These planes had seats for two passengers in front and one for the pilot in the rear seat.

The story went around that an elderly farmer wanted a ride but didn't want to pay the fee. So the pilot said if he and his wife

didn't say a word while he put the plane through its paces he
wouldn't charge him. After doing every maneuver possible—some
quite hair-raising—the pilot landed and congratulated the old
man, who was reported to have responded, "I almost spoke up
when the old lady fell out."

Aviators of note who attended that day included Harold
Pugh, the prime mover in getting Burlington's airport built and
in business. His wife had her own plane and flew for many years
while helping to run flying schools and providing services to visiting aircraft. Two brothers, Francis and Robert St. Jacques, gave
much input to the development of private and commercial aviation in Vermont.

Robert, who gave me my first ride, was killed crop dusting
during the war. Privately owned planes of many types came and
went during the three days, but I was able to attend for only one
day. I still have the ticket for that ride.

Soon after the field opened, Joe Rock and his wife arrived to
run the airport. He had his tool box, an old car and two new
Piper Cubs. He soon acquired a ten-year-old open bi-plane and at
times had two or three other models available for giving lessons
and joy rides. He took me for my second ride, along with his
wife, in the old bi-plane.

Joe's worst problems came in bottles. He learned to fly in the
Navy but never mastered night or instrument flying, an omission
that cost him his life some 20 years later. He gave me my first
lessons just before my 16th birthday. I wasn't quite legal, but he
wasn't quite sober. Mrs. Rock, a delightful lady and school
teacher, managed the $50 I gave her well enough so Joe was able
to get me ready to go off alone. He climbed out one day and
growled, "Go kill yourself."

I didn't, but the thrill of flying never left me after that first
few minutes.

The aviation-inspired euphoria of that summer of 1935 was
tempered by the death of my idol Wiley Post, along with the
writer and humorist Will Rogers. They were on a flight through
Alaska to Point Barrow and possibly on to Russia. Post had

bought a plane that had been wrecked and repaired. A wing from another plane had been fitted to it and floats from a third and larger plane had been attached, resulting in unusual flight characteristics. Nonetheless, the pair elected to go ahead with their plans.

Taking off from a small lake, the plane stalled and plunged straight down into the water, killing them both. An Eskimo ran 14 miles to Point Barrow with the news.

Post was never given credit enough for all he accomplished. After losing the sight of one eye, he practiced gauging distances and depth perception by setting out stakes to associate the distance between them from different locations. He was first to recognize what we call jet lag from his long-distance experiences of passing though the time zones with no set rest periods. Some of his flights were of 5,000-mile non-stop duration, but he had prac-

The "Winnie Mae" and J.F. Angier. A beautiful plane, quite aerodynamic for its time (1927) with wings and fuselage built of plywood. Improved by Wiley Post in 1935 to fly 350 miles an hour at 50,000 feet. Flown by Post around the world in 1931 and again, solo, in 1933.

ticed sleeping at odd hours at different intervals. On his solo flight around the world (1933), he had an early auto-pilot, but because of its mediocre performance he tied a wrench, which he held in his hand, to his finger so when he dozed off the wrench would fall and jerk his hand to waken him. His contribution to aviation medicine was not recognized until the advent of space flight, when the astronauts went back to study the several pressurized suits he designed for his high-altitude flights.

He learned how men and machines could adapt to function in the cold, thin air of the stratosphere. He was a man far ahead of his time but living in my time of learning.

1936, Toughening Up

Before my thirteenth birthday, my life was so busy it has seemed as if I missed having a childhood.

There were many chores for me, beginning at five years of age, and they grew in number according to my level of skills and abilities. There were two wood boxes to be kept filled, calves to feed, water to be carried some distance in five-gallon pails to young cattle and other livestock in various locations. Helping with haying, mowing lawns, doing field work with horses and, of course, doing milking chores made up my duties, commensurate with my age, strength and endurance.

Evenings and Sundays were my times to explore the woods, ski, ice skate, putter in the laboratory and shops or read if the weather was inclement.

After I started work for Mr. Shackett, it was understood it would be my responsibility to pay for my shoes, some clothes, sports equipment, entertainment or anything I could afford to buy myself. Pushing a lawn mower in the cemetery at 10 cents an hour meant working 15 hours to buy a pair of work shoes and 70 hours for my first pair of skis.

The Goodmans sent me their son's bike when he went off to school, and this multiplied my opportunities to earn money. The bike gave me mobility and speed to get around. It enabled me to pick up mail for people, carry water and milk to others and have time to take small jobs in my limited spare time. I learned to carry a pail of drinking water hanging down at arm's length while holding a tin pail of milk by its bail with the other hand on the handlebars.

The postmistress, Mae Squire, allowed me to open the door and take the mail I picked up for people out of their boxes when she was busy in her living quarters in the building. This saved me time, but more than that, it demonstrated her trust in me.

As more responsibilities were thrust upon me, my desire to put some of my own ideas to work in the running of the farm came to the fore. My uncle was demanding but kind. He appeared to be stubborn about any changes that seemed like a better way to get things done.

An example of that trait showed itself when I suggested we use straw on the wooden barn floor to let the heavy sled-loads of hay slide more easily. We drew hay from other barns and many haystacks in winter, using large double sleds that carried more weight than the horses could have pulled on wagons. The practice was to carry snow from outdoors to spread on the floor in two 60-foot-long strips. After unloading the hay, we had to scoop up the snow and carry it out before it melted and seeped down to the lower floor and onto the cows.

My plan was to use straw from its storage on the same level, then pick it up at any later time, and of course it could still be used as bedding for the cows down below. The sleds did slide on the straw as well as on snow, but my uncle was very reluctant to try it. He gave in grudgingly, and without his ever commenting on it, we used the method from then on.

It was in 1935 that "Bridget" came to board and work for us for her four years of high school. She was two-and-a-half years older than I and a very beautiful girl of 15. She was a hard worker, a good cook and a great help to my Aunt Emma. Because my contact with girls had been limited, due to not having my sisters around, I was in awe of Bridget and too shy to know what to say—so I said very little.

1937, School Days

Our school building, which housed the eight elementary grades and the high school, was located about 1,200 feet from my uncle's house. This was a lucky thing for me because quite often I would be coming in from chores to change clothes as the first bell was ringing.

There were times when the teacher would look at me over her glasses if my trap line had produced a skunk pelt or two. While I never received a direct hit from a nervous skunk, the odor from handling one did linger on. Another benefit of living close to school was being able to go home for lunch to get a good hot meal and read the newspaper.

School was a rather casual affair for me as I concentrated only on my favorite subjects and spent study hours poring through the encyclopedias. The books Professor Weld left in our house offered a vast store of information—a better and much more interesting education than school provided.

There was no time for sports, as I was expected to be in the barn 20 minutes after classes let out and all my free time was spent working. My uncle did insist on my taking extra time for school-play practice and later on—a half hour a week for dancing lessons after school. In addition to these concessions, he required me to attend catechism and go to Mass with my aunt, although he was not a Catholic. He was a man of high principles who adhered to the Ten Commandments and conducted himself all his life in a manner that set good examples and earned him the respect of everyone. He did not approve of extravagance, so it was necessary to tone down my interest in taking flying lessons, although $8 an hour for flying lessons was a bargain even in the mid-thirties. His greatest guidance for me was teaching me to respect and be polite to older people, especially women and girls. He permitted no crude or rude remarks about anyone.

Although sex was never discussed openly, it was plain in that household that sex outside of marriage was just not to happen. Modesty was practiced to an extreme. My grandmother chastised my father in the front yard when he was showing everyone the nasty gash on his knee caused by a frisky horse he was shoeing. "Pull down your pant leg, Frank. Someone may go by in a car and see you." She never showed an inch of flesh beyond her hands and face. During the day, she wore black dresses that swept the floor and a black bonnet covering her hair. At night, she put on a white nightgown and a white bonnet. Why she covered her hair was beyond me because she brushed it for a long time each night and morning.

No one in the family ever went half dressed, and I took great precautions to ensure privacy while changing clothes or taking a bath, but at 14, my curiosity was beginning to manifest itself. Bridget was becoming prettier and quite shapely. I began to notice her.

In my continuing study of aviation, General Billy Mitchell's accomplishments impressed me. World War I was less than 20 years in the past, and there were many veterans of that war still living. The importance of air power began to strike me as the coming prime weapon in future wars. Germany still seemed to be an enemy, so I fantasized about another war with thousands of bombers over Germany. Mitchell had mounted as many as 1,300 bombers and fighters in 1918 for a one day's strike at German facilities. His demonstrations fell on deaf ears at the Joint Chiefs of Staff even though he successfully sank two German battleships. The new battleship Osfriesland had been declared unsinkable and was the pride of the German navy. This was one of the ships turned over to the U.S. after World War I, and it was provided to Mitchell for testing. One admiral stated he would stand on the deck while bombers dropped their bombs he had such disdain for airpower. In July 1921, Mitchell's bombers dropped 2,000-pound bombs on the ship and sent it to the bottom in 20 minutes. The mentality regarding aviation in Washington was illustrated by President Calvin Coolidge's response to Mitchell's plea for more planes: "Why don't you fellows just take turns flying that one you have down there."

Mitchell's crusade eventually led to his court-martial and loss of his rank. But after his death in 1936 he was restored to rank posthumously and was recognized for his vision of the future of airpower. The admirals and "horse cavalry" generals in the Joint Chiefs of Staff hated to relinquish their antiquated ideas of warfare.

In his criticism of the Navy's habit of anchoring our warships in Pearl Harbor while the admirals enjoyed the island life and passed the time golfing and socializing, Mitchell described how dangerous this practice could be. He predicted an attack by the Japanese on our fleet that would leave us helpless to stop their expansion in the Pacific. Japan was rampaging through China and Manchuria in the early thirties and had plans to seize the rubber, oil and other resources of Southeast Asia and the Pacific Islands. The U.S. had disarmed and had no more than 300,000 men in all branches of the service, giving the impression we would be unable to exert any appreciable influence anywhere. Mitchell had the vision to see and comprehend what was to come.

In 1935, the Boeing Airplane Company, as it was called then, first flew the B-17 bomber. I had studied the development of the plane from the beginning, when it was designed in 1932. I realized it was far ahead of its time.

With Hitler in power, it seemed to me we needed to begin to prepare for another war. German aviation technology was surpassing ours, as Charles Lindbergh reported after his tours of German aircraft industries. Howard Hughes produced a superior plane in 1937 that was very fast and maneuverable, but the U.S. military wasn't interested. The Japanese soon came out with the "Zero" fighter that was almost an exact duplicate of Hughes' plane. America slept through the thirties.

1938 June-July

Among the individuals who contributed to my formative years were some fine teachers. I especially remember Miss Mary Dalton, Lyrace Flower Fontaine and Miss Butler. Marguerite Bottum started the first grade the same day I did, but she was the teacher, and I was a new student. The first mediocre teacher I encountered was in an early grade. She humiliated me in front of the class because of her lack of knowledge of history and events. We were required to give a factual report, once a week, on something of interest. My report had to do with the fact that Lindbergh was the sixty-sixth person to fly the Atlantic. She stopped me abruptly, remarking that everyone knew Lindbergh was the first. My research had showed more than 30 people were on a British dirigible that crossed the ocean twice in 1919, in addition to Alcock and Brown who flew a World War I bomber across from Newfoundland to Ireland that same year. She didn't allow me to finish the report, and I never attempted to substantiate my facts.

One principal was a dreadful, despot with an appalling lack of fairness. He was downright cruel to the boys, and to some girls, but he had a special animosity toward me because he disliked French/Catholics. My sisters Rena and Viola had to struggle to attend high school. They worked all summer to save enough for clothes, shoes and necessary equipment and books. Both of them managed to work for their room and board with good families near the school during the week but returned home Friday afternoons to help at home for the weekend. The dedication these girls had to remain in school and do well resulted in deportment that was impossible to criticize, but the principal managed to ridicule and attempted to belittle them. Many students left school rather than be bullied as did most of my class, which started out as freshmen with about 20 students and were graduated four years later numbering only 6.

We came to a standoff in my senior year when I discovered a longstanding discrepancy in his handling of some school funds. Each class had been required to turn over to him 10 percent of any money they earned, supposedly for a "sinking fund." My class held dances nearly every week to help pay for a new town hall. As business manager, I refused to give him the money. He had caused many students to leave school because of his fearsome, formidable attitude, but I had the evidence against him. He had no records to show how the money had been spent over the previous 15 years. He backed off, and we tolerated each other for the remaining months of my last year. The school house burned down that fall, closing our controversy over the misuse of funds. The "unavailable" records were lost in the fire.

My class had a very high attrition rate because of this man. On my return from the war, I visited the school with my Aunt Emma Clark. The man had the audacity to tell me how lucky I was to get all that "free" flying experience in the service!

My Aunt Emma Clark was a dear lady, an excellent housekeeper, hard worker and probably the closest female to me during my growing-up years. She had no children of her own but accepted the burden of raising her brother's son. Aunt Emma had a tough job—to replace my mother while not displacing her, and she did it very well. There were other ladies in the neighborhood who treated me exceptionally well. One—Mrs. Squire—made a suit of clothes for me when I was four years old. Another—Mrs. Sumner—a widow to whom I delivered a pint of milk each evening (the five-cent price was mine to keep) often showed me her house, pictures and other interesting items while grilling me very tactfully for gossip. This went on for several years, and I dutifully saved my nickel from each pint of milk. There could not have been more than two or three people in town who were not friendly to me.

There were, as in all small towns, two or three town characters who were very wise and profound. They also seemed to have a great deal of free time to sit on the store steps, chewing tobacco, smoking cigars and philosophizing. They made the mistake of trying to make fun of me, however, and although I was brought up to respect older people I had a low opinion of these loafers.

One day, while we were building a new barn, I was sent to the store after two kegs of nails. These kegs weighed 100 pounds each, but because of the heavy work I'd been doing my muscles were very well developed so 100 pounds presented no problem. One of the loafers bet me I couldn't lift one of the barrels over my head. There was just a narrow rim on each end to get a hold on with finger-tips. They wagered $5 each and told me I would owe them $10 if I failed, although I knew they wouldn't have five cents to pay me if they lost. I picked one up and raised it at arms length over my head, put it on the ground and then lifted it again. "You each owe me $5," I reminded them, but they were so chagrined they wouldn't talk to me. The store owner and a half dozen others who had been watching gave them a hard time, but we all knew they were deadbeats. They had failed to make me the town fool. It was good for my reputation, but my uncle reminded me when I reached home that gambling was wrong. "It certainly was for them," I responded.

Revelations

In my fifteenth year, we were to endure some catastrophic events that would change our lives and propel me from adolescence to young manhood. Before the calamities fell upon us, there was a period of enlightenment for me relative to my attitudes and curiosity about girls.

Girls at school and elsewhere did not wear very revealing clothes in those days. It was practically all guesswork wondering what they looked like without any clothes on.

Bridget was modest, always cheerful, considerate and busy with housework and 4-H activities. She especially enjoyed sewing and made most of her clothes. She never lost her temper but had a trait that was both amusing and endearing. She had a funny bone, and when anything started her laughing she had a hard time stopping. Bending over, unable to catch her breath, she would stomp her foot while repeating her only "swear" word, "Judas Priest-Judas Priest!" Of course, everyone was hysterical after a few minutes. It was a delightful performance and was one way Bridget brought great joy to the household.

My relationship to her was quite sedate due to my bashfulness around girls. We made ice cream together on the porch with an old hand-cranked machine and shared a few other chores. We took a few sleigh rides with our old but like-new sleigh behind one of the huge farm horses. There were group sliding parties as well as some ice skating and skiing. I never came really close to her until we took a few dancing lessons after school. Getting that close made my knees shake and my face red, but Bridget was very considerate and understanding.

The day before the senior prom (a very informal, come-by-yourself affair), we prepared for haying. Our neighbor on the next farm, Frank Merrill, was between hired help and asked me to milk his 30 jersey cows for him. That meant two milkings night and morning along with all the other work at home and the errands I was committed to up and down the street. My bike was indispensable. By noon on that day, just before my fifteenth birthday, the fatigue, dust and dirt from getting the haying tools out of old barns and sheds full of cobwebs and chaff was enough for me to ask for part of the afternoon off, and it was granted.

My secret swimming hole was about two miles on foot through fields and pastures, but riding my bike about four miles around the road put me within a few hundred feet of the hideaway. It was a very hot day, so the first plunge into the clear water was wonderful. The pool was a wider and deeper section of a brook with a sandbar in the center. Overhanging the water was an old tree that curved out horizontally over the pool with a fairly flat section that was comfortable to lie on. On one side across a fence was a wide, swampy, treeless area with always a few inches of water covering the moss and grass. No one ever walked across it.

On the other side was thick brush that I could see over, to the road where I left my bike. No one in sight, no easy way to approach undetected, the old tree was the ideal place to rest and enjoy. It was only the second time I had been swimming in the nude. I dozed off, a rare thing for me to do during daylight. Suddenly, I heard a horse nickering close by. He was tied on the other side of the fence, where he must have crossed the impassable (to humans) expanse of water and moss. A movement caught my eye, and my heart gave a great thump. A young woman had stepped into the pool about 20 feet away, and she was wearing no more than I was. Our eyes met at the same instant and we both must have registered shock. For me it was terror, for her it was anger. She crossed over at full speed, shouting all kinds of criticism, and grasping my left ankle she twisted so strenuously my body pivoted over and off the tree into the water. She still had a grip on my leg, holding it up out of water, and it seemed her intent was to drown me. Finally breaking loose, I grasped her by the hips to keep my balance as the edge of the sandbar kept giving way under my feet while she was standing on more solid footing. When we were stabilized, she had a grip on my biceps and I was still maintaining balance and a little distance between us by holding her by the hips.

There we were, face to face in four feet of water, both apparently startled by the sudden encounter. She was tall and athletic, with square shoulders and hips, all straight lines and angles but surprisingly powerful. No wonder she didn't hesitate to pull me off of the tree. While I was still speechless, she began to talk. "You're Francis, aren't you? I remember you from my last visit here when you were about eight or nine years old." Her name was Carol. She was a nurse, and she had come to visit her aunt, who kept the riding horse. I recalled her because her aunt had given her a new 1932 Plymouth while she was in nursing school. "I still have it." she told me, and as our conversation continued, she apologized for her reaction as she finally realized I had been sleeping or would have heard the horse splashing up to the fence. She suggested we disengage by turning away from each other to put on our clothes, which were stashed on opposite sides of the brook. "Now don't look back at me!" she warned with a slight smile. How could I resist a little glance? After all, I had seen most of her front; why not a glimpse of the other side? She continued to chat as she dressed behind a bush, while I was shaking so I could scarcely put my clothes on, to say nothing of carrying on a conversation. This was, after all, my first sight of a nude woman.

Peddling my bike home, it was difficult, impossible really, to keep my mind off what had happened to me. It was fortunate for me that it was Carol, older, from away and apparently not one to spread the story that would implicate both of us. She was intelligent enough to see that she wasn't being spied upon. I was innocent as far as she was concerned, and certainly I was innocent as far as I was concerned—at least up to that moment.

Arriving at the farm with over a half hour before the commencement of chores, it seemed a good time to relax and reflect in the shade, but Bridget spotted me about to stretch out on the lawn and called from her upstairs room. "Would you bring me my bath water, please?" She had had an appendectomy a few months before. Our bathroom had been very modern for its time when Professor Weld had it built, with a beautiful marble-topped sink and a fascinating water tank one flushed by pulling on an elaborate chain. However, there had been no practical provision to get water to the room, so we carried two five-gallon pails nearly full of water up from the kitchen stove reservoir and from a hot-water tank in the laundry room. I filled the pails and poured them into the bathtub, saving a portion in one pail for rinsing off. I had scarcely refilled the reservoir in the kitchen when Bridget called down to say the drain had not closed completely and most of the warm water had run out. There was not really enough hot water left, but I took what there was and made my second trip up the stairs. After adding the water and checking the drain, which seemed secure, I started down the stairs. The drain pipe was in the partition beside the stairs, so I paused to listen for the sound of any leakage.

Bridget's room was diagonally across the hall from the bathroom and at the head of the stairs. She started out of her room without a stitch of clothes on, saw me and shouted, "FRANCIS!"

Then she whirled as if to go back to her room but continued the spin and dashed into the bathroom. Many things flashed through my mind in those few seconds. It never occurred to me she would come out of her room uncovered. I felt remorse, truly embarrassed for Bridget, and apprehension for myself, as I knew if my uncle heard of this and suspected mischief on my part he would send me down the road. One practical bit of intelligence entered my brain. It was the revelation as to why girls wore bras and sometimes girdles. The contrast between Carol and Bridget was astounding. Carol was attractive, but her slim body was all straight lines and sharp angles while Bridget was a wonderful study in curves and roundness.

Two similar happenings within two hours left me stunned. Something I had looked forward to, when the time came, had been thrust upon me when I was totally unprepared. A huge dilemma with so many possible consequences weighed me down as I trudged through the lane to get the cows. Would this be the last time for me to tread these familiar paths? Here I was, innocent of wrongdoing but possibly facing shame and ridicule, certainly having no idea what it would be like to face Bridget at supper in front of my aunt and uncle.

Bridget made one of her famous cakes, an after-school routine. She bustled back and forth helping my aunt but spent more time than usual in the big pantry. Finally, she came out with the last dish and as she lunged for the table she burst out laughing, one of those occasional laughing jags. She bent over double, stomped her foot and started, "Oh! Judas Priest! Judas Priest!" until the tears came. We slowly came around to join in, but no one had the slightest idea what had set her off. I was baffled but guessed it had something to do with our encounter in the hallway upstairs. Apparently, she took the affair more lightly than I did, or perhaps she felt she had nothing to hide while I was aware that she had a great deal to hide.

Dressed and trying to get up courage to go to the dance, I was sitting on the porch visiting with my uncle when Bridget came out and started down the driveway to walk the few hundred feet to the Town Hall. She stopped, turned slightly and asked if I would walk down with her. Her short-term boyfriend, a student at the University of Vermont, was to come down about 10:30, and it was not unusual for boys or girls to go alone to the prom. It was all I could do to get down off the porch and join her, as I was still embarrassed and hadn't been able to look her in the eye. We made very little small talk, and neither of us mentioned the events of the afternoon. About nine o'clock, she asked me to dance with her—another silent interlude—but when we parted, she leaned close and said, "It's all right, you know." What a relief! True to form, this 17-year-old girl was considerate and compassionate even after what seemed to me to be a traumatic experience for her.

It was about time for me to go home, but as I edged toward the door someone spoke to me. It was Carol, in a long white dress and with a beautiful hairdo. She looked taller but didn't appear quite as slim with clothes on. My face must have turned red, but she said she would like to dance and asked if I'd be her partner as she had been away so long there was no one her age to dance with. She tolerated my awkwardness on the floor and kept up a steady flow of pleasant conversation as if we were old friends and nothing unusual had happened between us. Two girls, one of them about 30 years old and one just 17, had asked me to dance and were gracious to me after my seeing them nude—all in a matter of a few hours.

Neither one seemed to indicate she would tell anyone about the embarrassing events. Both of them accepted it as unintentional on my part. After a short circuit of the dance floor, I said it was time for me to go, as chores came early in the morning. "I'll give you a lift," Carol announced and started for her car, the same pretty little 1932 Plymouth convertible I had admired. She drove me home, where I fell into bed, totally astonished by the events of the day.

1938 July, FIRE!

During the last of June and through July, violent thunderstorms swept through the Champlain Valley. Some days there would be as many as two or three windy storms with spectacular lightening and crashing thunder. About a hundred barns and other buildings were destroyed by lightening strikes that summer in Addison County. People rushed to each scene as soon as they saw the smoke rising, to save livestock if possible but primarily to help save the house and contents. Fire departments from three neighboring towns usually responded but were often hampered by a lack of water and the need to race to another fire at another location. Many barn fires occurred at night, and they were more likely to be struck before houses or other structures because of their height.

Most livestock would be in pasture at this season, but horses, the main source of power in those days, were more likely to be tied in their stalls at night. We had been putting our horses in a small pasture at night for some time, but the storms often brought hail. This caused great pain to the animals, and they were terrified by the frequent flashing of lightning and the noise of thunder. For this reason, we quite often left the horses in their stalls. Many a hired man gained notoriety in the community for rescuing horses from burning barns at the risk of his life.

We had finished our first crop of hay before the rains started so had the benefit of more valuable early-cut hay. We were fortunate, as well, in harvesting our grain, which was stored in a separate barn. Feeling quite secure, we waited for the period of storms to pass.

On July 25, we took advantage of a sunny day and went for a picnic at the lake. Clouds were building up over the Adirondacks in the west as we returned home. One of my pastimes was to climb up into the peak of the barn to sit in a window opening and enjoy the pleasant aroma of the curing hay while looking out over a broad expanse of the valley to the west. The 50-foot-high perch gave me a chance to see to the back of our cow pasture, to determine whether the cows had come down to the gate or if I'd have to go after them as that would mean starting out about 20 minutes earlier than usual. I watched a large storm brewing, with ugly looking clouds, several miles away. The cows were coming toward the gate about a quarter mile away, so it seemed best to go after them immediately as the storm appeared so ominous.

It began to rain just as I reached the nervous cows. They hurried toward the barn while I followed, walking in the deep mud of the lane. Suddenly, the rain intensified greatly, and as about half of the cows were through the gateway to the barnyard, there was a blinding flash of lightning and a tremendous crash of thunder.

Some years later, Grant Parker, a good neighbor of ours, and his son said they saw the lightning strike the barn. He said the bolt of lightning was as wide as about one third the length of the barn. The cows inside the yard attempted to come back out, while the others were blocking their exit. I saw a large black cloud of smoke pour out of the window opening in the peak of the barn while large slates began sliding off the roof. The electrical discharge apparently had followed the steel horse-fork track the length of the hay mow, opening the ridge on the roof of the barn. The heavy slates from the roof whistled down to sink out of sight in the mud. One of the 16-pound pieces of slate could have cut a cow (or me) in two. After climbing the high fence beside the gateway still blocked by the struggling cows, I tried to run as fast as possible through the muddy yard to reach the door to the stable on the far end of the barn.

My uncle had just brought his milking machines into the barn and was unaware the building was on fire until the dense smoke came down to the ground, driven by the rising wind. "Call the fire department, and I'll get the horses," I shouted as I hurried to the horse stalls. He ran to the house for the phone. By this time the entire three-story building was filled with smoke, terrifying the horses. A strong wind had come up, driving the dense smoke down and across the farmyard, where my aunt was moving the car to what she thought would be a safe area. Meanwhile, my uncle had gone into the second floor of the barn to push his wagon out. On the first floor, burning boards were falling down hay chutes from the hay mow, igniting the ground floor, where there were several calves and a bull. The horses had balked at the smoke in the yard until I struck them with a two-by-four to make them get out the door. The calves had never been out of the barn and had to be pushed one by one down a ramp outside the door. As for the bull, I had no choice but to turn him loose, along with three hogs. These four animals took up residence near a fence and hedgerow, where they stayed for two weeks without wandering. Once those animals were out, I shut the doors and ran around the barn to the house. The barn was connected to the house by a three-story building that was already on fire.

The house was doomed, but neighbors had arrived to help salvage the contents. After some furniture had been removed, the storm reached its peak, with golf-ball-sized hail driven by a wind that flattened crops and knocked over quite a number of trees. People took whatever shelter they could find, while the hail broke windows, dented cars and broke some of the furniture from the house. It was quite calm after the hail and cloudburst of rain, so with the arrival of the fire departments we concentrated on saving the house or at least part of it. The fire was too intense for anyone to go inside, so just as the last big rafters of the barn collapsed, the house had to be abandoned as nothing more could be saved.

The loss of the house had to be most tragic for my aunt, as she had refinished each room over about a three-year period. She had painted and papered for weeks. We had a "Blue Room," a "Green Room" (mine), the "Bay Window Room", the "Girl's Room" and two guest rooms—all on the second level. Each room had its own character, and my aunt had lavished her labor and expertise on each one.

All the thousands of books and interesting things that had been such an important part of my growing up years were lost. My bike, boat and motor, tent, camping gear, nearly new skis, traps and the potentially dangerous flying machine were gone forever, along with my uncle's tool chest and the many useful devices needed to operate a farm. Most of the farm implements, horse harnesses and approximately 30 cords of wood, all carefully split and stacked under the approach to the upper barn floor, would take months and considerable cash to replace. A beautiful carriage and sleigh, perhaps used no more than a dozen times each, had been stored on the upper level of the barn along with two very well made farm sleds that would not easily be replaced. The sentimental and monetary value of everything destroyed could not be calculated. The loss of the books proved to be a burden for me the rest of my life.

With help from neighbors, we drove our cows to another farm to milk them. By that time, it was dark and still raining, the cows were bewildered and balked at being driven by strangers through the mud in unfamiliar areas to a different barn. I had been doing the milking at this farm for the elderly farmer, as he was between help. My schedule was to milk at home, then ride my bike to his place morning and night. We had to repeat the performance of moving our cows the next morning, an exhausting chore but we had no alternative.

By seven the next morning, John Clark, my uncle's brother, arrived at the scene of the fire with two men he put to work tearing out the interior of a building that survived the fire. Two more of his men arrived shortly thereafter with a truckload of lumber. By four in the afternoon, the men had put in a plank floor and constructed 12 stanchions to permit us to milk in shifts. We, of course, had to milk by hand, which we did for four months while a new barn was built. My uncle rented a house about a mile away from the farm, so we had a place to live while we took stock of the situation and replaced tools and machinery. We had to be able to resume cutting a second crop of hay between the thunderstorms that persisted on and off for most of the summer. We had no livestock feed for the coming winter and no storage, so hay had to be stacked outside. The corn fields had been laid flat by the storm but slowly recovered to a degree.

1938 September, Flood

We hadn't yet finished building the new barn[1] when the next calamity overcame us. On the twenty-fifth of September, 1938 a hurricane struck New England, causing great damage. Our new barn, not yet in use, came through very well, but our milking shed had a foot and a half of mud in it that had washed in from the barnyard. My uncle had bought a house across from the farm, rather than building a new one. The septic tank at the house floated up out of the newly dug and covered pit. Trees

---

[1] The new barn was completed the first week of December 1938.

were blown down everywhere and roofs torn off buildings. The storm was accompanied by torrential rain that caused widespread flooding. Our corn crop had partially recovered from the storm of July 25 when our buildings had burned, so it was heartbreaking to see it all flat on the ground again and most of it covered with mud. All through October and November, my father and I worked to salvage the corn as we had lost our hay in the fire, leaving us with just the second and third crops of hay for winter feed. The barn we had stored our grain and straw in burned as well, leaving us very short of everything.

The harvesting of the succeeding crops of hay went on into mid-November, and without a barn to store this winter feed, we stacked it in very high, beautiful stacks that kept it very well. My father's expertise in building the high, pointed stacks came in handy. His job, working for my uncle during this period, when we weren't haying, was primarily to salvage the corn lying flat in the fields. I helped him after school and on weekends, but he labored all day long, pulling up each stalk of corn, cutting it off and placing the stalks in bundles to be tied.

Along with going to school and working at home, I was involved in two projects going on at the cemetery. Any day too muddy to work in the corn fields gave me time to work there. We were still cleaning up from the great hurricane, and Mr. Shackett had built two large entrance gates and a very substantial iron fence across the front of the cemetery. He insisted that I would be the one to paint it all. It was a memorial to his wife, so it entailed a considerable amount of lettering in aluminum paint above the black gates and a heavy black, tar-like coating for the fence. The six-foot-high fence was more than 700 feet long, so the painting went on until cold weather arrived. I finished it just before he left for Florida but the cleaning up of the many downed trees and broken headstones from the hurricane kept me busy until Christmas. 1938 was my busiest year, but everything that happened taught me there is usually a solution to problems. I had lived and worked through fire, flood and storms that were real challenges, but I believe they built character.

1939, War in Europe

My first flying lessons were in May 1939, and on my birthday, June 11th I accomplished that goal of all teenagers: I earned a driver's license. I had been driving some since third grade and drove almost everywhere we went after I was twelve. Given my frugal upbringing, I didn't expect any great freedom on the open road but was surprised to be allowed to use the family car occasionally (once I had my driver's license) for some trips to swimming holes, a movie or a visit to my parents—not just for driving around. Mr. Shackett was not able to drive much as he had problems with varicose veins in his legs. Most of the summer he paid me to dress his legs, get his wood in for the cook stove, bring drinking water from a neighbor's well and pick up his fresh milk and groceries. Besides driving him to doctor appointments when I was free, I was allowed to use his car at times.

My uncle surprised me by paying me by the week as soon as school was out. Twelve dollars a week was more than most hired men were paid, $25 a month was more common. With our new barn, chores were easier but there was more overall work to be done, and more of it fell to me.

A four-day vacation at the end of August, 1939 allowed me to accompany Mr. Shackett to the state fair in Syracuse, New York. My first ride in a seaplane was the highlight of the first day at the fair. We stayed at a tourist home owned by a Polish couple who had several Polish guests as well.

They talked about the possibility of war between Germany and Poland. "Poland will fight!" they said, but I wondered, with what? Hitler and Stalin had just concluded a non-aggression pact that sounded ominous, as it seemed neither of them ever kept his word. As we drove home late on September 1, we passed through Saratoga at about 1 in the morning, just as the news of the German attack on Poland came over the radio. It was the beginning of World War II.

None of us could imagine what global catastrophe was about to unfold over the next six years.

The atmosphere at home was somber, and the house was quieter than usual because Bridget had left after her graduation. We missed her cheerfulness and good spirits, so the news of so many ships being torpedoed in the first few weeks of the war seemed even more discouraging. More work was the best remedy for me, and there was plenty of it.

The Piper factory in Lock Haven, Pennsylvania started offering its wonderful little two-place plane for $1,440, with only $440 down. Almost anyone could go to the plant, get checked out and fly a plane home. Of course, some prospects couldn't learn to fly that fast, but almost everyone interested enough to own a small, easy-to-fly yellow Cub was sent on his way with a map and a student-pilot's license. This was intriguing to me as my bank account was approaching that $440, and my plan was to go to Lock Haven right after my sixteenth birthday. However, due to events to come it was not for me to ever own a plane of my own, though I would live to fly nearly a hundred different types and models of planes.

1940

The news of the war in Europe was very discouraging. German U-Boats were taking such a toll of shipping it seemed but a matter of time before Hitler would be in control of every country on the continent—England as well. The fall of France was quite emotional for me, given my Norman ancestry. But it was to be expected because France had lost upwards of six million of her best young men in World War I, many killed and even more disabled. France suffered from a lack of spirit as well as effective manpower for governing and providing for the military. Pushing my lawn mower in the cemetery with no one to talk with about these events was quite depressing.

At about this time, Charles Lindbergh became involved with the "America First" movement, a group of people who wanted the United States to stay out of the war in Europe. Lindbergh had visited Germany and inspected its production facilities and operational training, and he was looked upon as an expert. Lindbergh reported what he had learned in Europe and stated that we should not become involved. He believed, as I did, that Russia was the greatest danger and that we would be better off to let Hitler deal with Stalin.

However, President Roosevelt was furious as this was the second time he had crossed swords with the popular flying hero—the first being when Roosevelt ordered the Army Air Corps to fly the mail. Lindbergh stated publicly that the Air Corps was not trained sufficiently and that the planes available were antiquated and not equipped for instrument or inclement-weather flying. After many fatal crashes, the debacle came to a halt and Roosevelt developed a years-long animosity toward Lindbergh to an extent that he withdrew the famous pilot's commission as a colonel, cutting him out of serving during the war.

Lindbergh's intent was to make the country realize we were not prepared, and we needed to shake off the methods envisioned by the cavalry mind-set of the Joint Chiefs of Staff and at least allow the Air Corps to prepare to defend us. With the attack on Pearl Harbor, Lindbergh offered his services but was rebuffed. He did perform valuable service, testing and improving many types of war planes and flew combat in the Pacific as a "technician."

The news became more alarming as Hitler commenced preparations to invade England. In order to ensure any successful landings across the Channel, Herman Goring, commanding the Luftwaffe, decided they must knock out the under-manned and under-equipped Royal Air Force. The RAF's successful Battle of Britain, which took place in the air, gave hope to the Free World and the United States began to aid England with supplies and weapons. Hitler gave up the battle for air supremacy just as the RAF had reached its limits. England was down to a few planes and a handful of pilots, but Hitler didn't know that.

The success of the British pilots, with help from Americans who formed the Eagle Squadron, resulted in the first real victory over Hitler, the "Battle of Britain." It was a thrilling episode in the history of air warfare.

It was easier for me to turn my attention to the farm after these encouraging reports from the war zone. There were very long days working at home as well as several jobs to take up my spare time: Mr. Shackett's chores, delivering mail to some neighbors, wood fires to start at a wealthy family's summer home for their hot water and the never-ending work at the cemetery. My relations with my uncle improved in spite of one setback over how to complete an addition to our new barn.

We needed a lean-to along one side of the barn to house calves and young stock. When it came time to attach the rafters to the roof of the main barn, we hired two men to help. My uncle decided to place the rafters below the eves of the barn roof, leaving an unsightly space—as if the addition were only temporary. My plan was to join the two roofs together to make a smooth junction that would not only look better but facilitate the sliding off of the great amounts of snow from the main barn. The two hired men also agreed it would add much to the appearance and be somewhat stronger. An argument ensued, until my uncle walked away saying with some bitterness, "Put the roof where you damned please!" I was somewhat remorseful because of our disagreement but pleased to see the nice-looking roofline. As was typical of the man, he never commented on the episode again, but it seemed to me he was very satisfied with my "kitchen-table architecture."

That winter, during Christmas vacation, we drew hay with our horse-drawn wagon from a remote part of the farm that necessitated traveling around the road to reach those fields. Something spooked the horses at the top of a steep hill appropriately named "The Chute," and they ran wildly. Once they were running at full speed nothing could have stopped them, as strong new guardrails kept them from leaving the road. There was a steep bank on the right side of the road, and I reached behind me where a double-bitted axe was a potential missile. I grabbed it and threw it over the guardrail and down the bank. By this time, my uncle and I each had a rein, trying to hold the runaways, but my uncle's line broke, leaving us with no control.

Near the bottom of the hill, the guardrail ended where we habitually turned into a gateway leading to our field. The drive to the gate was filled with frozen snow banks three or four feet high left by the snowplows. The horses were conditioned to turn at this point, and they attempted to do so, resulting in a sudden stop when the wagon struck the solid snow. The left horse flipped over onto his back, immobilized by his twisted harness. The other horse, directly in front of me, was stopped so suddenly I was propelled over his back, landing some distance ahead of him. I had managed to pass over him by a quick step of my foot on his rump as I flew off the front of the wagon. My uncle had been thrown onto the middle of the pavement, landing on his head then sliding and rolling for perhaps 25 feet. As soon as I could, I climbed the bank and ran to him.

He had a nasty gash on his head and had the wind knocked out of him so he appeared to have stopped breathing. Ignoring the struggling horses, I stopped the first car that came along and asked the driver to please take him to the doctor in Bristol, about five miles away. As we gently loaded him into the car, he started breathing again and regained his senses enough to ask, "What happened?"

Once he was on his way, I went back to the horses and wagon. Some men came along in a small truck and helped me free the horses from the tangled harnesses. They used the truck to pull the wagon out, and I made some emergency repairs. Then I drove the limping and subdued team home. They were in great pain and walked slowly with their heads down, while I was impatient to get home. The horses took several weeks to recover from their injuries.

When I got home, I ran to the house to get my aunt, and we drove to the doctor's office, where my uncle had been treated and bandaged. He refused to go to the hospital, so we brought him home. While he recuperated from his injuries, it was up to me to do the chores and run the farm while attending school as well. Our relationship became very close from that time on, and we came to rely on each other's judgment.

1941-42

Graduation from high school meant making decisions as to college, the farm and perhaps military service. We discussed the possibility of my buying the farm, but my uncle had decided he needed to farm for a few more years—to provide for a better retirement.

The Vermont School of Agriculture at Randolph Center offered a one-year course in agriculture that appealed to me and fit my budget. After looking over its farm and visiting with the faculty, I decided that it was the best choice.

My father, at age 70, didn't feel up to traveling by horse and buggy or sleigh during the winter. So it was arranged for him to stay at my uncle's during the week to help during the periods of extra work while I was away at school. He would drive his horse "Robin" up to the farm on Monday morning and stable it with my uncle's horses for the week. Saturday afternoon, he would drive back to his home. My sister Rena was staying at home to care for my mother, and I had planned to come home to work weekends, so all the bases were covered for me to be away at school.

Within an hour after arriving at the school, I had a job. The cook was a nice lady and needed someone to bring produce from the farm storage, vegetables from the horticultural building, butter and ice cream from the dairy and canned goods from the attic. Soon, the kitchen floor needed recovering and the dining hall floor had to be painted, so there was work for me most of the time. Several farms raised potatoes and hired "Aggie Boys" after school to pick up and bag the potatoes that were dug by machine during the day. In addition, older people around the school always needed wood put in, storm windows installed and other fall work done. This helped my bank account.

Before leaving home, I went to the bank in Bristol, to open a checking account to pay my expenses for the winter. While I was there, someone told me the bank had money for me from the time President Roosevelt closed all the banks in 1933. They paid me the 50-some dollars plus interest. After graduating from

Randolph, my checking account had more money in it than when I opened the account, thanks to all the work I was able to do in my spare time at the school.

The small school at Randolph Center was really needed in Vermont. It had a two-year program for boys who, for some reason or another, didn't complete high school. They were able to catch up by studying English, mathematics and other courses in preparation for the second year. The one-year men—high-school graduates—studied science, botany, genetics, mechanics and farm management while getting hands-on experience by doing chores, repairing machinery, doing forestry and maple sugaring. We worked with cows (Jerseys and Guernseys), horses, hogs, chickens and even oxen.

We used the oxen in the woods at sugaring time. We had shop classes, horticulture, orchard work, land surveying and tile draining of fields. Rules were strict: no smoking or drinking and everyone had to dress appropriately and conduct himself in a proper manner. It was a good experience for Vermont farm boys and helped many of them to become successful.

Pearl Harbor

On Sunday, December 7th 1941, some of my classmates and I were in my room, listening to the radio and rowdying around, when the news came about Pearl Harbor. A few said they would join the paratroopers. For me, it was time to think about getting into the Army Air Corps (which later became the U.S. Air Force), as no other branch of service would fit my nature.

My desire to fly had been with me since that day my mother and I saw my first airplane. It just seemed my country could utilize me to greater advantage doing something I felt able to excel in. There was one obstacle that could rule me out of flight training: a requirement of two years of college. When I applied for cadet training, I was referred to the glider-pilot training program, where I was told that the Air Corps would have to turn me down before the glider program could take me. Not being too enthralled with gliders and the use to which they would be employed, it was to my advantage to somehow pass the cadet exam.

At about this time, a directive came down that provided for a college equivalency test that would let me get around the two-year requirement. The test, given at Middlebury College, was not too difficult, but the added-on entrance exam for cadets was almost overwhelming and a real challenge for me.

My interest in physics helped me immensely but my lack of higher mathematics almost did me in. It was one of my good days, and I had a good enough score to get the attention of the recruiters who could then waive the college stumbling block. While waiting at home in late summer, I received a letter informing me I must be sworn in, in order to get into a quota of cadets. The only branch of service available was the infantry! I decided to take a chance, hoping they would not send me to the infantry instead of cadets.

On October 19, 1942 I took the oath. I was in the Army infantry, unassigned. After more delays, false starts and three trips to the Rutland recruiting office, I held my breath as a major made some phone calls and managed to get me into the next cadet quota.

A strange coincidence was associated with my swearing in. That evening while waiting for the bus home, I decided to treat myself to a seafood dinner, Lobster Newburg. My mind was filled with apprehension. Would flying be my contribution? Would I survive the training and combat flying? Would I be shot down? What did the future hold for me? There was a large mirror at the end of the restaurant, and I looked at my reflection, noting my trench coat especially.

Twenty-six years later, on the same date, I had just finished my military flying career by flying every aircraft in the Vermont National Guard. Meditating on my experiences and relative good fortune as I left the flight line for the last time, I decided to treat myself to dinner. I thought it would be a small reward, to make up for the sadness of leaving the Guard. Without thinking at all of my enlistment day and my apprehension at that time, I ordered Lobster Newburg. While savoring my favorite seafood dish, my attention was drawn to a large mirror at the end of the Black Cat Cafe in Burlington. It was then I noticed I was wearing a similar trench coat that the coincidence struck me. Same meal, same tan trench coat, emotional feelings, some sadness as well as satisfaction and thankfulness for having survived the years of flying. It seemed like an inevitable end to my military career, a unique moment in my life.

Perhaps it was a sign for me to be grateful, for the prayers of people who knew me then and some who did not know me at the time. A sign to be thankful that God had been looking after me.

On that last day at the National Guard, I had flown every plane and helicopter, the grand finale to my military flying career. It took most of the day. During my last years in the Guard, I would get quite stiff in the joints and my bad knee would be painful after an hour or so in the air. As a courtesy, one of the mechanics who always met the returning aircraft would reach in and pull my leg out over the side and give me a pull out the door. This last time after alighting on the tarmac, I told the ground crew it was my final day—I was leaving them for good. "Oh, no, Uncle John, why? What's wrong?" I responded, "Well, you guys have been helping me out of the aircraft after each flight for years. Today, I noticed you helped me to get in as well, so I guess it's time to quit." We had a laugh over that, but it was a sad moment as I sincerely respected and admired these skilled men and would miss them.

1942 December, Toil

While I was waiting for my call to leave for the Army Air Corps, a good friend, Julius Bottum, who farmed with his father up the road from us, decided to take a vacation with his wife and baby to Georgia, where he had managed a large farm and met his wife. He and his father came to see me about filling in for him during his two-week absence. It sounded OK to me, and my uncle agreed, as Mr. Bottum was a good friend and brother farmer.

Julius spent two days before he left showing me the routine. There were 52 cows to milk and feed twice a day and 10 registered Jersey cows on official test that had to be milked three times a day and needed to be milked by hand. Being on test meant they had to have their feed and milk weighed and records kept. Julius also had a valuable riding horse, in another barn that required special care.

It was a challenge to me to undertake what seemed an overwhelming amount of hard work. The routine went like this: at 3:30 in the morning, I drove Julius's new Buick to the farm and milked his cows by hand. Then I did a quick feeding of the main herd to keep them quiet while I milked them. Milking was followed by another heavy feeding of all the livestock. Then I fed the calves and retrieved the farm truck from the third floor of the huge barn. It was necessary to push the truck enough to start it down the high ramp from the third floor to jump start it by letting out the clutch at the right time and place to get the engine going. The upper part of the ramp was enclosed in a bridge, but the portion outside was covered with snow and too slippery to attempt starting. This necessitated getting the truck to start inside on the dry floor because there was no need to try it again out on the slippery hill outside. If it failed to start, the procedure was to coast down through the farmyard to the car garage and connect the battery to another fully charged battery to turn the cold engine over.

Once the gymnastics of getting the truck running were completed, I would load the milk cans up onto the high platform of the truck to deliver to the milk plant about four miles away and pick up the milk at another farm. If all went well, I was ready to stop on my way back for breakfast at home by nine o'clock.

About a half mile from the farm was an old barn with about 15 heifers that needed feeding and cleaning. These poor animals were tied in stanchions and were only released when I came to care for them. While I cleaned the barn and bedded them with straw, they had to get their once-a-day drink from a tub. The only way they could be enticed back into the uncomfortable stalls was

with the once-a-day feeding of hay. I tried to put as much of the
feed into the mangers as possible, but the next day it would be all
gone. This was the only flaw in the management of the farm, and
it distressed me considerably to see the animals spending the entire winter in such uncomfortable conditions.

After unloading the empty milk cans, I had to back the truck
up that steep ramp to have it ready for the low-technology starting procedure the next morning. The test cows had to be milked
at 11:30 regardless of the stage of other chores. Usually this
meant interrupting the barn cleaning—a major labor-intensive
chore. Huge amounts of loose hay had to be wrestled out of the
hay mow and down chutes to the feed floor, and there was a
noon feeding of hay to all the animals. The 52 cows were milked
at 4:30 in the afternoon, fed again and bedded down. Corn si-
lage had to be thrown down during daylight hours as there were
no lights in the silo. The calves had to be fed, the horse taken
care of and the hated Jersey cows milked by hand at 7:30.

Fortunately, Mrs. Bottum would have a substantial noon meal
for me. Unfortunately, Mr. Bottum slipped on the ice and broke
his leg the second day, leaving me with all the work to do alone.
Two days later, exhausted and unable to cover all the bases, I sent
word to Mr. Bottum in the hospital requesting (demanding) extra
help at least part time as there were not enough hours in a day or
enough energy in me to do all the work. This resulted in his en-
gaging a man to help clean the barn, spread the manure and
throw down the hay. He saved me about three to four hours a
day but could not be persuaded to work any longer. Being as it
was the last two weeks of December, the cold and snow made
everything more difficult. Nine o'clock was the earliest I was able
to get home for an evening meal, and this distressed my aunt as
we normally had supper at six. She said I was overdoing it, and of
course I was.

Julius arrived home by train with his family the evening before
I had to leave for Camp Devens. In fact, we didn't even see each
other, so close was our schedule. This phase of my farming experience taught me it was possible to do twice as much work

when there was a dire need. I sometimes wondered what would have happened if I had had a debilitating accident during that time. It was very stressful to work in a strange barn with so many animals depending on me while trying to not forget any part of the operation. Occasionally, I would wake up wondering if I had forgotten to feed or care for any of the livestock. Although this interlude took a lot out of me physically, it certainly put me in better condition to endure the rigors of cadet training I was about to face. Many cadet candidates were not in top physical condition and many washed out because they were unable to handle the stress due to living sheltered lives. I was ready.

1943 January and February, Cadets

On January 3, after my first train ride (not counting the one when my mother brought me home from the hospital), we arrived at Fort Devens, Massachusetts for a short processing before leaving for Nashville, Tennessee.

There were 11 of us, all country boys, mostly from around New Haven and Bristol, quite a number from a small rural area to be going into flight training. All but one were to be casualties, either to lose their lives, be shot down and captured or injured in some way. I was destined to be the last survivor of the group, many years later.

As the troop train, drawn by an old steam-powered, coal-burning locomotive, got under way, a sergeant came through the cars asking for anyone who had a Connecticut driver's license. Several recruits followed him like the Pied Piper. We saw them next in the KP car. Lesson No. 1—never volunteer.

We were all in civilian clothes, many of us in our oldest white shirts and jackets as we surmised they would not be worth much by the time they issued us uniforms. When my brother Carl left for service in 1940, we traded overcoats, and since he was going south to Savannah, Georgia, he took my light camel's hair coat while I kept his heavy, black winter coat. On his way South, Carl "sat through" the camel's hair coat on the train, ripping the back badly enough to make it useless. On my old train to Nashville,

Tennessee, ice formed on the windows and the window sill where I had rested my arm when I finally went to sleep. The train gave a sudden lurch when the brakes were applied, and most of us went flying out of our seats. My left sleeve was frozen solidly to the sill, and the old coat ripped at the shoulder. Just one of the coincidences of brothers going to war: We had each ruined the other's old second- or third-hand coat that would, no doubt, never have been worn again, anyway.

Two days later, the train pulled into Nashville with a load of dirty, tired candidates for the cadet program. A nasty southern non-com (sergeant) ordered us out with the greeting, "Another load of damn Yankees, a whole trainload of damn Yankees!" He led us to a large bin of coal. "Pick that up and take it over there," he commanded. It was very heavy and took more than 20 of us to lift and carry it. He had us empty all the coal out and put it back in by hand. This soured me on the military's senseless misuse of manpower during wartime.

At Nashville Army Air Base we were issued uniforms and given shots along with very thorough physicals. One of the most hilarious incidents of our stay there was triggered by the unfamiliar southern dialect. We were being moved through a room with only our trousers on, for checking heart, lungs and blood. It only required a pin prick on a finger for blood, but one of the men was having trouble understanding instructions. When the "medic" said, "les seeurfaangu" (meaning, let's see your finger), the candidate asked what he meant and heard the same request repeated in the same pure Mississippi drawl. Finally, exasperated, the man unzipped his pants. He must have thought it was a VD check.

These tests were followed by dexterity, balance and depth perception checks and then by written exams for several days. This resulted in nearly half of the men being eliminated as cadets. Those who failed were sent to gunnery school or to another branch of the service with much howling and gnashing of teeth.

My introduction to racial issues took place here as I witnessed the terrible treatment of black civilian and military personnel working at the base. Most of the men in my barracks were from New England, but a few at one end were from Alabama and Mississippi. Sitting on our bunks, we were discussing the treatment of the Negroes when I remarked it was strange that southerners hated the blacks but talked so much like them. About this time, silence fell on the group and all eyes were looking to something behind me. Turning around, I observed a belt buckle about eye level. The owner of the belt buckle was about six feet four inches tall and from Mississippi. "A've a good mane to haul off and kick yo' ass," he said, and he would have, too, had I not been surrounded by all "them dam Yankees."

In about three weeks, the survivors left for Maxwell Field at Montgomery, Alabama for two months of pre-flight cadet training. There were very tough classes, strenuous calisthenics, weapons training, marching and poison-gas exercises—always under pressure. The purpose of the constant harassment was mostly to see if the candidates could stand up under difficult situations. A large number from my class were washed out and sent to gunnery school at Biloxi, Mississippi. The phrase "I'm Biloxi bound" was heard often. Officer training permeated every activity, as successful completion of cadet flight schools meant a commission as well as those coveted silver wings. This carrot dangling on the stick was a powerful incentive to achieve, follow the rules and withstand occasional humiliation.

The upper classmen, those candidates a month ahead of us, were expected—in fact instructed—to harass us any time we left our barracks. To go to class or the mess hall and any other duty required us to assemble in formation in front of our respective barracks. One of the rules was that we must shine our shoes before each and every formation. One of the tricks our tormenters used was to get us to leave formation just before we were to move out and return to our barracks on some pretext. Upon returning, the upperclassman would ask if the man had shined his shoes. No time to go back, so this infraction would earn us a demerit. So many demerits added up to a penalty that could mean walking a tour on our time off.

A tour consisted of marching around a square at attention, in full uniform with a backpack, carrying a rifle for an hour. Some unlucky ones might have to walk as many as four or six tours on a weekend. It was wrenching to see the bus leave for "open post" in Montgomery, as that was the last chance and meant staying on base all evening and usually the next day as well.

The busses were always overloaded, and as we were allowed to return to base on one of the city busses, we experienced the embarrassment of seeing the "colored" people forced to the rear seats. The crowded city busses were very hot, and they didn't smell good, as many workers had to return home in their work clothes, carrying with them the odor of their workplace. One pleasant odor was from the local peanut butter factory.

At meal time, we "zombies" (underclassmen) had to sit at attention with an upperclassman on each side to distract us from eating. We had to sit on the very edge of our chair, keep our eyes fixed on a point on the wall across the room while eating square meals by lifting the food straight up and then horizontally to the mouth. This often caused food to be spilled on our ties or shirts, which led to more "gigs" or demerits. Woe to anyone who asked for the butter or any other food on the table as this resulted in, "MISTER! How did you know there was butter on the table?"

In other words, keep your eyes on that point on the wall. With 2,000 to 3,000 men in the huge dining hall at one time, it was an ordeal to get enough to eat. We "zombies" were put in a "brace," an amplified position of attention, nearly every time we encountered one of our tormenters. They often asked if we were "eager beavers," meaning were we committed to the cadet corps. We tried to be, but on becoming an upperclassman myself, I avoided most of the nonsense and concentrated on getting the newcomers to stand straight and tall.

I never gave out demerits and was known for my query, "Are you an Eager Beaver or an Evil Weasel?" Many months later, as I walked down a street in St. Petersburg, Florida, someone behind me called out, "I'm still an Evil Weasel!" It was one of my protégés, taking fighter pilot training at Pinellas Park. He thanked me for helping him get through cadets without blowing his stack and for making his ordeal at Maxwell Field a more pleasant and humorous one.

Most recruits in the wartime branches of service, especially the regular Army and Navy, soon picked up the foul-mouthed language so common at the time. To some of us, this disgusting habit was intolerable and often unavoidable, as well. It was my good fortune to be assigned to a barracks filled with quite a few cadets who were as repulsed as I was by the "f" word especially. If the offenders continued with their habit after being warned tactfully by some of us, they were, in effect, shunned and given the silent treatment. This had quite the desirable result, and some of the converts helped to set the example for others. Honesty was programmed into our everyday lives, allowing us to leave our valuables, watches, money (very little), on our bunks while in the bathroom or elsewhere. This was very comforting and aided greatly in building team confidence.

A graphic example of the code of honesty occurred when a cadet was found to have cheated on one of the final exams. Some 5,000 cadets were assembled in formation in front of a building with a balcony on the upper level, where the accused was brought out and had the charges read to him. Every cadet had to answer honestly to any question. An officer's word was his bond. The cheater admitted to his indiscretion, was stripped of his insignia of rank and heard his punishment read over the loudspeakers. He was discharged from the cadet program and transferred to the infantry on the spot. The irony of the whole affair was the fact the cadet had very good grades, was about to be graduated and sent on to flight school. He lost his chance to be commissioned and fight the war in the air rather than on the ground. The humiliation must have been a terrible burden to bear. We were all impressed.

1943 March

Pre-flight at Maxwell field was a monumental test of endurance—mentally, physically and emotionally. Some men, without proper upbringing or just lacking the motivation necessary to cope with the stress and adapt to unexpected changes, fell by the wayside. The fact that we had to be all volunteers rather than draftees no doubt played a part in our willingness to comply with every rule laid down and to press on to our goal. Perhaps it was better to have attrition at this point than later on.

After all the training and the responsibility thrust upon combat aviators, retaining a misfit could result in disaster for many others—not just the individual. The thing that impressed me the most was the large number of highly intelligent and self-assured young men I was privileged to be associated with. I often felt inferior, somewhat the "hayseed." There was no question that my long hours of working alone during my growing-up years had kept me isolated from valuable social contacts. Many of the really successful cadets lacked the interest in and knowledge of aviation I was fortunate to have, but they were, by and large, more intelligent and had better study habits than I did. Several of them helped me to get through the math courses.

The process of screening and evaluating cadets started at Maxwell, in sessions with psychiatrists who probed and uncovered cadets' traits. This was primarily to determine if a candidate would be officer material. After completing flight training, based on a man's profile or demeanor, a warrant of Flight Officer might be issued in lieu of a commission. If the student had performed especially well in flying skills, he had a second chance by receiving his warrant rather than being removed from flight status merely because he didn't measure up to the definition of "officer material." These profiling sessions helped determine who would become an aircrew commander in multi-engine planes and who would be sent to single-engine fighter school.

I learned later they had slated me to fly B-17s before my twentieth birthday.

Once we completed our classes and absorbed the principles of aeronautics, we went to the firing range to fire the .45 caliber pistol, .303 rifle and the .30 and .50 caliber machine guns, as well as learn how to clean and care for them. Most of us snickered at the old World War I water-cooled machine gun, but for all its age and appearance I found it quite accurate. The firing range was the most dangerous place I encountered, as most cadets had never fired anything more powerful than a BB gun. The recoil from an automatic pistol was enough to throw a man's hand up over his head causing him to pull the trigger again. I noted several holes in the tin roof of the shelter we fired from.

My first paycheck was for $21, but the pay as an accepted cadet was $50, less deductions for laundry and other incurred debts. Now we were to embark on our flying careers with a 50 percent increase for "flight pay," giving us the unprecedented compensation of $75 per month! Upon graduation from flight training, second lieutenants were paid $280 a month to fly and fight the war.

1943 April and May, Flying at Last

The sequence of events after pre-fight was for two months each of Primary, Basic and Advanced flight training. Primary for my small group of cadets was in the little town of West Helena, Arkansas on the Mississippi River. The airfield, Warner-Robbins Airport, was a square mile of level grass with a concrete apron at the west end for parking the planes. There were several hangars along the apron, and they were used for various purposes. One, with a low control tower on top, also held the manager's office. No radios were used, but directions to the aircraft were by a signal lamp that could be aimed quite accurately at an approaching plane. A red light told the pilot not to land while the green light meant it was clear to land.

Two groups of students would fly simultaneously, each using half of the field. Half the students would fly in the morning while the other half was in classes, with the two groups alternating each week. A civilian flight instructor would normally have five students, while the ground-school instructors might have about forty. Ground school included navigation, math, meteorology, radio and other necessary courses. We were introduced to the link trainer, a flight simulator, to safely practice blind flying on instruments.

Our training planes, Fairchild PT-19s, later replaced by PT-23s, had very few instruments as they were strictly fair-weather craft. The PT-23 was the same as the PT-19 except that it had a larger, radial engine. It could take off shorter and climb faster but didn't have more speed. The Fairchild PT-19s were beautiful, low-wing, open-cockpit types with six-cylinder in-line engines and were wonderful to fly whether the pilot had years of experience or was taking off for the first time. To me, flying was pure ecstasy.

My instructor was Mr. Weedmark, a superb pilot in his late twenties. He was tall and slim, reminding one of Charles Lindbergh, and we connected immediately. After our first flight, as we walked away from the plane, he remarked, "I have a sneaky idea this wasn't your first time flying a plane, but we had better not jump the gun. I know you can fly, but if I send you off tomorrow, they will look at me over their glasses." I had purposely tried to act as if this were all new to me, as the policy of the Air Corps training program was to not recognize a cadet's previous flight training. Weedmark, himself, had been unable to get into the cadet program because he had considerable flying experience. They were glad to have him as a civilian instructor, but their peculiar regulations kept him out of the military.

Perhaps they didn't want cadets to have to "unlearn" any bad habits, and quite possibly this was seen as a way to bring experienced pilots into other flight programs, as civilians, to save the expense the government would incur for long-time care and pensions. Weedmark decided we would play it cool by not accelerating my pre-solo training. These extra hours allowed him to give me more advanced training rather than performing the repetitious functions necessary before landing and taking off alone.

The school was owned and operated by a civilian group with a government contract to teach us to fly. The Air Corps kept a lieutenant called a Tac (tactical) officer on the base to maintain military discipline and see to the orderly carrying out of the ground-school training. There were also a few enlisted-men instructors for calisthenics and some classes including the Link Trainer introduction. Kitchen and household duties were taken care of by civilians, who provided excellent meals and clean quarters. The base was fairly new, with modern ranch-style barracks surrounded by well-kept grounds.

The owner-managers consisted mainly of two heavy-set, post-middle-age gentlemen who ran a tight ship on the flight line. Out of hearing, cadets sometimes referred to them as the two "old bullfrogs," but they were, on the whole, dedicated and fair. My instructor liked to "buzz"—the term for flying very low, just skimming the ground. It was a thrilling break from practicing stalls, spins, rolls and other maneuvers designed to develop safe and skillful control of an aircraft. One day, Weedmark took the controls, and down we went to about six feet off the ground, tearing past barns, outhouses, clotheslines and terrified farm workers. Occasionally a worker would throw his hoe at the plane, and on one occasion a chagrined student brought a hoe back to the field lodged in the fabric of his fuselage.

Weedmark headed down a road through some woods and encountered some farmers in a truck driving a herd of cattle. When he pulled up over the truck, the cattle scattered and ran off into the woods, no doubt creating a dilemma for the farmers. One of the farmers had seen and remembered the number of our plane, so when we landed the loudspeaker on the tower boomed out, "Mr. Weedmark and Mr. Angier, report to the tower." They chewed him out thoroughly while I waited my turn. Of course, it was the instructor's primary responsibility, but when I stood at attention before the "bullfrogs," my apprehension was genuine. "Mr. Angeer, how would you like to go back to Veermont and milk cows?" the chief honcho asked me. They just wanted to shake me up and let me know they had strict rules to follow.

My next encounter with these formidable people was very soon after the first episode, so I was fresh in their memory. We were required to practice simulated forced landings. The instructor would cut the power while we were concentrating on something else, and we were expected to choose the best available landing spot and bring the plane down to about 50 feet while the instructor evaluated our choice of field and how we set up the approach.

While practicing alone out over some flooded rice fields, I cut the power and was perfecting my approach more than selecting a field. The level, flooded rice plots would not make for a safe landing, but I had no intention of landing. Although I had applied carburetor heat and cleared the engine once or twice during the descent to ensure the engine would take hold when the time came to advance the throttle, it merely coughed and sputtered.

As the plane settled lower toward the green rice field, I worked the hand fuel pump, jockeyed the throttle and used body English to get the engine to respond. Soon the propeller was throwing green rice into the air and the tail wheel was dragging through the rice plants; a splash into the water and mud seemed impossible to avoid. Abruptly, the engine took hold and with the nose high and the tail still dragging I struggled to get free and flying again. Just as I reached the dike at the end of the field, it broke free and I thanked guardian angels, saints, the Blessed Mother and everyone I could think of.

There were several satellite airfields around our base, where instructors took students to practice landings and get out to talk things over at times. I selected one without visitors, to land and clean off the tail wheel and a few sprouts from the main landing gear. There was nothing I could do to remove the green stains from the propeller tips. About 20 minutes after I landed at the home base, the loudspeaker came on, requesting my presence at the tower.

A mechanic had called them to report leaf stains on my propeller, and they needed an explanation. A cadet's word was his bond, and he was required to answer any question truthfully. The old bullfrog that always looked at you over his glasses got right to the point. "Mr. Angeer, did you fly low enough to strike tree branches today?" "No Sir, I did not." He then reminded me of the cadet code of honesty and asked me again, and again I responded in the negative. It was the truth. He didn't ask about any rice field, but I often wondered if he worded his question to my advantage. It was close to disaster for me, especially coming at the close of my Primary flight training.

The tour of training at Warner-Robbins flight school in West Helena, Arkansas was a wonderful experience for me. The training, accommodations, personnel and environment were ideal, and of my three favorite airplanes in a long association with aviation, the Fairchild PT-19 was the best. Perhaps because it was my first real introduction to piloting, the thrill and satisfaction of accomplishment it gave me, and I'm sure others, instilled a great deal of confidence for whatever lay ahead.

Swooping down out of a loop or flying a steep, fast spiral around a point on the ground was exhilarating but learning to fly precise maneuvers gave a feeling of confidence. Those who failed to practice these primary flying skills often wished later on they had taken their Primary flight training more seriously.

Very few students washed out in Primary. Some discovered they had a fear of flying, some would become dizzy or sick to their stomachs. A few had dangerous tendencies, such as one cadet who apparently had political pull, or he never would have progressed to soloing. On his first solo, he landed on top of another plane, but fortunately both escaped serious injury. His instructor reluctantly flew a check ride with him and decided to let him go alone again. As he started to taxi out, his brakes were still set but he gunned the engine, and this caused the plane to go down onto its nose, splintering the wooden propeller on the pavement. More check rides and perhaps some pressure by his influential benefactor put him into the air again, much to the astonishment of students and instructors.

As he turned in front of me to land one day, I noticed he was slowing down and his nose was too high. Of course, he stalled and the plane started to spin, but at that altitude it made but two turns and there was no time to recover. He struck the ground nose first, the engine rolled away into a drainage ditch, both wings came off and the tail section folded over the fuselage.

There was no fire, and as I made a circle above the wreck I saw some farmers running toward him. Incredibly, he walked away and soon he was able to get onto a train for parts unknown to us.

Periodically, all cadets were profiled by psychologists or psychiatrists to help determine what type of combat aircraft we should be assigned to. My direction seemed to point toward multi-engine duty, and my reluctance to directly kill human beings ruled out flying fighter planes, if I could have my way. The strategic bombing phase of the war complemented my idea of winning the peace by denying the enemy his tools and the supplies to wage war. Depriving the enemy of oil, guns, planes, ships and production facilities seemed to be the shortest route to our objective.

In reality, many civilians were killed in strategic bombing raids and the surgical destruction of installations in Germany by precision bombing was offset by tens of millions of slave laborers who rebuilt the installations and replaced the materials in a relatively short time. Often, these labor battalions would be put to work before the fires of a bombing raid were put out. Members of my own crew, as POWs, worked to fill bomb craters and re-lay track within hours of a raid.

Social life at Helena, Arkansas was limited by our tight schedule, but the small city had an excellent cadet club, and people were very friendly and cordial. The cadet club was pretty much orchestrated by the leading belle of the county. Tina was efficient, ran a tight ship and didn't let any cadet be left out of things. I felt honored when she invited me to dinner at her parent's house and again when her father took me to a Chamber of Commerce lunch and presented me with a plaque in gratitude for serving my country. I thought it was a bit far-fetched, but they probably gave out plaques to all of us. I just happened to get a free lunch as well. They invited me to attend Mass with them and one Sunday introduced me to a Vermonter from Rutland who instructed at the base, although I never got to see him, as we were on different schedules.

The cadet club "Queen" seemed to pay considerable attention to me and drove home each weekend from college to manage the club's affairs. She probably thought because I was bashful the other girls were neglecting me, and she felt sorry for me. Toward the end of our stay in Helena, I took another girl who really was shy to the Saturday night dance.

She was a beauty but said she had felt dominated by Tina and had stayed away from the club for some time.

Tina turned into an iceberg, didn't speak to me even when I took a second helping of ice cream. She usually admonished anyone who was so greedy at the refreshment table. I called her from the train station at six o'clock in the morning when my group left for Basic training—just to say goodbye. "Don't bother," she said and hung up. Icicles, first class!

1943 June and July

It was a long, hot, dirty train ride to Walnut Ridge Army Air Field in Northeast Arkansas. The base was run by the military, but it was a dismal place to be in June and July with the heat and humidity almost unbearable. There was no air-conditioning in those days, so the only release was to be airborne. Classes were in "sweat boxes," so we all smelled the same. The water was heavily chlorinated, the food less than mediocre and the milk tasted of onion because the cows were pastured in fields infested with leeks. Pitchers of cold chocolate drink were plentiful in the mess hall, but there was very little chocolate in the water—no milk. The ice was the best part.

Our training plane was a Vultee BT-13 with a 450-horsepower engine, affectionately called the "Vultee Vibrator." It was an easy transition from the smooth-flying PT-19 but had enough instruments to help us become somewhat familiar with blind flying. The canopy covering both seats in tandem could be opened or closed while flying, and the students flew from the front seat as opposed to the rear seat during Primary. The exception was during instrument flying, when the instructor sat in the front seat while the student sat in the rear with a canvas hood over him to prevent his seeing outside.

We flew formation, cross-country, advanced aerobatics and night flying. My group of about 20 students took off on a night cross-country flight one evening at dusk to fly a triangle course through southwest Arkansas over to Memphis and back—a flight of about three hours duration.

The plane assigned to me was a real lemon. After spending more than an hour trying to get the vital systems working, the mechanics gave up and rolled out another lemon that seemed to pass inspection. Right after takeoff, there was a power failure over that part of the state that led me to assume I had flown into a cloud layer, since the ground wasn't visible without the usual lights.

After passing my first checkpoint, Newport Army Base, I looked back and saw the field lighted up and could see other lights ahead. The blackout was over. When I attempted to check in at my next change of course, my radio was dead; both the receiver and transmitter were out. I observed lightning ahead and soon was churning through my first thunderstorm, with bright, blinding flashes of lightning and considerable turbulence. The other students had passed through the area before the storm broke and were on their way home from Memphis.

The instrument lights in the cockpit grew dim and went out but I dug out my flashlight to see the instruments and check my map. Within a few minutes, severe turbulence bounced the plane several hundred feet up, and when it abruptly changed to a downdraft, my flashlight went flying down into the belly of the plane, several feet from my reach. As the plane rolled and pitched, the still-lighted flashlight was thrown about below me, causing more visibility problems.

In the darkness, with no electrical power, heavy rain and no way to orient myself, I opened the hatch to be ready to bail out. The plane was tumbling as I had no way of knowing which way was up or down.

It's impossible to direct a plane without a reference. I was about to unbuckle my safety belt when I saw a dim light that, at first, seemed to be above me because the plane was inverted. I rolled the plane over and could make out a change in features below me. Lightning flashes showed light and dark areas, meaning water and land—the Mississippi River, I hoped.

With this to go by, even in the dark and rain, I flew along the river and soon saw the lights of a city ahead that had to be Memphis. There was a Naval base on the south side of the city, and without radio or lights, I elected to land as there would be no traffic in that weather. I taxied to a far corner and waited for the weather to clear while idling the engine since there was no electrical power to start it again.

When the weather began to lift, I took off and followed the railroad tracks back to Walnut Ridge, where they had begun to be concerned about me. They soon knew what I thought about their sending me out into doubtful weather with a wreck of a plane. The lessons I learned that night helped me through many adverse situations for many years after. From then on, when I had the choice, I flew—just as I would gamble if I were a gambler: if it didn't look like I could win, I didn't go.

We had our first tragedy one dark night, when two cadets crashed and were killed. We had been operating out of an unlighted field to practice landings with only the lights of the plane. Using the "buddy" system, two students would fly over to the auxiliary field. One would fly the plane outbound and shoot his several landings. Then they would exchange seats, finish the exercise and fly back to Walnut Ridge. It was a method that allowed each pilot a chance to fly going or coming on the short cross-country, as well as gaining the experience of landing on an unlighted field. It was an extremely dark night, and the field we used was out in the country with no lights showing on the ground. The ill-fated cadets crashed on their way back—we never knew whether the pilots got vertigo or suffered from other causes.

Walnut Ridge was not a place to remember but a good one to forget. The temperature in our tar-paper barracks went to 109 degrees, and the wind blew dust inside. At night, my roommate and I would dampen our sheets with water and cover up with them to get the benefit of the evaporation. The BT-13s had had hard use and were not reliable, but we were lucky to get through the course without too many accidents. My first instructor, a frustrated first lieutenant, was so obnoxious and foul-mouthed he was replaced.

His replacement was very good, demanding but not devoid of humor, as I found out one day after goofing up our formation flight.

We took off in a four-plane formation from a remote field, and our leader turned toward me right after leaving the ground. This caused me to slow down to hold my position in the turn. We were very low over a river, and as the turn continued, I was forced lower and felt the warning buffet of a stall coming on, so I added power, and in spite of all I could do and still maintain flying speed, my plane slid past the leader. I broke off to avoid hitting any of the other planes. No one else had a problem as they were on the outside of the turn and could maintain speed while I was squeezed on the inside.

The instructor signaled for us to circle around and land, where we all shut down and gathered around him. He looked at me a while before saying, "Angier, let's see your left hand. Move it back and forth. How come you didn't pull your throttle back in that turn?" I felt like telling him how I was crowded on the inside of the turn, just skimming the ground and about to stall out, but cadets were taught to always answer, "No excuse, Sir." I think he realized the problem I had but let it go by remarking, "Well, Angier, I'm glad to find out your left hand still works." From then on, I concentrated on formation flying, and for the rest of my flying career it was one of my most proficient skills.

1943 August and September, Wings and Bars

Advanced training was at Seymour, Indiana, a delightful base set in the middle of corn fields and small farms. The food was wonderful, and everything about the base was clean and convenient. It was good to be back in the North again—to enjoy fresh air and cooler temperatures.

Our planes were brand new twin-engine Beechcraft AT-10s, with retractable landing gear, plenty of instruments and a lot of power for the size of the machine. They were a training model of the famous twin-engine Beech light transport but with only two seats rather than six or eight.

It was a thrilling plane to fly, was an ideal bridge from single-engine to multi-engine planes and had a wide range of performance. It was a time to be extremely careful on the ground as well as in the air, as we were very close to graduation. The silver wings and second lieutenant's bars were too close for us to screw things up in any way.

A captain from Mississippi was in charge of the instructors on the flight line. He had a mean streak and tried to get us into trouble in any way he could. We were required to march to the flight line in identical uniform (flight suits), and we took turns as cadet commanders to inspect each group and march in strict military cadence.

One evening, as we left the mess hall for night flying, we were each handed a large orange. It was my turn to inspect and march us down to another inspection by the captain. To insure uniformity, I insisted we all put the oranges in our left knee pocket of our flight suits. Even though each of us had a uniform bulge, the captain inspected one cadet and ordered an enlisted man to collect all the fruit and put it in a box. When I very politely protested, he told me I would not be flying but had to walk a tour around the concrete apron, with my parachute on, until the last plane landed. For five hours, I walked around the square, about a quarter mile each circuit. He was trying to get me into trouble, and he seemed bent on seeing at least one cadet wash out just before graduation. We hoped he enjoyed our oranges.

They apparently caught up to him and sent him into combat. During our four-day trip in the boxcars 17 months later, someone in our car began to panic and ended up going berserk. It was the same captain who had harassed the cadets. He had to be held down for the last two days in the boxcar, causing us all a great deal of trouble. He was turned over to the German M.P.s when we stopped in Munich, and we never saw him again. As he was a mental case, one could only speculate what the Germans did with him.

Seymour was a pleasant experience. Near the end of the course, we all flew down to Monroe, Louisiana for high-altitude tests. We would enter a tank-like structure that simulated various altitudes up to 38,000 feet to experience anoxia and determine our tolerance. At times, we removed our oxygen masks to perform tests and were subjected to "explosive decompression." This was accomplished by instantly changing the simulated altitude from above 30,000 feet to about sea level, which had an interesting effect on the human body.

One of our planes was left in Louisiana, due to mechanical problems. A few days later, I flew back with an instructor pilot to bring the repaired plane home to Seymour, and I had my second encounter with severe weather. As we flew across Arkansas, the sun was bright and the sky was blue. But suddenly we found ourselves between two huge thunderstorms. After trying to find a way through, the instructor told me to follow him. I lost sight of him right away in the heavy rain and dark clouds as an updraft carried me up nearly 3,000 feet. The natural reaction when a plane is rising rapidly is to nose down to slow the ascent, but this results in excessive speed, and many pilots have lost their wings because of this.

Fortunately, those of us at Seymour had just had a lecture on the proper procedures to follow when caught in the violent updrafts and downdrafts of thunderstorms. The only way to survive is to maintain airspeed within limits and resist the temptation to stop the roller coaster by trying to put the nose down.

In a downdraft, the technique is almost the reverse as the plane drops at a sickening rate, and the speed must be held up enough to prevent a stall. I remembered the lecture and held the airspeed constant although the natural impulse was strong to maintain altitude rather than airspeed. The violent up and down forces bounced me from 3,000 feet to over 7,000 feet time after time, until I had passed through the storms of the frontal system and flew through rain and hail for over a hundred miles. The other pilot said later he was glad we had recently been given sound advice for penetrating thunderstorms and admitted it was the worst weather he had ever encountered.

Graduation day at Seymour was the milestone we had all been striving to reach—gold bars and silver wings. Many of the new officers had family attending to pin on the wings, but none of my family could be there. A nice lady, a general's wife, pinned on my wings and bars. She told me she had pinned wings on her husband in 1926 at Randolph Field, Texas. The night before graduation there was an informal dance and party. A young woman I knew, "Mary Ann," from a neighboring town, came to see me a few days before and offered to help me "clear" the base, a long process of getting papers signed at each department, wait in line to get paid and settle all accounts. She had a car so we could get the job done in half the time with her transporting me about the base.

There was a graduate I'll call "Lucky" who had previous military service and never made a mistake. His uniform was always immaculate, and the creases were sharp enough to shave with. They said he even slept at attention. He knew all the angles and planned each detail of his everyday activities. At the party, he planned for the next day by persuading Mary Ann to drive him around to clear the base—leaving me to walk, carrying all my paraphernalia. Later, I had to get myself to the bus station with my two large bags holding my wardrobe and all my flight gear, including my new parachute. My orders were to proceed to Chanute Field, Illinois with a ten-day delay en route, which meant I could have at least three day's leave at home. My reservations on the train from Indianapolis called for very close timing, as it left in late afternoon of graduation day.

Lucky spoiled my day and made his train reservation on time, but as his train rolled south toward Mobile, he left his seat to go to the bathroom in the next car back. He left his uniform jacket neatly hanging by his seat, where my former roommate, Lt. Baker, could watch it while Lucky washed and shaved. The train stopped briefly, and when Lucky came out of the bathroom, the car he was in had been unhooked and the rest of the train was headed for Mobile, with his jacket holding his wallet and leave papers, still dutifully watched by Baker. Fortunately for him, his friend was able to tell the station master at the next stop what had happened, and Lucky found his valuables waiting for him at Mobile two days later. Lucky never made a mistake—at least that's what he always said.

Without a minute to spare, my taxi driver made a desperate attempt to get me to the bus on time, but it was already on its way to Indianapolis. My first leave to go home was going to be shortened by a day while I killed time waiting for the next through train—or so it seemed. My reservation was on the "Knickerbocker Special"—a fast train that followed the water-level route to Albany. My taxi driver was one of those patriotic types, so he raced off to catch the Greyhound and after about 15 miles, managed to pass it and wave the driver to a stop. I climbed aboard while the taxi driver threw my two heavy bags through the door and yelled, "Have a good trip, Lieutenant." A few minutes later, I realized I hadn't paid my benefactor.

The bus driver was running late and in a bad mood, so when we were within sight of the train station he said he couldn't stop there to let me out. He told me I could take a taxi back. The train was ready to leave, so in desperation I told him to let me out or else! About then the passengers set up a howl and convinced him to stop the bus. As I reached the train with my heavy bags it started to move, but a conductor told me to jump on, "Leave the luggage!" he shouted as he helped me through the door. Another trainman threw my bags into the next two cars and I was on my way home. Everyone seemed to be cooperating except the bus driver—and Mary Ann.

The Knickerbocker was a far cry from the troop trains. Pulled by a gigantic steam locomotive, it made the 700-mile run to Albany in nine hours, picking up water from a trough between the rails near Buffalo without stopping. The cars were luxurious, with comfortable seats and a lot of space in between the real easy-chairs. Three wives of friends of mine from the cadet program were heading back East after the graduation while their husbands had to travel west to new assignments. They took me in charge, packed pillows around me and let me sleep most of the way.

My sister Viola and her family gave me a fine breakfast while I waited for a slow milk train from Albany to New Haven. That used up my first day of leave. There was no phone at New Haven Junction, so I walked the mile and a half to my uncle's place and returned immediately to retrieve my luggage, which I'd stashed near the station.

My brother Laurence was most interested in my Air Corps gear when I unpacked it for all to see. Just before graduation, we had been measured by the Hart-Shafner and Marx people for uniforms, and they were a pleasure to wear. A nicely fitted grey overcoat, an officer's cap with the eagle crest and the popular overseas hat that folded flat made up the outer wear. Two dress uniform jackets (blouses) could be worn with the nice "pink" trousers (more of a grey gabardine with a tinge of pink) or the green trousers. Two gabardine shirts, one pink, one green, could be worn in place of the blouse for most activities, two sets of summer tropical worsteds, two dress shirts and two sets of khakis completed the uniforms. The whole wardrobe cost me about $500.

The flight gear was issued to us and consisted of two gabardine flight suits, the essential leather jacket, sheepskin and leather jacket and pants for the cold at high altitude, electrically heated suits (which I never wore), leather and sheepskin flying boots, GI shoes, gloves, leather helmet with goggles and earphones, oxygen mask, parachute and "Mae West" life preserver.

It was quite an array of equipment, all brand new and more property than I had ever owned as a poor farm boy.

A good uniform really does "do something" for any wearer, as I found out by visiting friends and old haunts. It gave me a sense of pride to wear it, and it seemed to make a person stand and walk taller, as well as generating a degree of respect from civilians. When I stopped at the dance in Bristol, a girl I'd dated before was there with another fellow, but she had me take her home—to her home, that is. It was my first leave, and I realized how hard it must have been for some servicemen to go overseas without a few days at home.

1943 October and November, Finally, B-17s

My leave ended all too soon. A late-night bus trip put me in Albany for the connection to the Knickerbocker early in the morning, providing me with a daylight view of the countryside on the way back to Indianapolis. Another bus deposited me in Champagne-Urbana, Illinois, a few miles south of Rantoul, where Chanute Field was located.

This assignment to the Specialized Pilot School was a stroke of good luck for me, because not very many new pilot/officers were sent there. It was the largest aircraft mechanics school in the country, so as we transitioned into the welcome B-17s, we had access to many classes that helped us to understand the systems of the four-engined bomber. Most pilots went directly to an Overseas Training Unit (OTU) for transition and crew assignments, thereby missing out on this all-important familiarization with the plane they would soon be flying into combat. This familiarization was a major advantage for me and was an enormous benefit in the next year to come. The better knowledge of the aircraft systems may have saved many lives for those of us enrolled at Chanute.

October and November were spent flying instruments, high altitude, night flying and many cross-country trips for navigation and familiarity with the Boeing B-17. The plane was a natural for me, and many times I gave thanks for being assigned to such a great piece of equipment. The four engines, one-hundred and ten foot wingspan and considerable weight of the plane did give the pilot a sense of power, but with a crew aboard, an even greater sense of responsibility. Before going overseas, a friend of mine and cadet classmate who was flying B-24s at Langley Field exchanged flights with me so we could experience the difference between the two. After flying the B-24, I was even more thankful, and he had tears in his eyes after flying my B-17.

Two cross-country flights turned out to be memorable. I volunteered (begged) to fly a visiting Dutch officer around the country to visit Dutch training fields. When we left Louisiana for Valdosta, Georgia, the weather looked doubtful due to the merging of storm systems over the entire eastern U.S. I tried to monitor the weather reports for our route, but there was some confusion concerning what was happening.

Low clouds and heavy rain covered the Southeast except for lower Florida. Since we could not be cleared to land at Valdosta, I requested permission to divert to Florida, but was ordered to fly north and try for an open airport. The rain produced one of the heaviest snowfalls on record for the Northeast, and the low ceilings closed one airport after another. We were trapped above, and in some areas within, the thick clouds covering most of the East. Enough fuel remained to turn back to Florida as we approached Wheeling, West Virginia, but we were still denied a clearance and told to head west. I made a decision to slow down, reduce power and try to extend our endurance in case the weather precluded our landing for an extended period of time.

We had been airborne for 18 hours when weather was forecast to lift in the Midwest. We continued to fly slow, to give more time for clearing weather, and about three hours later, Chanute was above the minimum landing limits. Fortunately, the plane assigned to us had been fitted out for VIPs, with not only a sofa and other amenities but an auxiliary fuel tank as well. If ever faced with the same dilemma again, I would have a radio "failure" before taking orders to go here, go there and be at the mercy of people on the ground guessing about the weather trends. Florida would have been a good choice.

My first "hazardous duty" mission came about due to several factors. My successful long-distance weather flight, the fact I had met the minimum number of hours for the course, and the fact I had learned how to plead my case enabled me to be selected to fly to Chicago one morning to pick up a group of nurses and deliver them to Ft. Myers, Florida. There were about a half dozen of the little dears and my crew of four, so they had to pass the "weight and balance" requirement. I told them it would be necessary for me to guess each one's weight in order to place them in positions so as not to upset the balance of the plane. I gauged each one's figure and tactfully made only mental notes, so as not to embarrass them. They never guessed that 800 pounds of pretty nurses wouldn't make a tad of difference to the balance of the B-17, but I had that opportunity to study each one's figure—and I took it.

It was a gorgeous day without a cloud in the sky, so the girls could see the scenery crossing Indiana, Kentucky, Tennessee, Alabama and a corner of the Gulf of Mexico. From eastern Tennessee, we had a wonderful view of the snow-covered Great Smokey Mountains. Our passengers took turns flying the B-17 in the copilot's seat and rotated to the nose section to look out at the world through the big plexiglass nose. It was delightful cruising above some of the most scenic areas of the eastern U.S. and to finally see the white beaches of Florida.

My passengers enjoyed the trip immensely, as I certainly did, and I almost took them up on their offer to stay a few days. The temperature had been about zero when we left Illinois, but when we stepped out on the tarmac, it was 80 degrees. We all had our winter uniforms on. The sweat ran down into my left shoe, but it didn't prevent me from getting a half dozen hugs. I was scheduled to be stationed at MacDill field near Tampa within a few weeks but never did see those pretty nurses again.

The introduction to a four-engine plane was not very taxing because we had been progressively challenged as we went through the cadet program. The high-altitude experience was unpleasant but was absolutely necessary since we would be flying combat in the rarified air above 25,000 feet. Airplanes handle differently in the thin air, but the oxygen mask was the hardest to get used to. It was uncomfortable to wear and always smelled as if we were breathing the same air over and over. It was hard to believe the day would come when it would be necessary to wear the mask for 10 or 12 hours, giving time for the stubble to grow and become extremely irritating. Perspiration due to stress or exertion made the contraption difficult to keep in place. The system had an eye-like indicator below the instrument panel that let the wearer know if it was working—not a thing to stare at, but an occasional glance could prevent a catastrophe. The men in the unheated parts of the plane had to constantly guard against the oxygen hose freezing up, shutting off the lifeline.

I learned a technique for flying the heavy bomber with less expenditure of energy than we all started out with. It took a fair amount of strength to move the controls, and many pilots complained of sore stomach muscles from holding the control wheel back during landing and other maneuvers. Rather than tug on the wheel, I used the elevator trim tab control (a large, thin wheel close to the right side of my seat) to take pressure off the elevator during landing—a method I used for most all of my years of flying. Trim tabs are small surfaces at the rear of each control surface, rudder, elevator and aileron. If the pilot has to constantly hold rudder to keep the plane straight or maintain pressure on the wheel to keep the wings level, he can relieve the pressure by adjusting the appropriate trim tab.

At Halloween, the nurses at Chanute invited only the pilots to a party. The "ground pounders" on the field were somewhat put out by this exclusion, but we had little to do with them anyway. The nurses had costumes, refreshments and dancing. The affair was quiet, relaxing, and there were no incidents, a fact the ladies said pleased them because the non-flying personnel tended to drink excessively and become unruly.

For Thanksgiving, we turned the tables and invited the nurses to the officer's club for a nice meal and socializing.

1943 December, Side Trip

In mid-December, my orders came through, posting me to MacDill field for OTU (Overseas Training Unit). It seemed my moving about coincided with the seasons. I had escaped Vermont's severe winter and the awful heat of the South—except for Walnut Ridge—and with winter setting in, I was to escape again to the warm climate of Florida. My time en route was six days, so allowing for two-and-a-half days on the train, I could look forward to some time to visit. I thought of Mr. Shackett and others who wintered in St. Petersburg and thought it would surprise them and give me an ego boost to show off my uniform and officer's bars.

The train was very comfortable, and after napping most of the first night, I went for breakfast. The conductor came through and announced the next stop was Corinth, Mississippi, just over the line from Tennessee—a stopover on some of our cross-country flights from West Helena, Arkansas. I asked him when the next train came through Corinth, and when he said in forty-eight hours I made a quick decision.

Amelia Kessler was a really nice girl I had met at the cadet club in Jonesboro and thought I had said goodbye to for the last time before leaving Walnut Ridge. She had shown me the name of Roger Layn, an acquaintance of mine, carved into a table at the club. He had preceded me in the cadet program and was from near my home. My name had been written on the picture of the BT-13 plane we flew at Walnut Ridge and hung in the club. Amelia had an interesting and quiet personality, as well as being exceptionally good looking.

A quick computation indicated there was time to go to Memphis, take a train to Jonesboro, visit Amelia and her landlady and get back to Corinth in forty-eight hours. The station was just a dirt-floor shack with a lean-to storage shed in back and looked quite deserted in the dawn's early light. However a thin, sharp-faced man appeared and convinced me my two large bags with my valuable belongings would be safe in the shed and, yes, he would be there to unlock it two days later. With some misgivings, I parted with all I owned in the world. With no insurance, I would have a big bill to pay Uncle Sam if I lost my flight gear.

There was no bus to Memphis until afternoon, so I inquired in the small town whether anyone would be going to the city. Word spread quickly, and by noon everyone knew me and my needs. Corinth and northern Mississippi had been a hotbed of the Confederacy during the Civil War, and Yankees had not been welcome for many years afterward.

But there could not have been a more helpful and friendly people, and although no one was going to Memphis, it gave me a wonderful feeling about everyone in the community. The bus appeared with luggage piled on top, three spare tires on the rear and a too-small engine sticking out in front—a product of the 1920s. The road turned into a soft sand surface, and going up one of the hills the wheels started to spin and sink into the sand. Without a word, the bus driver stopped, opened the door, and everyone piled out to push until we crested the hill.

It was nearly dark when we arrived in Memphis, and the train to Jonesboro was across the river, due to leave in about an hour. I hiked toward the bridge, thinking about parting with several dollars for a taxi to Arkansas, but I was delayed by an incident in a short alley. Two big "rednecks" were giving a young Army private a going-over. Suddenly they had a mad Frenchman (well, French-American) on their hands. It took less than five minutes to convince them they had better leave—one of them with a bloody nose. I checked out the soldier and gave him advice, but the fracas had put me behind schedule. Right away, a truck piled high with what looked like melons stopped and offered me a ride if I didn't mind sitting on top of the load to cross the mighty Mississippi. They took me right to the railway station, where I boarded a Toonerville Trolley type of train, with a wood-burning stove in each end of the car. Again, the friendliness of the people surprised me.

The short visit with Amelia was pleasant, a reminder that the dreary tour at Walnut Ridge had one redeeming factor. We had only three dates that hot summer and her companionship was a contrast to the dust and heat of the base. This last visit was mostly to thank her and her roommate Ruth for being so gracious. In addition to providing some nice home-cooked meals, they toured the city with me and called on Amelia's cousins: Ruby, Pearl, Opal and Crystal!

After an uneventful trip back to Corinth, I began to worry about my luggage locked up in the shed at the station. The train whistle sounded through the early morning darkness, but there was no light at the station and no sharp-faced Tennessee "cracker" with a bunch of keys. The train stopped just as I was about to break into the shed, but I heard the jangling of keys and saw my good mountain man lugging my two bags toward me in the darkness. I didn't kiss him (he hadn't shaved for a few days), but I did give him three dollars instead of the one bill I'd planned on. He even smiled a little bit.

I settled into one of the comfortable chairs next to a big, pleasant man and rested until a porter came through announcing breakfast. I asked the man if he was coming along, but he said no, he'd been robbed in Cincinnati and was without funds. We introduced each other, and I insisted he come with me, so we had a chance to get acquainted.

His name was P.A. Kale, an attorney from Ohio, and was on his way to his winter home in Sarasota, Florida. We visited quite a bit as we rolled along through Mississippi, Alabama, Georgia and Florida. He would have been hungry before we reached St. Petersburg had I not persuaded him to have meals with me. After the train backed into the station, I realized he needed to get to Sarasota by ferry or have his wife drive a long way to retrieve him, so I loaned him an additional 25 dollars. I had not the slightest worry he would repay me, but it would have been worth it if he had not. He returned my favor by mail in a few days and later on sent me a package (which I never received) while I was a POW. I appreciated the gesture anyway.

Years later, my wife and I were invited to his home on our honeymoon, and he and his wife and granddaughter treated us in grand style. The granddaughter had been a nurse in the Pacific theater, had seen too much of the wounded and dying, and had a breakdown—another casualty of war, in a category that was and still is hardly remembered by the general public. Mr. Kale made one more kind gesture a few years later by writing a fine letter to our son John soon after his birth—an important message filed away in a trunk for many years.

A vehicle was sent for me from MacDill Field, but it deposited me at Drew Field instead, as they were not ready for more flight crews at MacDill. A small cadre of us was relegated to tar-paper shacks on a field commanded by a frustrated signal-corps general who hated the Air Corps and everyone in it.

He insisted on the protocol of the 1920's: no fraternization with enlisted men, full and correct uniforms on and off base—even going so far as to send captains and majors out on the streets to enforce his rules. To be caught fraternizing or out of uniform could mean a court-marshal. I soon was spending my time at the flight line to keep out of sight of the "wire cutters," as we called the signal corps people. There were Martin B-26s on the field that towed targets for the bombers at MacDill. Before long I wrangled a copilot's place on those beautiful, fast planes.

The game plan for target towing was to fly up and down the west coast of Florida over the Gulf of Mexico, towing a bright yellow sleeve on a cable for the B-17s to shoot at. We would fly north for a while, with the bombers firing out to sea, then turn south and repeat the performance.

It was somewhat boring, but taking off and landing the B-26 was interesting. It was called "the flying prostitute" because it's very short wing seemed to offer no visible means of support. The Drew Field planes carried no superfluous weight, giving quite an advantage over the fully equipped combat-ready versions that needed full power throughout the takeoff roll and a high speed for landing. Everything had to be working at optimum level, including the pilot. The B-26s at MacDill had a reputation for trouble leading to the phrase, "One a day in Tampa Bay." Before long, the Martin Company added six feet to the wingspan, giving the pilots more confidence and by war's end, the B-26 had the lowest loss rate of any of our bombers.

1944 January, MacDill Field

Training for overseas deployment was very intense at MacDill as the number of available pilots had increased to such a level there were not enough airfields and planes to go around. The situation was solved by using returned combat planes for training and flying three eight-hour periods a day, which resulted in inadequate servicing of the combat-weary B-17s.

The required rebuilding or replacing interval of the engines was increased from 1,000 hours to 1,500 hours. The result was increased engine failures and many aborted training missions as well as the loss of several planes and crews due to crashes. Most losses were at night or in bad weather, quite often due to the failure of more than one engine. We soon learned to shut down a malfunctioning engine and head for base because the strain on the other engines usually soon led to another failure.

The routine was very stressful, and we lived with constant fatigue. We lost two crews whose members were close friends of mine in crashes. Lt. Barber and some of his crew lived in our barracks until they went down near Bradenton late one night. As they were letting down to return to the field, the plane suddenly rolled over and dove straight into the ground. Barber and his copilot Lejone were a great pair of gentlemen—one rather loud and flamboyant, the other pleasant, well educated, reserved but friendly and extremely popular. There were others we didn't know as well, but it caused us great sadness to see ten young men with their lives ahead of them die in a fiery crash.

The training consisted of gunnery over the Gulf, bombing targets anchored in Lake Kissimmee, Lake Arbuckle and Apopka and ground targets at Mullet Key, Sebring and some remote areas. There were navigation flights that provided experience for the navigator primarily, but also for the bombardier, as he would use his bombsight on one target after another as we made simulated bomb runs along our course.

One example of a multipurpose mission might be south from MacDill along Florida's west coast, making practice bomb runs on bridges, road intersections and the occasional moving ship. All this time, the navigator had to keep track of our position as we changed course every few minutes.

The radio man kept busy tuning to stations along our way while the gunners were for the most part bored stiff—although I tried to keep them occupied by changing stations with other crew members to give them the experience of replacing someone. The engineer monitored the instrument panel and the fuel consumption. The route around Florida took us past Ft. Myers, Key West, Miami and up the east coast past Jacksonville or sometimes Charleston and back to Tampa. It was usually a nine- or ten-hour mission. Other navigation flights took us to Atlanta, Memphis, New Orleans and once to Pittsburgh. Most of these were at night or in inclement weather, to give us good instrument training.

One night, we had to bomb the target in Lake Kissimmee by flying a cloverleaf pattern, with several planes each taking a turn to bomb, one behind the other. It was very hazy, with a dim moonlight, making it extremely hard to see the target. We had nearly finished dropping our 12-bomb load by midnight when just before "bombs away," I glanced up from my instruments just in time to see another B-17 heading straight for us from slightly to the left of our nose. The four engines of the other plane seemed to be just outside the windshield, and the thought flashed through my mind that we were all going to die in less than a second—in a tremendous explosion. I slammed the control wheel forward instinctively, throwing us into a vertical dive so suddenly that the engineer was thrown up into the roof just behind the windshield, a machine gun in the waist was torn loose and everyone went tumbling upward and forward in the plane. It was the most violent maneuver I had ever experienced. We all heard the earsplitting roar of the other plane's engines and heard a sound we discovered later was some projection on the other plane as it tore off the antenna that was attached to our vertical fin above the rudder. No one else had seen what had taken place, as the copilot was looking to the right at the time, everyone else was busy, and normally I would have been watching the direction indicator that was tied to the bomb sight. I closed the throttles somewhat and concentrated on recovering from the steep dive while everyone tried to get back into position, wondering what had happened.

There seemed to be no major damage and the engineer regained consciousness. I closed the bomb-bay doors and headed back to base, explaining to the crew what had happened and what might have happened but for the grace of God.

Back at MacDill, it was raining hard, the runway was barely visible, and not knowing if we had any damage to the controls, I needed to use extreme caution. I told Sam, the copilot, to watch the instruments while I kept the runway in view. He was to give me the air-speed reading every few seconds and watch the altimeter. As we passed through 1,100 feet, Sam grabbed the control wheel and yanked it all the way back, nearly stalling the plane. He thought he was reading 100 feet instead of 1,100! Some time after we landed, the other crew came in—all quite white faced. They were really shaken up but didn't know what had happened out there in the bombing pattern. No one saw our plane. After I described to them what had taken place five miles above central Florida and how lucky we were to be alive, they claimed we damaged one of their bomb-bay doors! Twenty men and two planes could have been lost.

Shortly after this near-disaster, Operations scheduled another night bombing mission to central Florida. Thundershowers were reported all over the area, with rain and turbulence, but despite our protests we were told to go. The rain was coming down as we taxied out for takeoff, and before starting our run I called the tower to report very poor conditions for a group of planes to venture out. It seems the training command was under pressure to make themselves look good in terms of the number of crews ready for combat.

We were cleared for takeoff, and I started climbing up to 25,000 feet, trying to avoid the thunderheads in the dark by watching for the lightning flashes. Occasionally we blundered into a storm cell and experienced severe turbulence, but on reaching our altitude we found the storm system extended even higher, and, of course, there was no way to see the target. As we wound in and out among the towering thunderheads, the rough air tumbled our directional gyros while the magnetic compass just whirled around. We were without direction-finding equipment, and the radios in those times were quite primitive, so we received only static during electrical storms.

After an hour of buffeting winds and being tossed about, we agreed we could not determine our position. There appeared to be less lightning ahead of us, so I headed for it and soon had much smoother and clearer air but realized we were lost. Flying down to lower levels without seeing any lights on the ground indicated to me that we were over water, but what water? Inching our way down with landing lights on, we soon could make out waves, but it could have been the Gulf or the Atlantic Ocean. In the more stable air, we soon had the compass working, and I chose to fly northwest, with the presumption that if we were over the ocean, we would make landfall on the east coast. In the same strategy, should we be over the Gulf, our heading would take us to the Florida panhandle or the beaches of Mississippi, either way we should strike land, and we did, at a point just north of Jacksonville. The storms had moved off to the south, so it was not difficult to make our way back to base.

Three of our planes had not taken off, three more landed at other airfields and one went down in the Gulf. A massive air search went on for days with no sign of the wreckage or crew. However, seven days after the accident, a plane spotted a man in his life vest, floating in the waves. Incredibly, he had survived but required lengthy recuperation. One lucky guy!

Several other incidents marred our progress through MacDill's training program for combat, most of them due to the poor condition of the planes we were provided with. It was my habit to look out at the landing gear just before takeoff, just to make sure the tires were inflated properly. Due to the great weight they supported at all times on the ground and because they were subjected to severe punishment on landings, tires could and did fail.

One afternoon, preparatory to taking the runway, I called for Sam, the co-pilot, to check the wheel and tire. "Right wheel and tire OK," answered Sam, but I felt what seemed like a bumping on the right side and had heard a clanking noise about 20 feet back. Engineer Howard Lang must have heard it too, for he was pressing his face against the window to see behind us. "Hold it!" he shouted. A large piece of the right wheel rim had broken off and was lying on the pavement just behind us. The gap in the wheel allowed a large bulge of the tire and tube to protrude and strike the leg of the landing gear as the wheel rotated. No question but even taxiing a short distance would cut the tube on the broken rim of the wheel, to say nothing of what a takeoff roll or a landing would surely do. A flat tire could allow the wing tip on that side to strike the ground or throw the ship into a tight circle with serious results. We were fortunate to catch the problem on the ground.

A much more dangerous event occurred in the oldest plane on the field when a makeshift hydraulic oil tank, located in back of my seat, exploded just as we were about to take off. Sam, the copilot, loved to smoke, and he agitated me by being prepared to light up as soon as we were in the air. My rule was no smoking under 1,000 feet or above 10,000 feet, but Sam had his lighter out at the ready. Suddenly, the tank burst, throwing the highly flammable hydraulic oil all over the flight deck, covering the three of us, coating the windows and all of the interior. Our flight suits were saturated with the volatile fluid, and it would have taken only a spark to blow us all up. Sam sat there with his lighter in his hand. Lang, in his position behind our seats, had taken the brunt of the deluge. Instantly, I cut all switches to prevent any spark, but then we couldn't call the tower, as the radios were cut off as well. Finally, one of the men in the rear got out and flagged down a vehicle to alert the tower that we needed to have the plane towed off the runway and we would need help to get the oil cleaned off of us. It was a terrible mess, and again, had it happened in the air, it would have been the end of us. From then on, the rule was: no smoking—period!

The emergencies, accidents and other incidents at MacDill were stressful and dangerous, but all in all, the experiences helped us along the way to becoming skilled airmen, better able to deal with whatever was to come. Personally, it conditioned me to handle surprises.

Due to the frequency of engine failures, I developed a plan—using Vermont foresight. If an engine failed while taking off to the southwest, I would head for the small St. Petersburg airport that lay dead ahead across Tampa Bay about eight miles. Likewise, leaving on the Northwest runway, Pinellas Field lay about nine miles ahead, while a takeoff to the north, our most common, gave us a straight shot into Drew Field, later Tampa International. The idea was to avoid making a turn at the low speed of takeoff, and further, should a second engine fail at such a low altitude, there was no alternative but to belly in, so the surrounding airfields were an ace in the hole. On the west side of the field was a 12,000-foot runway that we never used except to park airplanes on. It was built for the B-29s, but when they started flying, it was discovered the large bombers didn't need that much runway.

1944 February, OTU (Overseas Training Unit)

The push was on to get as many bomber crews ready for overseas deployment in as short a time as possible. The Eighth Air Force in Europe was attempting to destroy the German Luftwaffe in the air and on the ground in preparation for the invasion. Fortunately, the production of American planes had reached an astonishing volume, a steady flow of aircraft matching the huge numbers of newly trained pilots and aircrews.

As the new planes arrived overseas, well-worn combat planes were sent back to use for training, hence we experienced many malfunctions. A dubious benefit was the opportunity to train mechanics "on the job," so to speak, while the most experienced technicians went on to service the combat aircraft.

In the rush to staff the many training fields for OTU, misfits were all too often placed in positions for which they were not qualified. We had tolerated one operations officer who used poor judgment in flight training and was extremely rude and overbearing with the personnel. One morning, with his shiny new captain's bars on, he decided to lead a formation flight to "weed out" a few clumsy pilots, as he put it.

He led us down the Florida coast and back at very low altitude even though there was turbulence at that level, due to the build up of puffy cumulus clouds. This caused much bouncing up and down of the aircraft, creating a dangerous situation as it could easily result in a collision. As we passed over the Ten Thousand Islands at 1,000 feet, there were several near misses, causing several pilots to loosen up the formation as contact with another plane would no doubt send one or two aircraft plunging into the water with no chance to bail out. The captain started a harangue, yelling for us to tighten up. About that time, concerned for self preservation, I dropped down about 500 feet, advising the crew to watch for other aircraft getting too close above us. My position in the formation was on the leader's left wing, so we were immediately missed, causing the captain to explode with every foul, insulting remarks he could think of. He not only chewed me out then and there so everyone could hear but carried on the tirade in the debriefing room. He aimed all of his vehemence at me, calling me names no one else ever had.

Finally I got up to leave, walked up close to him and said, "Captain, your remarks are uncalled for and unbecoming of an officer. I took action today as a safety precaution in an unsafe situation that should be reported." He leaned close to my face and shouted, "You're a sad excuse for a pilot! Tomorrow, we will fly a cross-country formation. You will be on my right wing, and if I see any sloppy flying on your part, you will face a court martial and be dropped from the program."

"Closed up tight". One reason there were collisions, especially when the air was turbulent and a cause of greater pilot fatigue.

Next morning, we took off with the captain in the right seat of the lead plane, where he could keep an eye on me, and he got an eyeful. In almost no time after takeoff, I was bolted to his right wing with my wing overlapping his and my propellers spinning very close to the trailing edge of his wing. We were eyeball to eyeball about 60 feet apart. His crew all watched wide eyed from the windows, probably thinking we would collide any minute, but I had no intention of crashing into the lead plane. Our cruising altitude was 20,000 feet, and I was confident I could hold my position.

The white-faced captain stood it for the first four hours and finally signaled for me to move away, and as we made no response he called over the radio requesting us to loosen up a little, but I just tapped my earphones to indicate we were unable to understand him. When we landed seven hours later, I apologized to each of the crew on the captain's plane for causing them so much apprehension. They said that was the best formation flying they had ever seen. For the captain, I had a well-earned cold shoulder to present, only asking him what kind of a report he planned to write. For the remaining two weeks of our stay at MacDill, he never once looked me in the eye or spoke to me.

Original Crew at MacDill Field, Florida in front of the "Memphis Belle". Left to right standing:

T/Sgt. Howard Lang, engineer, top-turret, Illinois (KIA)
1st Lt. Earle Beyeler, bombardier/navigator/radar operator, Idaho
Replaced later by F/O Robert Maitland, Bombardier, Pennsylvania
1st Lt. John Francis Angier, pilot/aircraft commander, Vermont
2nd Lt. Samuel Cashman, copilot, Kansas
2nd Lt. George Yep, navigator, China
Replaced later by 2nd Lt. Samuel Plestine, New Jersey (KIA)

Kneeling, left to right:
S/Sgt. Maynard Judson, tail gunner, Rhode Island (KIA)
S/Sgt. Charles D. Osborn, waist gunner/armorer, California
T/Sgt. Robert Tunstall, waist gunner, Massachusetts (completed missions before we were shot down)
T/Sgt. William Thomas, radio operator, Florida
S/Sgt. Edwin Van Tine, ball turret gunner, New York

Just before we left MacDill, the battle-weary Memphis Belle was brought to our field for a training plane, and I flew it a few times. They had just finished filming the movie about the plane and Bob Morgan's crew, who were the first to complete 25 missions in the Eighth Air Force.

Before the movie was made (the same name as the plane), she had been on a bond-selling tour of the country, which added a great deal more wear and tear on her. I managed to have my crew's picture taken with her, but the developer cropped it so the name and nose art of the "Memphis Belle" didn't show.

Ironically, when Morgan returned to the States, his now-famous romance had cooled, but he remained friends with the girl from Memphis for many years.

1944 March, Langley Field

We were all packed and ready to leave for overseas when the orders were changed, resulting in our crew splitting up temporarily. Beyler, the bombardier, was sent to Boca Raton for radar school, my four gunners traveled by ship to England. The navigator, engineer, radioman, copilot and I took a train to Langley Field, Virginia to fly and study radar bombing and navigation techniques. This was another stroke of good luck for me as it meant much more flying time while being trained as part of a lead "pathfinder" crew. Sam, our copilot, had made several hundred dollars playing poker the last night at MacDill but lost much more on the train. This was his usual mode of operation: get paid, win a bundle, lose a bigger bundle, then borrow until next payday. He owed me 50 pounds by the time we were shot down.

Langley was an exciting place. The new (to me) radar equipment was amazing and made flying missions much easier because we had the ability to see features on the ground or water through darkness or bad weather.

Along with my skeleton crew, a radar instructor with three or four navigators would accompany me on our six-hour missions so they could practice navigation and bombing techniques. We were required to remain above 25,000 feet for five hours, making runs on specific targets such as bridges, buildings, ships and other ground features. Electronic devices on board calculated how accurately the results would have been had real bombs been dropped, allowing the instructor to check the proficiency of his trainees using the marvelous new radar equipment.

Our targets were spaced up and down the east coast and as far west as the Allegheny Mountains, giving the radar operators sufficient time and distance to practice navigating to our destination city and finding the target as well as positioning our plane at a proper bomb-release point. Washington, New York, Boston, Pittsburgh, Asheville, Charleston, Jacksonville and Atlanta were our most frequently visited areas.

We were designated a Sea Search Attack unit, and our duties included flying a triangle-shaped route from Langley to Charleston, then to Bermuda, to Atlantic City and return. This route consumed about 11 hours and entailed intercepting any ships on the surface along our route. Our part was merely to pinpoint any ship's location to the people who would check to see if any friendly vessels were expected in that area and would take the appropriate action.

About half the missions took place at night, and fortunately we encountered storms only twice. During the daylight hours, we avoided the mostly localized thunderstorms, as the equipment did not function in those conditions. Cloudy, rainy weather gave the best practice as the radar showed the contrast between built-up areas as bright light while water and some terrain, such as extensive forests, showed up dark. On water, a ship was depicted as a bright spot on the dark background. Five-mile-thick clouds presented no problem to the radar, and climbing up and letting down through the overcast not only gave me practice for flying in the weather so typical of England but gave me a very satisfied feeling of confidence in my abilities.

Occasionally, we had visitors to the base, people who developed and manufactured the radar and related devices such as the little gadget that recorded the predicted strikes on our targets so the operators couldn't cheat. I enjoyed taking them up on a mission so they could see their handiwork in action.

They would appear in business suits at the flight line so had to be fitted with flying suits, oxygen masks, helmets and headsets.

Someone else took care of those chores, but I briefed them on the use of parachutes, how to monitor the flow of oxygen and how to communicate with us. They rotated from the radar room in the radio compartment to the nose of the plane to study the matching instruments there. Most of them had never flown in anything but passenger planes and were a little unsteady as they walked around, plugging into oxygen lines in different parts of the plane. I instructed the crew members to watch out for them, to make sure they didn't push a wrong button or pull a wrong lever. It would have been difficult to explain how one of them opened a door at 25,000 feet.

One morning we climbed up through rain and clouds for a few thousand feet before breaking out into bright sunlight. It was a beautiful spring day with hundreds of tall, very narrow clouds building up, reaching from the top of the undercast to probably 30,000 feet. I called them baby thunderheads, and they were scattered all over the sky, with clear air in between. It was exhilarating to fly between these towers, the most spectacular sky-scapes I had ever seen. My passengers were ecstatic, showing more interest in the flight between the cloud formations than the functioning of the equipment they had come to study. Virginia had the most beautiful clouds that towered upwards as the day progressed, with the strongest ones developing into isolated thunderheads. The clouds shining in the bright sunlight, with small rain showers following along in the shadows beneath them, were truly nature's works of art.

Across Hampton Roads lay the Naval Air Base, where lucky pilots flew the highly maneuverable Hellcat fighter planes. Returning from a mission early one morning, I decided to get a closer look at them. The pilots soon spotted my slower B-17 and began to line up for simulated attacks. As most of my fuel had been used up on the night's mission, the plane was fairly light, weight-wise, giving me a surprising advantage to turn, dive, climb and change speeds safely. While the gunners on my plane trained their machine guns on the fighters, I went into a steep dive and, by dropping wheels and flaps, was able to drop down almost vertically. As the Hellcats went speeding past in a wide turn, I pulled up wheels and flaps, added full power, and before the Navy pilots could get into position again, I was in a nearly vertical climb that I was able to hold until the airspeed dropped to 70 miles an hour.

Of course, my playmates were unable to fly slowly, so in seconds I was once again in the vertical dive and reversed direction, easily again confounding the fighter pilots. I could turn in a short space at very low speed while they would go looping out over half a mile to change direction. Never once did a Hellcat get into a position to fire, but they were in our gun sights at all times. It was great sport and showed what a B-17 alone was capable of under attack. The mock combat surprised me as much as it did the Navy boys.

The balmy spring weather and ocean breezes made any time off most pleasant. There were three forts in the vicinity, one where Jefferson Davis, president of the Confederacy, was imprisoned. And there was still animosity toward black people and Yankees (make that "damn Yankees") in 1944 among some of the old families of Virginia, but all in all, servicemen and servicewomen were treated cordially. A group of us were invited to a policeman's ball in Norfolk and a concert later with very talented singers, especially one 12-year-old boy who had a wonderful voice.

A fellow pilot decided to buy a car, even though we expected to leave shortly. It was a like-new 1935 Dodge sedan, and he felt it was worth having his family pick it up and store it for him after he left for overseas. I guess you could say he was an optimist. He drove us to the affairs in Norfolk as well as taking us on trips to explore the old forts. One evening, he and I took two nurses over to Norfolk by ferry and drove to Virginia Beach to ride the roller coaster and walk on the seashore. Everyone had changed to summer uniforms, tropical worsteds—so it really felt like spring.

The nurse I was with had just settled into the seat of the roller coaster with me when I saw my copilot Sam Cashman looking at me with a big grin that usually meant I was getting into trouble.

As the car started up the incline, a wall of water struck us, a cloudburst that came out of nowhere and dumped six or eight inches of water right up over our shoes. There was no method of stopping the ride, so by the time we finished we were soaked to the skin and our nice, sharply pressed summer uniforms looked as if they had just been taken out of a washing machine. No wonder Sam had grinned; he had seen the storm coming.

"Big Gas Bird" (951) at Langley field, Virginia.

Madeleine and Francis in the nose of a B-17 at Duxford, England 1976

Not wanting my friend with the car to spoil his evening or get the nice upholstery wet, the nurse and I decided to take the trolley car to the ferry and get to our respective quarters to change clothes. The water in the streets was up to the step of the trolley car, and people were walking in knee-deep water. Upon arriving at the nurse's barracks, we were pulled inside by the "housemother," who sent us to separate rooms, took our clothes and in a little over an hour had dried and pressed them for us. My expensive tropical worsteds came halfway up my calves and I could scarcely button the shirt so I packed them up and sent them home.

Months later, when I returned home from overseas (seventy pounds lighter), the shrunken clothes fit me just right, but they were too small to wear at Langley.

One interesting feature of Langley Field was the huge dirigible hangar that in the early thirties had held two of our largest airships at one time. It was used for servicing patrol blimps during the war, but they seemed lost in the huge building. It was said it was large enough to create its own weather, at certain times producing small clouds of vapor up under the high rounded roof. Lighter-than-air ships had always fascinated me, but I was unable to wrangle a ride in a blimp.

1944 June, Home and Farewell

On D-Day, the sixth of June, my crew and I returned to Langley Field from a sea-search attack mission to find a four-day leave waiting for us and orders to prepare for departure overseas. We were briefed on the necessity for secrecy and advised not to indicate the date of our imminent departure to anyone and to post-date letters to be mailed after we left. There was a message for me from a young woman, "Pat" whom I had met in Florida, saying she was in nearby Newport News and would like to see me.

Pat had been informed in February 1942 that her husband was missing and presumed killed in action during the attack on Pearl Harbor. She had been awarded his insurance money ($10,000) and invested it in a store in Clearwater shortly after receiving it[2].

Pat had a child who was going to start school in the fall, so it seemed like a good time for her to take a vacation to visit friends she had made in Washington, D.C. I accepted her offer of a ride to Washington for a head start on my way home. As we passed the airport near the Capitol, I dashed in and found I could get a

---

[2] After V-J Day, her husband showed up long enough to demand the $10,000 "or else." He'd obviously hung out in the Islands until the war ended, and he would have been charged with desertion if apprehended. Pat wrote to me in October 1945 asking what she should do as she feared for her life. I told her to contact the military and keep out of his reach until they put him in his place. I never learned the outcome of the affair.

seat on a plane to New York immediately. She was somewhat disappointed as she expected me to at least go to dinner at Hogate's, one of the city's finest restaurants, where she had worked at one time. We quickly made a date for me to ride back to Langley as our holidays ended on the same day. Thanking her profusely, I ran to the plane and was on my way home. There were no connections late at night by air to Burlington, but I got on a train and woke up in Albany. From there, the only transportation was on a milk train that took all day to get to New Haven.

With only three days of leave, after deducting travel time, I was busy visiting friends and relatives. The most difficult goodbye was to my father and mother since they were still at the old house without amenities and my mother was failing. My sister Rena was helping them as my mother could no longer walk without assistance and my father, at age 74, was limited to three or four days of work a week. Mother was sitting in a chair in the yard at the same spot we had seen my first airplane, and she mentioned that event.

Although it was a couple days before my twenty-first birthday, my father went with me to Middlebury, and we had two beers, the first and last I ever had with him. My mother was seeing her second son off to war and would live to see two more of us go. She was remembering young men who went off in the First World War and failed to return.

My goodbyes to girlfriends were purposely casual. There were no serious relationships and the relatively few girls I had dated were all nice girls and good friends, but I went out of my way to discourage any close ties. No need to have strings attached not knowing what the future might bring. It was just as well not to have emotional concerns while carrying out my duties. It was sad to leave home and friends, but I did have an eagerness to get on with it, especially because the invasion was underway and there was an urgency to do everything possible to end the war.

My second commercial plane ride left Burlington, stopped in New York and put me in Washington by late morning. On landing, the pilot ground-looped the plane with much screeching of tires and nearly dragged a wing tip on the ground. But no great damage was done—except for waking up a few passengers. Probably his first day.

A quick phone call brought Pat to pick me up with just enough time to arrive back at base before my leave was up.

New orders awaited me and my crew: check out our new B-17G in the morning and depart the next day. We were restricted to base, and no phone calls were allowed, so I wondered how to thank Pat for providing me with transportation. An army saying, oft repeated, was "see the chaplain" whenever in trouble. The chaplain let me use his phone so I could thank Pat and apologize for not reciprocating in some way for her generous transportation that gave me more leave time at home. It had been my plan to take her to the officer's club for dinner, but she wasn't allowed on base due to the scheduled departures for overseas.

951 at Langley, ready for the flight to the United Kingdom.

The day after arriving back at Langley from our visits home, my skeleton-crew and I flew 951 (the last three numbers of our plane's serial number) on a four-hour shakedown flight. It was truly ahead of its time.

Besides the radar equipment for navigating and bombing through clouds, it had an absolute altimeter, giving us the exact height above the ground. An instrument landing system was installed, providing the capability of landing in near-zero visibility. But unfortunately there were only two airports in the world with the necessary corresponding equipment on the ground. In addition to the special devices on board, the new plane had only 16 hours flight time when I signed for it. And it flew like a dream. We would be leaving on our great adventure in style.

When we returned to 951 with our gear and baggage, I was amazed to see men unloading boxes from a large GI truck into our new plane—containers of food rations, supplies, three crated radar sets, mailbags and tool boxes were being crammed into all available space. Two "passengers" also appeared—radar mechanics, hitching a ride to the U.K with their tool kits as well.

It seems the "chair-borne" generals had decided that all planes headed for the combat zones could be used as freight carriers. Knowing the B-17's characteristics, I could see they had loaded our plane to a serious weight and balance condition. Several hours were spent redistributing the load by moving some of the heavier but compact pieces toward the front of the plane as a tail-heavy-condition was extremely dangerous. It took some arguing and tricky slide rule calculations to satisfy me. Even then, before we took off the next morning, my crew unloaded at least a ton of heavy boxes and left them in a neat pile on the hardstand.

Pat said she wanted to wave us goodbye when we took off, so an hour before we started engines, the good chaplain called her and relayed the time and the runway we would be using. Just outside the base boundary was a sand dune near the road that crossed our takeoff path. She was conspicuous in a bright yellow dress on that rise of ground, and I left no question as to which would be my plane.

Sam, my copilot, used to raise eyebrows whenever I took off and called for gear up just as the wheels left the runway. My thinking was: If anything happened at that stage, we needed to have the wheels up right away as there would not be room to land back on the runway and a crash landing, or "belly" landing, was safer with the wheels up. Another plus was that by trimming the ship to the most aerodynamic configuration, by getting rid of the drag of the landing gear, we gained a safe climbing speed much sooner. Rather than climbing right away that morning, we picked up speed, just skimming the runway, so when we passed that sand dune our speed was approaching 200 miles per hour. I tipped a wing in Pat's direction so she knew who we were, and she waved her scarf to give me a great sendoff from Langley Field, Virginia. I climbed out over Hampton Roads, turned east toward Chesapeake Bay and crossed back over Langley at about 4,000 feet. We could just make out the yellow dress.

To the War Zone

Once on our way, Sam opened our orders, which offered three options to "proceed to the U.K". We could go by way of South America and Africa or Goose Bay, Labrador to Greenland and Iceland or directly across the Atlantic by way of Gander, Newfoundland. We were all eager to be on our way, and the high, ice-covered mountains of Greenland held no allure for me nor did fog-shrouded Iceland. Each additional landing in strange areas with doubtful weather was just another hazard as some unlucky crews were to learn. The southern route had tourist appeal, a chance to see several other countries, but would take much longer. The opportunity to fly along a portion of Lindbergh's route 17 years after his historic flight seemed like a mandate to me—a small boy's dream come true, a challenge for a young man.

Our first stop was in Manchester, New Hampshire for winter gear, long underwear. We flew above New York harbor to view the Statue of Liberty and over Willimantic, Connecticut where my father was born. Here was where a decision was made that would haunt me for the rest of my life, to dust off the old home town as most pilots tried to do, or forego the thrill of a lifetime. It was a chance to show the taxpayers what they were getting for their money. Less than an hour away was my home town of New Haven, Vermont. The temptation to go up and dust it off by flying our new, beautiful, silver B-17 over my old home for friends and family to see was powerful enough for me to head for the Champlain Valley.

But soon we could see ominous black clouds over the White Mountains of New Hampshire, and a quick call to Manchester confirmed that a frontal system was moving in and the weather forecast was dismal for our arrival there.

We could have gone to Vermont, taking a chance the weather there would be tolerable, but getting into Manchester later in the day might involve a long detour to the north while the thunderstorms passed through. With the greatest reluctance I turned back and continued to Manchester. The weather didn't seem as bad to me as the meteorologists had predicted, but the opportunity was lost. Even the next forenoon, as we left for Gander, the temptation was strong. But again weather interfered, with reports of fog and freezing rain in Gander. It was a great disappointment but some consolation when considering the great amount of paperwork and explaining to be done if I had bungled this important flight.

There were incidents of crews getting into trouble over this traditional lark, resulting in the crew being broken up and reassigned as well as, sadly, crews being killed by a pilot being carried away with his daring-do. A friend of mine, Bill Good, had a pilot who went out of his way to fly over his hometown in Pennsylvania, where he put on a spectacular performance. He was reported and, after landing on Long Island, was arrested. His crew was broken up, sent back through training and reassigned.

I have often fantasized just how my fly-over would have been accomplished. Perhaps a quick pass over the lake near the Champlain Bridge, where my uncle would quite likely be fishing, then three or four passes from different directions over the village to show off the plane to the best advantage. What a beautiful sight for anyone lucky enough to see 951 flying overhead at three or four hundred feet. We have all missed opportunities, but to us pilots headed off to war, this aerial "visit home" was a hard-earned entitlement and privilege.

This poem by Edgar A. Guest best describes this tradition.

Dusting Off His Town

I have it from his mother: 'tis the custom with them all
When they're finished with their training to fly home and pay a call
Not as earth-bound fellows do it, nor as sailors home from sea,
But as pilots of the heavens in the cause of liberty,
And before he leaves for battle and can put his school books down,
He must do that bit of solo known as dusting off his town.
Now the trick that's known as "dusting" is the swooping from the skies.
Where his mother's sitting watching with the sadness in her eyes,
He must rouse his home-town people with that terrifying roar
Of a bomber rushing downward, bringing friends to every door,
Where they stand aghast to see him goggled, capped and dressed in brown,

A lad they've known from boyhood back and dusting off his town.
Those acquainted with the practice know the final rite is paid;
Know the boy is off to danger when that hasty trip is made.
With the morning he'll be flying to some battle post afar
Where the skies with flack are troubled and the fearful hazards are,
So just pray the Lord to save him and his pluck with glory crown
And just wish him happy landings when he's dusting off his town.
　　　　　　　　　　　　　　　—Copyright, 1943, Edgar A. Guest

　　With our winter underwear safely aboard, we flew over Bar Harbor and the length of beautiful Nova Scotia. I had Beyler, my best friend and triple-rated crew member (he was a bombardier-navigator-radar operator) come up front to see the wonderful landscape. We were flying fairly low when we passed Grande Pre, the home of "Evangeline" the young woman who was separated from her lover when the British dispersed the French families from Nova Scotia. We both mentioned the place at the same instant. Beyler had to get back to his radar screen as we would soon be over water and close to Gander, Newfoundland. It was raining heavily as we approached under a low ceiling and finally saw the runway, where we landed just as it started to freeze.

At Gander, we had our bomb-bay auxiliary fuel tank filled with 1,500 gallons and topped off our regular tanks to give us a total of 4,400 gallons of gasoline. This was enough to take us about 4,200 miles under normal conditions, but we were overloaded by about four tons (more mail was loaded at Gander) and we were assigned an altitude of 9,000 feet, which would shorten our range somewhat. My preference was to climb to 25,000 feet to be above the weather and take advantage of the B-17's greater speed at high altitude, thereby saving time as well as fuel. Operations people at Gander informed us that traffic in both directions over the Atlantic required adhering accurately to flight levels, so we were stuck with 9,000 feet, which put us in weather the entire trip.

Our takeoff was interesting. The runway was somewhat rough, we were very overloaded, and there was no wind to shorten our takeoff roll. At the far edge of the field was a ridge, a roadway, and just out of sight beyond the road, a power line. Fortunately, I had walked over to look at the terrain and saw Gander Lake several hundred feet below, so we had an advantage, in that I could lift off, clear the power lines and pick up flying speed by going down toward the lake. This was trading altitude for speed. I had never taken off with such a heavy load but we left the ground just in time to clear the obstacles and dove down slightly over the lake to gain climbing speed.

Our course was described as the "great circle route" that would take us on a curving path to the north rather than a straight line across the Atlantic. The curve of the Earth shortened the route because we passed over the area where the circumference of the earth is less than if we traveled from point to point. For the navigator, this meant following a series of "rumb" lines with a change of course every few hundred miles.

As we climbed up from Gander, we could see a vertical wall of dark clouds to the east and a few small icebergs offshore. This was our last view of the surface until we were on the other side of the Atlantic as our flight level was in a massive stretch of clouds. At times, we would be between layers of clouds but never able to see the sky or the cold water underneath. The navigator had wanted to try taking a celestial fix but didn't get to see a star the entire trip. He had to rely on dead reckoning, which proved to be quite accurate.

Back in the radio room, in his cubbyhole, Beyler kept his set warmed up, but we had retracted his radar dome to cause less drag. When he needed to take a fix we could lower it, giving him about a 300-mile range at our altitude. His part would be to guide us once we approached Ireland as he would see the geographic features on his screen, and I had a small corresponding screen on my instrument panel.

Our fuel consumption was an alarming 650 gallons per hour until we reached our cruising altitude where I could throttle back and get our plane on the "step", so to speak, much as a power boat skims along better at higher speed rather than wallowing nose high at low speed. My concern with improper placement of the excessive load at Langley and Gander was justified. To maintain a proper center of gravity, the plane needed to be slightly nose heavy, which we had accomplished as best we could. My procedure in the use of the autopilot was to leave the elevators out so I could control the attitude of the plane manually. This allowed more efficient control of speed and altitude. When turbulence tosses the nose of the plane up while on autopilot, speed drops off and there is a noticeable mushing effect. Turning control of the aircraft over to the electronic wizardry of the autopilot was standard procedure for some pilots on long flights. This always disturbed me and there were cases of the pilots dozing off if they didn't have anything to do. I had no worries about Sam, he slept most of the way, as did our two passengers. The two navigators and Thomas, the radio operator, needed to be alert. Howard Lang, the faithful engineer, stood between the seats for most of the way where he could better see the instrument panel and turned down my suggestion for him to find a more comfortable place to relax for a spell. He was very dedicated to his responsibilities.

There were a great many things to keep track of as the flight progressed. Flying in weather required that the pitot tubes be heated as they could freeze up causing our air speed indicators to stop functioning. It was impossible to fly on instruments without an air-speed indicator. Many planes have gone down because of this oversight. It was my habit to check frequently to see if, indeed, the heaters were on.

Fuel management was of primary importance. We had been consuming 620 to 670 gallons per hour on our climb to cruising altitude, but this steadily dropped as we used up more and more of our 13 tons of fuel. The last hours, we coasted along on about 150 gallons per hour.

About one third of the way into our flight, we encountered ice. It had been snowing for some time, but soon the super-cooled surfaces of the aircraft began to collect a white rime ice. It covered the windshield, the leading edge of the wings and control surfaces on the tail. The windshield was no problem, as I was flying on instruments and there was nothing to see in front, but the wings and propeller hubs soon had a thick, white coat. We had on board a strong spotlight on a cord that could be aimed at the wing's leading edge and could be carried back to the radio room, plugged in and aimed through the roof window at the 19-foot-high vertical stabilizer. When the ice built up a few inches, our de-icing boots could be inflated to crack the ice so the slip-stream could carry it away.

Ice on the propellers was taken care of by a system much like a car windshield washer except it used a glycol liquid anti-freeze. When the system was activated, the glycol was thrown out by centrifugal force, removing the ice. Ice caused many of the early attempts to cross the north Atlantic by air to end in failure. As ice accumulated on the wing, the extra weight was not the only concern. Ice changed the shape of the wing until there was insufficient lift to hold the plane up.

At times, pilots have felt a pervasive loneliness and apprehension as flight progressed further across the expanse of the cold north Atlantic. Severe weather, mechanical malfunction or the pilot's inattention for a few seconds could send the plane downward in an uncontrollable plunge through the darkness. Quite a number of aircraft were lost in these ferry operations without a trace, leaving others to speculate on what those last moments were like for those crews. Bailing out would be suicide because even if the decent were successful, the cold water would allow perhaps no more than a few minutes before death in the crashing waves. Attempting to ditch the plane would afford no more than an extra two or three minutes—if you survived the crash.

My thoughts went back 17 years to Charles Lindbergh, alone in his small primitive plane as well as to the 1919 first flight across by Alcock and Brown in their clumsy World War I bomber. The progress of aviation in those few short years amazed me. Sending fairly inexperienced crews across the ocean in brand new, expensive (for the time) airplanes was an enormous display of confidence on the part of our military planners. Some of us had been reluctantly trusted with the family car only three or four years before. Of course, survival was a powerful incentive.

Just after we passed south of Iceland, the wet, sticky snow that caused the build-up of ice tapered off and although it was still a little dark because of the clouds, a slight pink glow appeared in the northeast. Soon we were flying between layers of clouds into the morning of a new day. Somewhere, northwest of Ireland, I looked down through a hole in the undercast and saw a patch of water. I was mentioning this to the crew when there appeared a black rock with a pointed dome shape perhaps a few hundred feet high. I told everyone to look down to the left quickly, but only one or two saw the strange rock with waves splashing up its sides. It was several years before I saw a chart marking that isolated rock in the sea. This strange protuberance is called "Rockall" and must have seemed strange to the discoverers as there is no solid land within about 150 miles.

Allied traffic was prohibited over neutral Ireland except for a narrow, three-mile-wide corridor to Northern Ireland. It was across the narrow waist of the northern county of Ballyshannon on Donegal Bay. Our navigator George Yep reported we should be approaching this landfall and asked Beyler to crosscheck with his radar, which could show the outline of the coastline ahead of us. George was right on the money and from there on Beyler could guide us easily across the Irish Sea to our destination at Holyhead, Wales. There was a base in Northern Ireland called Nutt's Corner, open to Air Corps planes that might be short of fuel or whose crew might just want to catch a glimpse of an Irish colleen. One 457th pilot landed there but damaged the plane. Probably some explaining had to be done about that.

George Yep had our great circle course plotted directly to Holyhead, Wales, but the wizards who controlled the ferry flights to the United Kingdom insisted we should fly across Ireland to pass over our field at Nutt's Corners. This resulted in a deviation to the south, then east, with some loss of time. Next time, I would continue on the direct approach to Holyhead.

We were welcomed to the U.K. by a tower operator who informed us in a crisp British accent that we were expected, but that they were recovering planes from various missions and there would be a delay in our landing. He was quite apologetic but had to ask how much petrol we still had and how many hours could we remain airborne. We had calculated there were at least six hours left in our tanks, but I reported three hours just in case. We were stacked 2,000 feet apart vertically over Holyhead and were called to lower levels as space permitted. Beyler guided us in a race-track pattern about eight miles long and four miles wide over the field. This was easy for us as we could see the ground patterns on the radar screens.

Near the end of three hours, the tower called with a weather report calling for visibility over the runway of a half mile and ceilings of 100 feet, expected to decrease rapidly. He advised there was drizzle and fog, as well, and they were, at that moment, looking for an alternate field with conditions "more kind to us." I immediately informed him that we had radar aboard that could let us land at minimum conditions and were currently in a position for approach. Meanwhile, Beyler had measured the height of land under our flight path to the runway and advised we could descend another 100 feet, which I did confidently. We broke through some low clouds, and I saw a horse standing on a hill right under us. I flew down the hill and caught a glimpse of the runway. "I have your runway in sight," I told the tower. "We don't have *you* in sight," they replied, so Sam put on our landing lights while Beyler retracted the radar dome as we could not land with it extended. We were the last plane to land that day as the field was shut down by the fog and rain.[3]

After the paperwork and getting the crew fed and quartered, I headed for a Quonset hut for some rest, as I had been up and busy 16 hours before our departure from Gander. The 13-and-a-half hours in my seat, flying 951 across the Atlantic, added up to almost 30 hours without sleep. As I walked to my Quonset hut, the setting sun was visible through the thick haze as a red ball nearly on the horizon. When I got up, the sun was still red and either coming up in the west or my sense of direction was off. In a few minutes, it was clear the sun was sinking in the west again just about where it was before I went to bed. I had slept nearly 25 hours.

The next day, we had orders to go to a base near Liverpool. Halfway there, we encountered a frontal system with turbulence and hail that sounded as if each stone was denting the aluminum skin of 951. Heavy rain blotted out visibility, and the lightning was blinding. A quick 180-degree turn put us on course back to Holyhead, where we examined our new plane for hail damage. Fortunately it was OK, and we were able to set out again the next morning.

It seemed we might not ever get to Glatton, the location of the 457th Bomb Group, due to our being shifted around from one base to another. In addition to the pressure to give up 951 at each stop, we were told the plane needed to go to a modification center. I tried to argue that this plane was equipped and combat ready for Pathfinder duty and we had been trained for that specific type of mission. Overruled, we were sent to an orientation

---

[3] The flight from Gander, Newfoundland to Wales was 2,100 miles and took 9 hours plus another 3 hours circling over Holyhead.

course near London, while the plane was sent off without us. But on our return to Alconbury, there was 951 in its same configuration. Only negligible changes were apparent.

By the last week of June, I was told if I insisted on flying 951 I would be accommodated. I would fly, but the commander of the mission would be in the right seat. Fine, let's go! It was a fairly easy indoctrination to combat, so next I was informed that another group needed a radar-equipped plane for a mission and I was to take 951 to that base, fly a mission and return to Alconbury. This went on until the 457th people called to see why I hadn't reported to Glatton with the rest of my crew. Four of my enlisted men had arrived nearly two months ahead of me and had flown as replacements on various other crews. There was no choice: 951 would be based at Polebrook, where most of the maintenance work was done on the radar-equipped planes, while my skeleton crew reported to the 457th. Number 951 was farmed out to other groups on a need basis. It would be early August before it arrived at Glatton to stay.

For my first mission with the 457th, I was sent to Polebrook, and there was 951, ready to go, with a nice captain as copilot to give me my "indoctrination flight." Later on, I picked up 951 to bring to Glatton for a 457th mission. This was interesting because I flew alone from Polebrook to Glatton as no copilot was needed to retract the wheels, which stayed down for the four- or five-mile trip. One humorous aspect was my calling for landing clearance at Glatton before taking off from Polebrook. Driving over to Polebrook from Glatton by jeep, the driver had to get out and open a gate across the narrow country road as the road was not fenced off from the pastures. The officers on my crew were housed in a Quonset hut with about eight bunks, four of them newly vacated by a shot-down crew. Parts of the base extended into and between private English homes with just a flimsy fence to mark the boundaries while the wings of some B-17s protruded over the fence above gardens and clothes-lines. The people were wonderful and tolerated the Americans very well, but I soon noticed they were exposed to quite a bit of American slang and foul language from U.S. servicemen—especially the rowdies from some of our big cities.

These individuals bragged and threw their money around. This was not a fair way to act in front of the English citizens who had been without sugar, coffee, oranges and other good things for years. They did not have surplus money as everyone had to sacrifice for the war effort. It was hard for us to tolerate the rude and loud troops.

I have to say that the flight crews tried very hard to be polite and friendly to our war-time hosts. While the ordinary people were easy to get along with, the snobs, barons, earls and counts proved to be abrasive and overbearing. When titled people put in an appearance at an airbase to get their pictures in the papers, it took great forbearance on our part to be civil and diplomatic. Some of these people complained about the noise of so many planes while the people around our bases counted the planes going out in the morning and again when the survivors returned later in the day. They empathized with us when

My older brother Carl Angier spent 3-1/2 years overseas. He was in the first contingent of the 8th and 9th Air Forces in England, participated in the North African campaign and was based at Foggia, Italy until the autumn of 1945.

there were substantial losses.

My brother Carl was at Polebrook in 1942, with the first cadre of the 8th Air Force. When the 8th started flying missions, Carl and his group of ordinance people helped start the 9th Air Force.

In November 1942, they went by ship to Casablanca, Africa as the nucleus of the 15th Air Force.

After Thanksgiving dinner on the ship, they went on shore to find the airfield still under control of the Vichy French and Germans. Once the area was somewhat secured, Carl's small group proceeded to prepare for the arrival of the bombers and fighters of the 15th. Our North African forces moved to Oran to Algiers to Tunis and Tripoli before locating in Italy until after the war ended.

A very dear friend, my idol back in school—Joe Trudo, was at the same airbase at Foggia, Italy as Carl, but they never met as it was a gigantic base, and they worked in different areas. I often thought of my brother while I was in England, as I walked the same ground he had. His three-and-a-half years in the war zone, handling and loading the bombs in all kinds of weather, was the tough duty he put in for his country.

Five crewmembers on a half day off by the fence along the old North Road, in back of my hut, Glatton, England: Thomas, Osborn, Angier, Judson, Lang.

It didn't take too long to get acquainted with Glatton (actually located in the hamlet of Connington) and the routine. It was located about 65 miles north of London, along the Old North Road leading to Scotland. Each of the four squadrons had its own living area, consisting of several Quonset huts and a miserably cold, concrete bathroom that had no heat and quite often no hot water as well. Two mess halls, one for enlisted men and one for officers, a dispensary, administration buildings, motor pool, fire station and maintenance buildings made up the areas apart from the airfield, hangars and parking for the aircraft. Around the three runways ran a perimeter track, along which were the revetments, small round pads of concrete where the B-17s were parked and waiting.

A mission commenced with a green flare fired from the control tower, signaling the pilots to start taxiing to the active runway. It was a complex procedure. We waited in our revetment for a certain numbered plane to pass; this was our cue to take the perimeter track until we came to the plane we were to follow to takeoff position. There we waited for that aircraft to take the track, and so on, in our order to take off. All the while, the brakes of all the planes screeched in a nerve-wracking sound that carried even farther than the noise of the engines. This was a trademark of the B-17.

The famous November fogs arrived early in 1944, but there occurred many mornings all summer long when the fog was so thick it was necessary for a ground person to line up the plane on the runway with a flashlight. Once the plane was aligned with the center of the runway, the pilot held his brakes and ran up full throttle. The directional gyro was set to the heading of the runway and was the pilot's only reference during takeoff. I would watch that gyro while Sam tried to see the edge of the runway lighted up somewhat by the exhaust flame. The engineer scanned the instruments to detect any hint of power loss and to monitor engine temperature, oil pressure and a multitude of other gadgets.

Once we were rolling down the runway in the total darkness of early morning, it would take a major malfunction to halt the takeoff. When the approximate halfway point was passed, it was too late to stop; the takeoff and the climb would have to be initiated and continued. The end of the runway could not be seen through the fog. Every man on board was holding his breath, keeping his thoughts to himself and wondering if the four engines were strong enough to lift the weight of the plane, fuel and bombs.

It was a very intense time, an epic of suspense and fear, that moment between death that was seconds away and a feeling of reprieve as the plane lifted off and we were flying. These takeoffs in zero-zero conditions tested men and machines and converted many an atheist, as well as generating heartfelt thanks on safely leaving the ground even though we were on our way to other dangers. Most of my missions flying the pathfinder aircraft were in bad weather—the only reason there was a need for the radar equipment that could find and hit the target through five or six miles of weather.

Each bomber setting out on a mission was itself, a gigantic flying bomb. The TNT of years past was replaced with RDX, an explosive with three times the power of the old ones. All the bombs except the very dangerous incendiary and antipersonnel bombs carried this powerful new ingredient. This ordinance we were entrusted with, to deliver to the Nazi targets, was added to the nine tons of highly inflammable 100-octane gasoline. The combination was more perilous to the crews than to the enemy, exposing us to the danger of certain death in a crash or collision. Each bomb had a fuse on each end, either one of which could detonate the bomb on contact. A small propeller at each fuse was designed to spin off as the bomb fell, uncovering the fuse. Safety wires were inserted to prevent the propellers from spinning off due to wind flowing through the bomb bay en route. I never allowed our safety wires to be withdrawn until the start of the bomb run. An unarmed bomb could withstand a moderate hit and a relatively short fire while still in the plane, but the violent jolt of a crash or collision could set them off to add to the conflagration of the instant explosion of the 3,000 gallons of fuel. We were riding a volatile projectile, vulnerable to many external and internal forces beyond our control.

As we made our way across enemy territory to the IP (Initial Point), where the bomb run would begin, vigilance for pending fighter attacks was our first priority. Meanwhile, the four gunners in the rear of the plane were tolerating the intense cold of 50 below zero and colder, guns and oxygen masks froze up, and the constant roar of all the engines in the group built up to over 120 decibels of penetrating sound. Tension and fatigue increased as the day-long mission progressed. Once the bomb-bay doors opened after the planes turned at the IP, the running of the anti-aircraft gauntlet commenced. There could be no deviation along the flight path to the bomb release point because the accuracy of airspeed and altitude would determine whether the bombardiers were able to hit the targets or not.

It was relatively easy for the gun crews on the ground to predict where to put their fire. With our doors open, it was obvious to them we were on our run and would not change course. Their procedure was to fill the corridor ahead of us with concentrated "flack," as the anti-aircraft fire was called.

All guns were brought to bear on a box about 2,000 feet wide and about the same depth, along our flight path, with gun batteries as far as seven or eight miles on either side pouring thousands of shells a minute into our midst. Each shell was fused to explode on contact, in proximity to an object or at our altitude. The black puff of the explosion had a bright red core initially, and shrapnel was thrown in all directions up to a distance of 90 yards. These pieces of cast iron broke into jagged segments ranging in size from that of a section of orange up to an occasional piece as large as a dinner plate. Most often, the fragments were in between these sizes but hot enough to burn through a parachute. If the shell exploded inside or against the aircraft, the concussion was usually enough to disable the plane and kill at least some of the crew since they were dispersed throughout the fuselage. The steady boom of the anti-aircraft explosions could be heard above the noise of the hundreds of engines.

Every crew member tried to make himself as small as possible. Some were able to smuggle extra flack suits aboard to place around the exposed parts of their bodies, but the bombardier had to be hunched over his bomb sight in the very front of the Plexiglas nose. My faithful engineer Sgt. Lang always tried to place a piece of armor plate on my seat to protect that part of my anatomy, and I lowered the seat to where I could just see out the windshield. It still felt as if I were a big target for the shrapnel. Flying through the flack barrages was a terrifying ordeal and generated a fear that was impossible to shake off.

During these dangerous times, the burden of waging war against a determined and ruthless enemy by those who believed they had to win at all costs was driven home to us. It seemed futile sometimes. The Nazis were extravagant in their use of military manpower as well as exploiting slave laborers. Much of the funding for the war effort came from confiscated money and material appropriated from the Jews and conquered countries. All available resources were expended because they believed they would eventually control the world. The Allies had to prevail or be dominated by people who cared only about themselves. The young airmen kept flying and dying and hoping our efforts were having enough effect to shorten the conflict.

The barrage from a heavily defended area was often described as thick enough to walk on, and the one "benefit" was that no enemy fighters ventured into their own flack zones. When the heavy load of bombs was released, the planes bounced up, requiring some skill to maintain control while avoiding collisions with other planes in the formation. Usually we turned right or left as soon as "bombs away," but the big guns on the ground continued to track us, and all too often the Luftwaffe would be waiting for us to emerge from the flack barrage. They looked for damaged aircraft to pounce on before our P-51s arrived.

Crews observed the ships going down and tried to count the parachutes, all the while watching for damage to their own craft, extinguishing fires and helping the wounded. Looking ahead to the black puffs of deadly fire, it seemed impossible to survive an entire run to the target. We all looked death in the face and many actually experienced it.

Everyone hoped the strike was effective after all the planning and expenditure of resources, and those who survived felt more astonishment than relief for having lived through it all. Artillery could hurl shells but a few miles to damage the enemy war effort, but the Air Force carried bombs more lethal than artillery shells hundreds of miles into the enemy heartland.

1944 June and July

The air battle over Orainienburg was heating up. Some 2,400 heavy bombers were to participate in one of the largest air assaults against Central Germany, including RAF Lancasters planning a daylight raid. Groups from the 15th AF in Italy were also scheduled to participate, but both of these forces were withdrawn leaving the 8th AF to carry out the mission.

Over 1,400 bombers were launched from our bases in East Anglia to strike about 14 targets in and around Berlin, a large number of aircraft to maneuver in space roughly 60 miles in diameter from the city center. Some 1,400 fighter escorts patrolled the routes of the bomber formations that stretched from horizon to horizon. Once over central Germany, each task force broke off from the bomber stream to take up a course to its area of operation.

The combat wing I was flying with that day was among the last to reach our IP, the start of the bomb run, in the vicinity of Orainienburg just northwest of Berlin. We could see tremendous black clouds of smoke rising thousands of feet up from the synthetic oil plants we were scheduled to bomb.

It was apparent that one of the groups ahead of us had missed its aiming point and started fires in the oil complex. The anti-aircraft guns of this heavily defended area were putting up an intense barrage for the B-17s and B-24s to fly through.

As we continued down the bomb run, planes ahead of us were falling four and five at a time, some trailing sheets of flame and smoke and others spinning wildly with pieces flying off. We observed several chutes disappearing directly into the dense smoke of the burning target area, their white canopies sharply outlined against the black, billowing smoke. Added to the terror and despair of these fallen crewmen was the knowledge that hundreds more bombs would be falling into their apparent landing area. Some of them would, no doubt, fall into the great fires started by the preceding groups of bombers. It presented a ghastly scene to us as we continued our passage down the bomb run.

Suddenly, we saw a B-17, obviously out of control—perhaps with the pilot and copilot incapacitated, swing out of a formation miles ahead of us and start a slow 180-degree turn directly toward us. The burning plane was approaching so rapidly (our combined speed was approximately 400 miles an hour) that we could not take effective evasive action even if we abandoned our bomb run. When the head-on crash seemed seconds away, the B-17 exploded, apparently with its bombs still aboard. The violence of the blast shook our plane so severely we feared it would disintegrate. We flew through the fireball and debris. The destruction of the B-17 was so complete there appeared to be no large pieces, although our ball-turret gunner claimed to have seen three of the engines pass underneath us. Many small parts of the wreckage struck our plane and glanced off, except for a piece of metal that passed through our propeller blades and lodged in the frontal area of the number-three engine.

At this time, the bombardier reported he was unable to see the target due to the heavy smoke. He huddled with the navigator to plot our course to our secondary target, an aircraft engine plant some 30 miles to our right. There was a flurry of activity in the entire forward section of our plane. The engineer was looking for serious damage from our near miss with the derelict plane. My copilot, the commander of the group I was flying with that day, agreed with the bombardier's assessment of visibility and gave the order to abandon our run and take up the new heading for the secondary target. Because of the heavy traffic in the area, he suggested dropping down 2,000 feet to avoid other groups attacking targets to the east. This put a burden on me to complete the turn to the new heading while descending and maintaining the proper speed for the bomb run. This also meant a quick recalculation for the bombardier, to enable him to achieve any accuracy at all from a lower altitude.

All the scrambling was for naught because I suddenly had to dive steeply to avoid a group of B-24s crossing our path at their customary lower altitude. Most of the group we were leading, fortunately, had time to follow my maneuver, but a few threaded the needle of passing at right angles through the flight of B-24s, putting us out of position to establish our run to the secondary target, as it was less than seven or eight minutes away.

The decision of the air commander to change altitude had caused confusion and a near-fatal encounter with the B-24 group. His next order was to go for a target of opportunity—no small undertaking with the sky full of 10 or 12 groups of 36 planes each. Most of us had an aversion to dropping bombs on residential areas, so we had ruled that out. While the bombardier and navigator studied their charts, I led the group in a wide circle until the bombardier and navigator came up with a new target: what appeared to be some sort of factory complex. They selected a geographical point on the ground for the IP, to commence our run. This was fairly uneventful, but after "bombs away," we were unable to turn toward our route home because we found ourselves 2,000 feet directly under another group with their bomb-bay doors open, an indication that hundreds more bombs were about to fall. We turned sharply to get out from under the rain of bombs about to be released by the group of 36 planes above us.

By flying to the east of Berlin and then northwest to the Dutch coast, we managed to avoid the other formations, all trying to reach the English Channel first. The white cliffs of Dover were a beautiful sight in the afternoon sun. We could descend to a warmer level, take off the miserable oxygen masks, rub the stubble on our chins, rearrange parts of our anatomy and relax. As I had been flying with another group, it took me a while to get back to home base, so I missed the coffee and doughnut from the Red Cross girls. We were each issued a ration of whiskey at the end of each mission, but I always passed mine on to my crew to save up for any special occasion they might think up.

There were few days in July 1944 without missions, due to the good weather, the invasion of France and the task of knocking out the Luftwaffe in the air and on the ground. The Germans were critically short of fuel, as we struck often at oil plants and storage areas. To conserve fuel, planes and pilots, the German air forces monitored our formations, looking for weak spots—gaps in our fighter escorts or sloppy formations. As their high-flying scouts relayed information to the airfields, decisions were made as to which of their fighter units were best positioned to be launched for an assault.

As many as 80 to 100 planes would be assembled ahead of the selected group of bombers. By this phase of the war, most of the pilots were young and inexperienced, so they were herded into a huge gaggle by old-timers who had fought in Spain, England, Africa and Russia. They had not survived those many air battles to be shot down by a kid from Brooklyn in a P-51, so they employed their skills to shepherd the swarms of planes into position for a massive attack. The professionals stood guard on the periphery of the melee to watch out for the bombers' escort fighters.

We had intruded about 200 miles into enemy territory, and although we were aware of our escorts being delayed by bad weather, we could observe the makings of an attack. The enemy had but one chance at the bombers due to the light fuel load they were rationed. The game plan was to make a head-on attack through the bomber formation, giving a rate of closure of nearly 600 miles an hour—too fast to aim and fire—so they rolled over upside down to facilitate a quick diving escape.

This maneuver avoided undue negative "G" forces for the attacking pilots and presented the plane's heavily armored underbelly, which resisted our .50-caliber guns. As they approached

their massive target of 36 heavy bombers, they fired all of their
ordinance—rockets, machine guns and cannon—into the bomber
formation before pulling down to return to base before their fuel
ran out.

It looked as if they had selected us to be their victims, and
things were very tense. Each of our aircraft had 13 guns—or more
than 400 total for the group—but not all of them could be
brought to bear on targets in front. Some might have a chance to
fire on the survivors after they had passed through. Suddenly the
swarm of Me-109s and FW-190s started down, and it became apparent the group ahead of us would bear the brunt of the attack.

We observed about 40 to 50 enemy planes going down, many
on fire, some disintegrating, others barreling through the B-17s
as usually happened if the pilots were killed or wounded. One
FW-190 came at us on fire, finally exploding just off our right
wing. The pilot bailed out just prior to the explosion and seemed
to be in flames, but we had no time to watch for his fate. There
was no celebrating the loss of half the attacking fighters and their
pilots. Some, no doubt, parachuted to safety and took a bus back
to base, but 17 of the B-17s, each with 10 crewmen aboard, went
down during the battle. They were over 400 miles from home
base. The sky was littered with planes, parts of planes, bodies and
burning debris. All the wreckage swept past underneath us to
litter the ground for four to six miles, with many fires caused by
nearly 70 destroyed aircraft. Some 220 airmen went down—in
parachutes if they were lucky—or in the burning planes. Returning from our mission later in the day, we were able to see, at a
distance, numerous fires from the wreckages still burning on the
ground.

Our group had the close-up view of a clash of arms that reminded me of the cavalry charges in the old days, but these were
modern, desperate battles with much farther to fall than from a
horse. We were witness to the loss of our fellow aviators from a
vantage point that allowed the total scene to unfold before us.
For some, it was too great a spectacle to erase from the mind in a
lifetime. As for myself, I had decided there was little I could do

to change fate. What was to happen, would happen. I knew it was time to do the job laid out for me; this was what I had been prepared for in training.

One Sunday morning in early July, an order came down to bomb transportation facilities at Châteaudun, France. The Germans were retreating and were bringing up supplies to delay the Allied push after the fall of St. Lo, using the roads and rail lines. Châteaudun was a junction of road and rail centers, bridges and marshalling yards, a busy crossroads as well as a bottleneck, and since it was in France there was no doubt there would be civilian casualties. I dreaded this mission, the only one I participated in that involved France. The towns of northwestern France had been subjected to savage ground and air attacks since the invasion, with considerable loss of life to non-combatants.

Warnings were sent covertly to the Underground to warn the inhabitants, and leaflets were dropped prior to the approach of the bombers; still, I had a mental picture of families leaving their churches at about the time of our strikes. The Germans, of course, had been alerted by the leaflets but had very little time to prepare a defense, so the anti-aircraft fire was light and sporadic.

Our bombardiers released bomb loads with pinpoint accuracy, resulting in extremely light damage to the city. We had been able to see the roads black with vehicles during the raid, but crew members reported that they were scattering into the fields as the bombs fell. The bridges and railroad-marshalling yards were put out of use. Much to my relief, I never again had to attack any part of France.

Mission Briefing

We lived with stress 24 hours a day as we fulfilled our role in the efforts to bring the war in Europe to an end. Stress manifested itself in many ways beyond the ordeal of combat. When the order for a mission came down from Eighth Bomber Command, the tension began with the myriad details of organizing our group to fit into the overall complex plan. Before midnight, meteorologists were studying weather, updating maps and perusing the reports from the weather aircraft far out over the Atlantic—where the weather for the continent made up. Other aircraft were launched to get a view of the actual weather in the vicinity. Intelligence (G-2) studied maps and reconnaissance photos of the targets to be struck. Usually the task force of bombers would number from 1,500 to 3,000, and a determination would be made of how many to send to the several targets—600 to an aircraft plant, 800 to oil facilities, 400 to a rubber factory and whatever was estimated to allot to transportation centers for maximum effect. With luck, we could have from 150 to 180 squadrons of escort fighters. The thought of more than 40,000 men in the air over the Continent at once seemed at times to be an excess of manpower committed to savage battles. A maximum effort by the Eighth Air Force combined with the Fifteenth Air Force from Italy, together with our fighter aircraft and whatever the enemy could put up on one occasion totaled in excess of 60,000 airmen.

Information for the pilots to carry on the mission—concerning routes, targets, times for each phase of the operation, codes and colors of the day for identification—was printed on rice paper, to be eaten in case of capture. Usually our captors didn't wait around for us to have our rice-paper lunch! By 0100 hours, lead crews were awakened for early briefing at 0200. Breakfast would be scheduled for 0300, main briefing at 0400, aiming for takeoff at 0600 if all went according to plan. Weather or changes in up-to-date information at higher headquarters could result in delayed departures. Tension increased as the details were worked out and disseminated to the crews.

The briefing had an atmosphere of drama as the commanding officer strode in dressed in full regalia, swagger stick under one arm, and the room snapped to attention. He would wave the men to "at ease" before pulling back the curtain that covered the map of the Continent with the red lines depicting the routes in to the target and back. He usually gave the reasons for the targets selection as well as a "pep talk" to buoy up our spirits-nice try! A "milk run" was a short, fairly easy mission, but almost invariably the revelation of the target brought verbal expressions of dread, astonishment and disbelief, especially if it showed a strike at the same location we had attacked the day before or one of the more heavily defended areas. Still, once in a while, the crews were elated to be able to hit back at a place that had taken a heavy toll on previous strikes.

Once the briefing was over and the CO had left, it was time to gather all the gear. But almost every man stopped between the briefing room and the locker room at the quite crude outhouses. This was nature's way of relieving the tension as well as avoiding the need for a bowel movement at 30,000 feet in 50-below temperatures. Frostbite on the buttocks was the price to pay for that.

Everyone in his right mind put on heavy winter underwear under regular pants and a shirt followed by a heated suit, fleece-lined leather pants and jacket, heated gloves and fleece-lined leather boots over GI shoes. Then the collection of equipment had to be meticulously checked over. Oxygen mask and parachute received close scrutiny, as did the Mae West life preserver, flack suit and steel helmet. A leather helmet with built-in earphones, goggles and microphone, escape kits, the rice-paper flimsies and sunglasses amounted to a lot to carry to the plane. I never wore the heated suit or bulky fleece-lined jacket and pants as I felt too encumbered while flying—especially since I never left my seat during a mission.

I did wear my leather A-2 jacket over my gabardine flight suit with its many pockets to hold papers, glasses, escape kit and gloves. It was absolutely essential that each crew member be responsible for collecting all the necessary gear and getting it to the hardstand, where the plane waited. I always wore my uniform cap until we reached 10,000 feet, when I handed it to the engineer who helped me into the leather helmet and oxygen mask.

As we returned, Lang handed me back my cap when we had passed the altitude where we no longer needed the oxygen mask. The steel helmets fit over the leather helmets, but because of their weight no one put them on until we could see the anti-aircraft fire.

The noise along the perimeter track was deafening as ground crews revved up engines to check them out a last time. This was a dangerous place. In the darkness and blackout it was easy to walk through the arc of a spinning propeller—make that *halfway* through. Fatalities occurred from this danger, and injuries caused by vehicles were common because an approaching truck or jeep could not be heard above the noise of the aircraft engines. Stress and danger were not peculiar to the time spent in the air. The chaplains moved about the area ready to hear confessions and give communion should anyone feel the need at the last minute. Some Jewish boys were observed receiving communion, getting all the help available. It seemed better to be flying in the state of grace, whether in combat or just being in the air.

It was time to climb in and set off on another great adventure, to accept the ultimate challenge. This was always a test of learned skills, remembering a thousand details that could mean life or death. For some, it would be that last day on earth, for others excruciating pain as fellow airmen tried to keep their wounded alive in the cold thin air for hours on the withdrawal from enemy skies.

I walked out on each of the slippery, wet wings to check that all the gas caps were secure. Guidelines advised opening each cap to see that the tanks were full of fuel, but most of the ground crew chiefs were somewhat insulted by this advice; for myself the recommended procedure increased the possibility of leaving one or more of the caps improperly fastened. After checking the plane over inside and out with the ground crew, we boarded our aircraft. Some of us could wear a back-pack parachute while most of the crew, who had to move around more, wore just the harness but needed to buckle on the smaller chest-type pack if needed. Settling into my seat with my chute on, I buckled my seat belt and adjusted the seat for as much comfort for 10 or 12 hours as possible.

The "Mae West" life vest had to be strapped on before the parachute. If landing in water, the chute harness had to be unbuckled before inflating the vest. This was accomplished by pulling two short lanyards that activated CO_2 cartridges allowing the gas to enter the compartments of the floatation device. If the vest was inflated too early, it would be impossible to release the heavy chute harness because of the air pressure from the vest.

The hose for the oxygen mask had to be connected to the system and checked for proper functioning. The radio wiring had to be connected to the microphone and earphones, but before attaching these umbilical cords, the heavy flack suit had to be in place, as the hoses and wiring had to be on the outside of this steel and canvas device that hung on one's neck like a hated excess weight but had only to save a life once to be appreciated.

The bombardier installed his bombsight, the navigator spread his maps and instruments on his small desk and radio checked his equipment, while the gunners installed gun barrels and ammunition belts. The copilot and I started our long checklist. The green flare from the control tower signaled us to start engines, a procedure that required continuing with the checklist, not that I couldn't remember the sequence but just to insure nothing was overlooked.

After all the switches and controls were adjusted, I called, "Energize one," the order for Sam to hold down a button that would start a heavy flywheel located behind each engine. Just as the sound of the spinning flywheel indicated it had reached the maximum speed, I called, "Mesh one," and Sam pushed the button that caused the inertia starter (the flywheel) to turn the engine. Actually, I had developed the habit of calling Sam to energize Number Two engine before meshing One—a saving of several seconds as we progressed to all four engines. Each engine would cough and shake in its mount before settling down to a smooth roar. Ground personnel stood close by with fire extinguishers while we continued with the firing up of all four engines.

Once the engines were running smoothly, there was some relief from the tension that had gripped us since before going to bed the night before, knowing most of us would be awakened to begin the grueling preparations for another mission.

Another flare let us know it was time to taxi, but each plane left its hardstand in a certain sequence, according to the position it would fly in the formation. The heavily loaded planes lumbered out onto the perimeter track that circled the runways, bringing that shrill penetrating sound to the countryside, the nerve-wracking squeal of the brakes that could be heard for miles. To steer the plane and keep from overrunning the plane just ahead put great strain on the brakes. Local inhabitants never complained about all the loud sounds of our engines and brakes.

The takeoff was a sobering affair. Each man knew all four engines were needed to lift off and climb out, so they listened carefully to the sound of the straining power plants. A mechanical failure, a wrong move by the pilot as he intently guided the plane along the narrow, dark runway or the effect of turbulence from the planes taking off ahead could lead to a disastrous crash with small chance of any survivors. Breaking ground with sufficient flying speed is another stressful hurdle to overcome in the making up of a mission.

The climb up to assembly altitude was fraught with many dangers. In the 40 or so minutes to climb to assembly, with thousands of planes in the air over East Anglia, there was great danger of collision in the fog and clouds, and it happened all too often. This was one of the most draining of all the events of the mission and for the pilot, extremely exhausting. To be in the clear above the clouds was a tremendous relief, and the sun would often be coming up by the time we reached our altitude, renewing our spirits. At times the group of thirty six plans had to circle the homer beacon over our airfield for up to an hour waiting to fit into its place in the bomber stream. The constant turning while keeping formation was very tiring and it was with considerable relief to level out and commence our journey. At that point, we could relax somewhat until we approached the enemy coast. It was a short respite from the epic suspense we had endured for the past several hours.

Each bomb group consisted of four squadrons, with three squadrons participating in the mission while the fourth stood

down. Occasionally, the group was called upon to put up a
"maximum effort" that required all four squadrons for the mission, with the fourth one assembled in a "composite group"
made up of squadrons from two other groups. We especially de-
tested these operations because the fourth squadron would normally have had the opportunity to repair its planes while the
crews rested during their day off from operations.

The normal configuration for the combat group would have
the lead squadron flying to the left and below the high squadron
while number three was stationed to the left and below the lead.
We usually maintained a 1,000-foot difference in altitude, with
the lead a few hundred feet ahead while en route but then con-
solidated the formation on the bomb run to achieve greater accuracy and a more concentrated bomb pattern. It required great
skill and patience to get each individual plane into its proper position in its right squadron.

Each mission was unique and impressed each crew member in
a different way. The severe cold high in the sub-stratosphere was
punishing for the crews, especially those in the rear part of the
plane. There was some heat in the pilot's compartment, just a
token amount piped into the nose, while the radio room was the
warmest place on board as well as the quietest due to insulation.
The ball turret and waist gunners could not have survived the
long hours of the cold without the electrically heated suits. Removing a glove to clear a gun usually resulted in frostbite; oxygen
masks froze up, shutting off the supply, if not monitored closely.
At five or six miles up, death was only a few minute away if the
flow of oxygen stopped.

A nerve-wracking sound aggravated us soon after penetrating
enemy air space, as the Germans attempted to interfere with our
communications and radar. Weird, grating, penetrating sounds
came through the earphones for hours, and even though we
maintained radio silence it frequently became necessary for orders to be transmitted regarding changes of targets or other per-
tinent information. Broadcasts from home base came into the
radioman's receivers, to be relayed to me if necessary. But direc-

tions from the task force commanders had to come through my headset. The jamming interference made it difficult to understand messages.

One unexplained sound that came through the jamming that puzzled us was our national anthem played over and over amid the other sounds. We never learned if it was from the Free French Underground to encourage us or a German trick they might have thought would make us homesick. Regardless, although the noise was hard on the nerves and ears, we had to keep a listening watch.

Fighter attacks were becoming more infrequent as our escorts of P-51s began arriving in greater numbers and the critical shortage of fuel kept more Luftwaffe planes on the ground. As the noose tightened around Germany, the enemy pulled more and more anti-aircraft guns back to the fatherland, resulting in much greater concentrations of firepower. Each bomb run had to be flown through much more intense barrages as we approached targets. More than once, the 457th Group had losses of 25 percent—9 planes out of 36. As our ground forces battled their way across France, the haven behind our lines provided a degree of safety for badly damaged planes unable to reach the English Channel. Whether they crash landed in France or bailed out, it was better than ending up in a POW camp.

The English Channel and the white cliffs of Dover were always welcome sights as we left the aerial battlefields over the Continent. We experienced many emotions, thoughts of our losses of men and planes, the injured and dying some crews were carrying home, the awful destruction we had left on the ground and the relief to be within sight of our sanctuary.

There were concerns, to be sure. Would the weather hold until we were safely on the ground? Was there some hidden damage to the aircraft to cause a crash as we touched down? A deflated tire could be a hidden defect to wreck a plane on touchdown. Vigilance had to be maintained all the way to our base as an occasional Luftwaffe fighter or bomber could return with us to knock us down or bomb our runways. Usually it was during periods of foggy or inclement weather, giving the enemy cover to sneak in to do mischief, that these incidents took place.

A number of downed B-17s had been rebuilt in Germany and were used to join a formation on the way back, hoping to shoot down a number of planes before breaking off or possibly to go all the way and dump a load of bombs on an airfield or other target. If a B-17 attempted to join us and we didn't recognize its markings, we would challenge it by shooting off a flare that signaled for it to send up a flare with the proper colors of the day. If the intruder failed the challenge, our orders mandated destroying it, which would be done with the fervent hope it was not a lost, friendly plane hoping to be led back to England. A number of aircraft being ferried from the States to the war zone lost their way and landed in France, providing the Germans with brand new planes in perfect shape as well as another crew that would never attack the fatherland.

For the last hundred miles or so as we descended to more comfortable levels, the engines could be throttled back, saving fuel as we coasted downhill anticipating shedding the heavy gear we had been wearing for many hours. Oxygen masks irritated our faces, the steady noises in our earphones annoyed us, straps of the parachute harness cut into flesh, and the heavy flack suits felt like millstones around our necks. The steel helmets over our leather helmets grew heavier as the day progressed, and the pilots began to experience fatigue from the long hours at the controls and from managing their part of the overall mission.

The sun was in our eyes going out in the morning and forenoon as we flew east and southeast, and again it caused us strain after the strike as we turned and flew into the afternoon sun. We needed relief from the stress, tension and weariness of a long day never experienced by most people. There were no foxholes in the sky and five or six miles to fall if we lost our magnificent flying machines. We couldn't climb out, open the hood and make repairs. Our survival was tied to the functioning of a complicated piece of equipment in which we had to have strong faith.

All crews who returned to base had another tedious task: re-living the day's operation at debriefing. Intelligence personnel and operations people bombarded us with questions as to what we observed regarding planes shot down and the number of parachutes, gunners' claims of kills, performance of our escort fighters and a general overall report from each crew. Intelligence would later compare the answers to these questions to come up with the most accurate accounts. Pictures of the bombing results were taken from some of the planes while individuals trained cameras on planes going down. This mass of information from 36 crews was all compiled and used in the planning of future missions.

It helped the ground maintenance crews to make repairs if we took time to describe what we felt happened to our aircraft. Patching a bullet or flack hole didn't solve problems. The path of the projectile had to be studied to see what internal damage it caused. A nick in a fuel or oil line, a scuffed electrical wire or control cable had to be attended to, hopefully to avoid trouble on a subsequent flight. These dedicated men often worked all night regardless of weather to restore each plane to a safe condi-tion. British hangars were no wider than 100 feet, a shortcoming they solved by limiting the wingspan of their planes to 99 feet. This shortcoming required all our maintenance to be accom-plished outdoors.

Frequently dwelling on my good fortune to be stationed in re-gions with fairly comfortable climates, I gave thanks many times for not being in England to fly in winter weather. Ice on the ground, ice on the planes both in the air and on the hardstands made winter operations more hazardous. I was to experience se-vere inclement weather in Poland and Bavaria as a POW but avoided having to fly in it.

Old Half and Half was a unique B-17 because it was made up of two aircraft put together. It was involved in a collision on the ground when the brakes failed, totally destroying the rear half from the wing to the tail end. It was painted the old olive drab color of early models and married to the rear half of a shiny newer plane, one whose front section had been totaled. It looked odd, hence its name, but it had peculiar flying characteristics.

No one liked it because it tended to fly only in a straight line and required considerable strength to maneuver. I found that by relying on my old method of flying by trim tab rather than struggling with the direct connections of the controls, I could make it serve as a lead plane but it was not suitable for formation flying. I flew it successfully, leading the high squadron, my favorite position.

Old "Arf and Arf" was comprised of two different airplanes pieced together— the front half was olive drab and the rear was silver aluminum.

After my unceremonious departure from the 457th, Old Arf and Arf, as we called it, collided with another B-17 over the Channel and was cut in half again by the propellers of the other craft. Sadly, all of its crew members were lost, but the other plane made it to the ground. I learned about the tragedy many years later and experienced a wave of nostalgia.

The contrast in the methods of the Eighth Air Force and the RAF Bomber Command became something of a moral problem for me as well as for others as we worked to bring the war to an end. The British adopted a pattern of carpet bombing that systematically destroyed huge areas of German cities by raining bombs from every direction of the compass in an effort to discourage the citizens. In 1940, Germany tried to break British morale by bombing their cities, even to the point of total destruction, as in Coventry. It didn't work; it strengthened the people's resolve. More than four years of attacks on German cities failed to break German morale, but British Bomber Command persisted to the very end.

Our approach was precision bombing of industrial and military targets in daylight. The British flew under cover of darkness and aimed for a whole city rather than a factory as we did. If the RAF bombers attacked an industrial complex, more than likely large areas around the target were also damaged in their efforts to destroy the primary target. It should be noted, however, that when our lead bombardiers missed the target that group's entire load of bombs was wasted.

American losses were unsustainable early on, and Churchill tried to get us to abandon daylight operations, but as more long-range fighters became available for escort, our losses decreased percentage-wise. Our strategic bombing denied the enemy his resources to continue the war and resulted in relatively few civilian casualties. The greatest loss of life in our attacks was quite likely among the forced laborers working in our target areas, a deplorable situation but unavoidable.

RAF bombers attacked from all directions at different altitudes. Their Lancaster bombers took off individually all night long rather than flying in formation as we did. This method caused the German anti-aircraft fire to be dispersed over the whole sky and kept the defenders busy from dusk to dawn. This was in contrast to our method that allowed the much greater concentration of enemy firepower to strike our formations on the bomb run, causing the heavy losses we endured. On the other hand, the RAF had collisions in the darkness and occasionally dropped bombs on their own planes flying at lower levels. In addition, German night fighters equipped with radar caused severe losses in the darkness.

Some pinpoint bombing such as the "dam busters" who dropped sophisticated skip bombs to knock out power dams were carried out at great risk due to the low altitudes flown on these missions. Lancaster bombers were real workhorses and carried tremendous loads while the smaller twin-engine Mosquitoes with only a two or three man crew could carry three loads of bombs to Berlin and return to base in the time it took our ponderous formations to make one trip to Berlin. This remarkable plane, built mostly of plywood, could outrun most German fighters. Several other RAF light bombers wreaked havoc on many diverse enemy targets by flying at low levels, often in bad weather. The navigation facilities used on these daring sorties could theoretically put the attackers on the precise coordinates of the target. The RAF crews were in their sixth year of war in 1944 and were extremely professional at their business.

The majority of the people looked on the bombing of German cities as justifiable retribution for the destructive raids on Warsaw, Rotterdam, London, Manchester, Coventry and hundreds of other cities. The cruel V-1 and V-2 rocket attacks, beginning in 1944, lessoned the Allies' resistance to bombing populated areas. The V-1, or buzz bomb, was a fairly crude affair powered by a pulsating ramjet engine with a speed of about 400 miles an hour. Some were shot down by waiting RAF fighters, but usually they flew until they ran out of fuel, and wherever that happened, they dove abruptly into the ground. The *put-put* sound of the engine gave us time to spot the missile's approach and take shelter if it seemed headed our way.

The V-2s were much more sophisticated than V-1s, with a celestial guidance system that allowed them to hit a target in any area such as London easily. The rocket-powered missiles climbed to over 70 miles and came straight down, so there was no sound or warning of any kind. Tens of thousands of civilians were killed by these weapons, and considerable damage occurred to cities in England, Belgium and France. Thousands of bombing sorties were flown against the launching sites with little effect, as the sites were quickly moved from one location to another. These weapons caused the Allied air forces tremendous expense while tying up planes and men needed for the destruction of Germany's ability to wage war on two fronts.

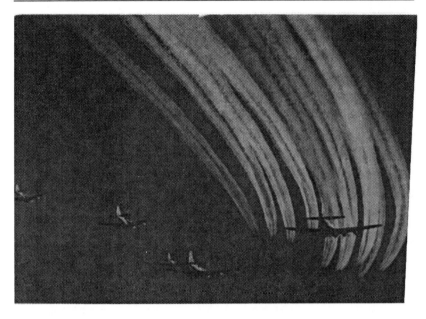

Contrails were beautiful but an annoying condition for pilots to contend with.

1944 August

On August 4th, two incidents of interest occurred.

The 356th Fighter Group had squadrons of P-47s flying at 38,000 feet near Bremen when the crews spotted a large number of Me-109s and Focke-Wulf 190s below them. The P-47 could out-dive any other fighter, so when the German planes tried to escape by diving to treetop level, the P-47s followed, shooting down 15 of the enemy without loss. Two 109s were destroyed without a shot being fired. As they were driven into the ground, one hit a large oak tree while the other crashed into a field and exploded. This showed the advantage of getting our escorts up to extreme altitudes, where they could better observe our bomber formations, spot enemy fighters and use their high-speed dives to advantage.

This same day, "Aphrodite" radio-controlled expendable B-17s were launched against submarine pens and V weapon sites along the coast of France and Belgium. Conventional bombs had little penetrating effect on the thick concrete protecting the pens. By filling the bombers with heavy loads of explosives, it was hoped to put the submarine bases out of use by flying the planes directly into the targets by radio control. The pilot would take off, get the plane on course and hooked up to the radio controlling "mother" ships flying on each side. The pilot was to bail out of a hatch cut into the roof of the pilot's compartment to be picked up by boats waiting in the Channel.

On a later mission, Joseph Kennedy, brother of future President John F. Kennedy, was killed when his plane blew up prematurely. Anti-aircraft fire was more effective on these experimental missile-type planes because they approached the targets at much lower altitudes.

In August, we seemed to have an increase in collisions, crash landings and bizarre incidents. On August 23, a B-24 trying to land in poor visibility crashed into a school and a café near its base, killing 58 people, 35 of them children. A B-24 collided with a B-17 during assembly, with the loss of both crews—an indication that one or both aircraft did not adhere to the strict flight paths prescribed for inclement weather. The two types of planes had to be from different air bases. An engine failure could cause a plane to deviate, but many times newly arrived pilots had not had enough instrument flying time to be able to deal with the rigors of climbing up through miles of fog and clouds. One B-17 was abandoned over enemy territory for some reason, but it flew alone and empty for over three hundred miles, finally bellying in somewhere in Wales. No one knows the reason the crew decided to leave the aircraft. It was graphic proof of the stability of the B-17.

Early in the month, our 951 was finally assigned to the 457th. I had taken off from Polebrook, where the 351st Group had furnished the radar planes for the 94th wing. When they told me to land at Glatton after the mission, we had no idea 951 would stay with us although it was disappointing for my crew not to have it assigned specifically to us.

In August 1944, the Fireball Outfit began use of a diagonal blue stripe for Wing identification. Aircraft 951, the plane I flew to England, was transferred to the group still carrying 351st codes and was soon to be lost on 17 September. Note extended radar dome in place of the ball turret.

Most groups by this time had acquired their own H2X or "Mickey" ships, as they were now called. Polebrook had been host to several celebrities, among them, Jimmy Stewart, who flew missions and was operations officer for the 351st Group when it flew B-24s, Walter Matheau, Andy Rooney, other journalists and, of course, Clark Gable, who was declared a major and flew a mission as a gunner. Other Hollywood types passed through Polebrook, some to photograph a bit of history and others to get into the act for publicity.

A number of B-24-trained crews arrived and were mistakenly assigned to the 457th. They were given the choice of being sent to a B-24 unit or taking transition training in B-17s at Glatton. They all elected to stay and were delighted with the B-17s. Also, when the Eagle Squadron was transferred to the Army Air Corps, many of its members wanted to fly the bombers, giving some of us the opportunity to give them transition flying, a most rewarding experience for me. All of them had flown single-engined fighters but adapted quickly. A few became good friends who offered me an honorary membership in the Eagle Squadron.

There were many acts of heroism in the skies over Europe during the summer of 1944 that were not witnessed by anyone. Men struggled to survive, to help their wounded comrades and keep a damaged aircraft flying only to lose the battle and go down to a fate one can only imagine. Ball turrets were observed separated from the aircraft and spinning down, a metal ball with a man trapped inside knowing he faced a violent death with two or three minutes left to think about it. Some unsuccessful bail-outs caused terrifying last moments. Some parachutes were on fire, others snagged on a part of the plane, dragging the victim along as the plane continued its long plunge. There were planes that broke up or exploded before a parachute could be put on, throwing crewmen out without that second chance a parachute provided.

Making it to the ground did not guarantee survival. A considerable number of airmen were killed by crowds of civilians or irate farmers with shotguns or pitchforks, but only rarely did the German military kill an American.

Perhaps this was because hundreds of thousands of Germans were in POW camps in the U.S. where they reported good treatment and a good chance of arriving home safe and sound. In one instance, a German civilian shot a U.S. pilot in the head after he had surrendered, but he was turned in by his neighbors and executed after the war. These Christian people treated the murderer no differently than if he had killed one of their own.

Many strange and bizarre accidents happened, not surprisingly, given the myriad circumstances presented in the numerous actions by so many individuals. In an unusual mid-air collision, one B-17 landed on and became attached to another B-17. The pilot and copilot of the plane on the bottom were believed killed in the savage fighter attack just before the collision. The pilots in the upper piggy-back plane discussed their precarious situation, and as there seemed no way to disengage the planes, they elected to work together to, at least, get back to friendly territory.

This presented a strange spectacle to all who saw this strange flying object. Once over familiar land again, the pilot gave the crews the option of bailing out or taking a chance on landing. As I recall, just a few elected to remain on board as the two pilots brought the planes down, and all survived. This was one of the most bizarre accidents of all time, and it demonstrated the skill of those pilots and the structural strength of the B-17s.

During the summer, a flight leader of a fighter squadron was hit in his P-51, causing the engine to seize. He glided down and was about to bail out when he spotted a beautiful section of one of Hitler's wonderful autobahns. He made a long, straight approach and set his plane down but deliberately ran it off the highway, planning to burn it to deny the Germans the use of a rebuildable P-51.

However, his wing man, a second lieutenant, had followed him down and, not seeing any sign of enemy vehicles, decided to land and pick up his captain. As he came to a stop, he set his brakes and threw out his seat cushion and parachute while urging his flight leader to jump in. Sitting on his passenger's lap, the young pilot could reach the controls although he had to scrunch down a little to close the canopy. They took off without any opposition showing up, so the cocky young pilot had the audacity to turn back and shoot up the downed aircraft, leaving it a blazing wreck. By buzzing along just over the treetops, they made it back to base. If they had encountered enemy fighters or damaging ground fire, they'd have had no parachutes to bail out with. An amazing performance at great risk but one for the history books.

My own moment of notoriety came on a mission to the vicinity of Saarbrucken, close to the French border. Due to a malfunction, our bombs failed to release, and rather than make another run on the same target, we decided it made more sense to choose a secondary target in an industrial complex that was directly ahead of us. We were well covered with fighter escorts that day, and other formations of bombers were within our sight all over western Germany. So with the agreement of the crew I was with that day, we made a run on a marshalling yard near Mannheim. Half of our bomb load made a direct hit on railroad tank cars, but the other half still hung up in the bomb bay. Without closing our doors, we continued eastward toward Ludwigshafen and successfully unloaded the rest of the bombs onto an airfield, with practically no resistance. We flew back to England in close proximity to a friendly group of B-17s without incident.

Every evening a German radio propagandist with a British accent, called "Lord Haw Haw," would broadcast what was—to us, anyway—a comical report of the day's operations. That evening, he reported, "A lone Terrorflieger flew out of the west today and struck at Mannheim and Ludwigshafen. A hospital and many public works of art were destroyed." It seemed to us there was a lot of smoke for a hospital and statues, but we felt the Luftwaffe might be short of fuel at that airfield.

Finally given the go-ahead from headquarters, probably at the suggestion of General Jimmy Doolittle, our fighter escorts were given permission to go down on the deck as they returned home. They shot up hundreds of planes on the ground, over 1,000 locomotives and any other targets that moved—or didn't move. This was very dangerous business, as it was usually a disaster to be hit at such a low altitude with no chance to bail out and usually not enough time to belly-in. This action practically finished the Luftwaffe except for a handful of ME-262 jets that survived to fight in the last days of the war.

One of the dangers that caused me considerable apprehension was "friendly fire." With 400 guns in a single formation, there was a lot of steel flying in all directions. During a fighter attack and in the ensuing excitement, with each gunner trying hard to shoot down any enemy plane in sight, there were bound to be some hits on our own bombers. As a gunner followed his target, he could easily hold his finger on the trigger for a fraction of a second after the enemy plane either broke off the attack or was hit. Quite often a few of the 50-caliber projectiles would strike a nearby bomber, usually resulting in slight damage—but occasionally a crewman would be wounded and sometimes the bomber would go down. My friend Carl Hedin was struck in the elbow and wounded by one of our 50-caliber projectiles, but others were killed by the friendly fire. Our fire power was awesome, as each gun spewed out hundreds of rounds a minute.

The deadly pieces of falling shrapnel from anti-aircraft shells must have been a dreadful hazard to everyone on the ground. Europe was littered with this trash as well as hundreds of thousands of spent machine gun bullets that had to eventually fall to earth.

Blind Date

In late August, an opportunity came for me to enter upon a little social life, for a change, under unusual circumstances. A good friend came to me and said he was in a bind inasmuch as he had a blind date in Peterborough and had been made Officer of the Day, an assignment of considerable responsibility. Blind dates had never been my thing, but being in the mood to get out and having nothing scheduled for the evening, I agreed to fill in.

"Meet her at seven in front of the city hall. She is red-haired and will be wearing a green scarf," my friend advised me over his shoulder as he hurried back to his duties. Wow! a redhead. I wondered if I could handle this, as I was out of practice.

Seven o'clock came and went but no redhead. However, two nice-looking girls were standing near the front steps of the city hall, where the music and dancing was about to start. I inquired if they had seen a girl with a green scarf waiting for a date. No, they hadn't. But a girl of that description had asked one of them to meet a tall, slim American airman in front of city hall. Imagine that. A blind date with both parties missing. We introduced ourselves, and it seemed they had decided to come down together as neither one cared for blind dates. The best-looking one was Allison Byington, who favored being called "By." The other girl was her cousin Beryl, and we went into the dance hall together.

While the band was playing "Boogie Woogie Boy" (too much jitterbug for me), I stood with By in front of two massive oak doors, and as I leaned back against one, it suddenly unlatched, pitching me end over end down a flight of stairs. No harm done, no broken bones but By rushed down to see if I'd survived. Such was our first encounter, embarrassing for me and quite humorous for By, once she had ascertained I'd suffered no injuries. We danced a few times to the wonderful swing music of the time, "I'll Be Seeing You," "I Walk Alone," "As Time Goes By" and "You'll Never Know." It was hard to take my eyes off By, and all too soon Beryl suggested it was time to go home and said that, if I cared to, they would like me to walk back with them.

We parted at the house where By lived with her aunt and uncle. It was still early and fairly light due to the latitude of the country, where the nights were quite short, but I wondered if I could find my way back to city hall through the unfamiliar streets. Transportation back to base was waiting when I finally made all the right twists and turns. On my subsequent visits to By's home, she led me through the blackout, wheeling her bike but rode it back home through the darkness.

How she could cycle through those streets in the dark was a mystery to me. She had a small blackout light driven by a generator that threw a faint reddish glow for a few feet in front of the wheel. On my last visit, she insisted I ride her uncle's bike to follow her when it was time to catch the truck to Glatton. She started back, riding her bike and guiding her uncle's precious machine beside hers. By's green eyes could see through the darkness, and her sense of balance was amazing.

By was about my height, a year older and very attractive. She was modest but had a lively personality and a sense of humor that made conversation easy and delightful. Not once while we spent time together did she give a hint of an argument nor did her countenance change if she disagreed about anything—no suspicious glances and a smiling, disarming way of keeping a man within the constraints she insisted on. Some of my comrades at a 457th party and later at the dance hall discovered they must stay within parameters when they took their turns to dance with her. If their hands started to wander, she had a way of breaking off the interlude in a charming way with a smiling, "Thank you, we must do this again sometime." Those same guys seldom came back to "do it again," and those who did remembered to play by the rules—By's rules.

1944 September, the Serious Part

By the end of September, my adaptation to combat had allowed me to assess my ability to cope with the violence and uncertainties of our operations over the Continent. Like most of my fellow pilots, I had occasionally meditated on how combat would affect me, mentally, physically and emotionally. In fact, at an early age, about the time I started to read, it seemed to me as if another war in Europe was inevitable. If circumstances led to my participation in a war, it was my hope even then that my part would be played out in the air. By the time I was 10, when Hitler came to power, I had read a great deal about the air war of 1914-18 and the rapid development of aviation during the war years. It hardly entered my mind that I might have to serve in some capacity on the ground in a future war.

During flight training as an aviation cadet, I was extremely thankful to be lucky enough to be flying instead of serving in the infantry. It was luck that I was able to circumvent the rule that cadet applicants must have two years of college and it was luck that I was in that narrow age group of young men who were considered for flight training. Having good role models as I was growing up was luck, but the ultimate good fortune was to complete flight training without washing out—or worse, being killed or crippled in an accident—as happened to all too many of us. Further good fortune for me was the opportunity to acquire many more flying hours in the States before going overseas by being selected for "pathfinder" training.

The violence of the fighter attacks on our bomber formations and the magnitude of the anti-aircraft defenses over the targets were much worse than we had ever imagined. The great numbers of air crews lost in the 8th Air Force exceeded the losses of any other branch of service. With average losses of three percent on all missions, it was statistically impossible for a crew to complete the 35 missions required for a tour.

Prior to 1944, air crews had one chance out of three of surviving only 25 missions. With 100 crews in each group, the loss rate indicated no more than 33-1/3 missions could be completed. Of course, some did complete the 35 but only because some crews were lost on the first or third mission. Another factor to be considered was the reality that practically no group ever had or maintained the required 100 crews to make up four squadrons. Nearly 9,000 8th Air Force bombers were shot down, with the loss of 80,000 airmen in slightly more than two-and-a-half years of operations in Europe. I was among the roughly 27,000 to fortunately survive the shoot down and become a prisoner of war.

A rocket from a fighter plane caused this damage.

Each man had to deal with his fear and his own thoughts of what might befall him. We thought of crippling wounds, being shot down and captured, mental breakdown or the ultimate fate: death. There were countervailing forces at work. There were opportunities for promotions if one excelled in the performance of his duties, medals to cover one's chest to show family and friends. But the most compelling force was the desire to survive and be reunited with loved ones.

All of these incentives served as catalysts to make us all strive to get the job done. There was little chance to display cowardice, for once the order came down to the group from headquarters, there was no turning back; the wheels of organization turned relentlessly. The 8th AF never turned back because of enemy action or human failure. Weather, at times, deteriorated to the point where it was determined there would be no way to recover an aircraft after a mission was completed. This resulted in the mission being "scrubbed" or a recall if the task force had already taken off. Not once did the German effort cause the bomber streams to turn back or break off the strike.

After my first few missions, I decided there was nothing I could do to change my fate. My course of action was to do my work as skillfully as possible, keep my crew informed and trained as well as being meticulous in the inspection and care of our aircraft. This relieved my mind of apprehension to some degree and left my fate in God's hands. I fervently hoped to survive but stopped dwelling on the alternatives.

As a crew, though, we practiced possible scenarios and ways to try to deal with them. Occasionally, due to bad weather, we had a little time off and I would get the crews into their positions in a parked B-17 and give a theoretical happening over the intercom. It could be ditching in the channel, a wheels-up crash landing, a fire in some part of the plane or some other calamity. A few times, to simulate darkness, I required them to be blindfolded.

Two engines out, on fire, badly damaged and still under attack. No place to go but into the North Sea.

Pilots and crews seemed to have great loyalty to the type of plane they flew, and many good-natured arguments took place as to the qualities of each type of aircraft. When the smooth-flying P-51D fighters started arriving in the ETO, (European Theater of Operations) some of us were envious but none of us criticized the plane or its pilots, as they provided the most effective escort service for us on our long missions.

The most controversial comparisons were, of course, between B-24 and B-17 pilots. A popular ditty went around: "All the Forts to Berlin, the newspapers say, while the B-24s hit the Pas de Calais." This insinuated B-17s were entrusted to fly to targets hundreds of miles from home base while B-24s didn't get out of sight of England's shores. The B-24s (Liberators) did have greater range and bomb-load capacity but lacked the ability to absorb serious damage from flack and fighters. The B-24 Liberators were not as maneuverable at higher altitudes and usually flew a few thousand feet lower. Because the Forts could sustain punishment that would knock down many other types, they often did fly deeper penetrations into Europe and made their way back. Some Forts returned on only two of their four engines, and a few made the last leg to base on one engine by trading altitude for distance.

General Adolf Galland, commander of Luftwaffe fighter units during most of the war, was asked on one of his visits to 8th Air Force reunions to compare the two widely used bombers. His answer was quite humorous: "My pilots had to almost be horsewhipped to attack B-17s but we loved the B-24s. They burned beautifully but were a triple threat—they dropped bombs on us, they shot at us and finally fell on us." There may have been redeeming qualities for each plane, but all the crews were very brave men. No one could argue about that. The ridiculous manner in which the low-level raid on Ploesti, by B-24s, was planned and ordered to be executed certainly brought out one of the greatest displays of courage in the history of the air war.

On September 10th, on our mission to Gaggenau, a waist gunner Alexander McCahon, was badly wounded in the leg. His crewmates kept him alive for the hours-long return flight by applying tourniquets, maintaining his flow of oxygen, keeping him warm and encouraging him. His leg was so badly torn up he spent over two years in hospitals steadfastly refusing to allow them to amputate. It was many years later that we became acquainted, and he remains a dear friend.[4]

The most spectacular sky-scape I ever witnessed from the air occurred one morning when our task force was flying at an extreme altitude in an incredibly clear sky. The bright sun reflected off of a thin layer of cloud, actually ice crystals, high above us, in a way that turned the whole sky into brilliant silver light. The sun reflecting off the shiny aluminum bombers enhanced the brightness of the scene. In the stratosphere high above us, the sky was a dark blue, while the air around us was so clear we could see the snow-covered Alps to the south and looking back, the light blue North Sea.

I had never before been able to see so far. Almost the whole of central Europe stretched out under us to the far horizons. The light was dazzling, and there was less need to worry about enemy planes at our great height so many of us who appreciated the spectacle could relax somewhat and marvel at the natural beauty of the scene. It was a surrealistic experience beyond my ability to fully describe.

In contrast to that beautiful day of clear skies, there were dark days when the sun was hidden and visibility was almost nonexistent as we threaded our way through layers of dark clouds. These were the depressing times because the murky darkness lowered our spirits. The danger of other formations intercepting ours required the full attention of every crew member, while the navigators had to work diligently to maintain our location, as we changed course often to avoid the heavy clouds. Being in penetrating clouds in a large formation of aircraft was a nightmare everyone fervently hoped would never happen. When it did, it was easy to lose sight of the next plane, quite often resulting in the breakup of the formation. Everyone tried to keep the adjacent ship in view, hoping to break out of the cloud in a short time, but such intense concentration by the pilots could not be sustained for very long.

---

[4] His crew (Ellsworth's) went down 10 days after he was wounded.

My worst experience with this dangerous situation was sheer terror. We'd climbed steadily on a course to the east, attempting to clear a great rounded mass of weather ahead of us. The task force commander should have turned right or left to search for a different target, as some of our planes had reached their limit to climb in the thin air; instead, he led us on up and up until we were engulfed in the air mass of a frontal system. I had little hope of penetrating this weather system but led my high squadron on a straight, level course, although the lead squadron had disappeared completely. It was my hope that everyone would maintain a constant speed and altitude until we broke out, but the crew notified me the other planes had disappeared in the thick, murky mass.

The natural instinct is to put as much space as possible between you and the other planes. Each of us used his own technique to escape the chance of collision. Some bolted straight ahead, depending on speed to escape; others turned one way or the other, while some elected to dive away from everyone else.

No matter where we turned, there would likely be someone else in that space, so I continued straight ahead through the bumpy, white cloud—realizing there was a violent storm underneath that would make even an escape by parachute a chancy action. Just when it seemed it was time to turn or start down, we spotted dim light head, and soon we were in the clear.

The east side of the cloud formation was slightly rounded but almost vertical. Visibility was limited, but someone called out, "Bandits!" and there were, indeed, a flock of planes just ahead of us. From the type of loose flying they were doing, I guessed these were young, poorly trained Luftwaffe pilots, but we had no desire to find out for sure.

I rolled the plane over into a nearly vertical dive, remembering our mock dogfights with the Navy flyboys at Norfolk and how the B-17 could dive with wheels and flaps down to a lower level in a very short time. Because of the steep slope of the cloud mass, we soon exceeded the safe speed for wheels and flaps down, so they were retracted and I allowed our speed to increase

to the red line. The fighters made a half-hearted attempt to follow us but were soon lost to sight in the very dark, hazy atmosphere under the storm we had climbed over.

After recovering from the terrifying vertical descent, we flew
back through heavy rain without spotting our group and hoped
they had come out of the ordeal safely. Counting our losses that
evening, it was impossible to determine whether collisions in the
clouds or enemy action had caused three planes to be unaccounted for. It was a whole series of miracles that more were not
lost. Only a few planes managed to get together and rally for the
flight home. Most crews dropped on targets of opportunity or
jettisoned their bombs in fields or into the North Sea. This frugal
Vermonter carried his load back to base rather than waste it.

It was sad to see so many of our flying fortresses falling from
the sky, taking many close friends down to an unknown fate.
Many planes crashed on returning from missions for various reasons—most often, as the autumn weather worsened, for trying to
get back to base in poor visibility under low ceilings. Formations
had to break up under such conditions, creating an "every man
for himself" situation. My crew fared better than some, as we
could choose the best option from the many that were presented.
We usually returned with more than average fuel remaining, due
to our lead position, which required less jockeying of throttles
and allowed us to use more efficient power settings. One crew
chief accused me of not participating in the entire mission because I always had more fuel left than most others. I believe this
was the same crew chief who some forty years later presented me
with a bill for $400,000 for losing "his" airplane. More fuel
meant we could stay airborne longer waiting for clearer conditions or go to a field some distance away that reported better
weather.

If all else failed us, we were left with the one chance to regain
our home field, sneaking in under the low ceiling, dodging haystacks and chimneys and hoping no one else was using the same
procedure. Two or more planes homing in on the radio beacon

simultaneously would always be on a converging course although limited radio advice from the tower helped us to space ourselves.

One system that worked well for me in formation flying and conserved fuel was to let the weight of the plane do some of the work. When a pilot noticed he was falling back in formation he usually jammed on more throttle until he regained his position, but by that time he would be gaining too much, so he'd feel he had to pull the throttles way back. In addition to burning more fuel, this shortened the life of the engines. Just as the cruise control in an automobile jams the pedal to the floor after the vehicle has started up a hill, waiting until the plane is falling behind requires applying excessive power. If I was falling behind slightly, I allowed the 30-ton plane to lose a few feet of altitude, resulting in a slight gain in speed.

By the same token, overrunning the plane ahead could be remedied by climbing just a bit. A three- or four-foot change in altitude was usually all that it required to use the energy it took to raise or lower more than 30 tons. If I had to make these changes more than two or three times, I would then change the throttle setting very slightly to compensate. This was a less tiring and frustrating method of flying in formation, but no one in Operations listened to my suggestion until Colonel Rogner took over the group.

He listened, but I never knew if my idea was adopted as my unplanned departure occurred soon after.

On September 17, an invasion of Holland was carried out, involving airborne troops and paratroopers, to be followed by armored divisions and later by infantry. The operation was named "Market Garden" and was dreamed up by the unpopular British General Bernard Montgomery. He had sat all summer at the "pivot," as he called his assigned area for the invasion of Europe. The Allies committed a huge number of combat units in the hope of cutting off the Germans in the north, allowing our armies in the central and south to push on through France to the German borders.

As it turned out, our forces were landed in the midst of a powerful German army corps on maneuvers and were cut to pieces. We lost our airborne and parachute forces as well as the advantages we had expected.

Montgomery was, in my opinion, egotistical, abrasive and always insisted on taking credit for any success and blaming everyone else for failures. An example of his audacity was his remark after the Battle of the Bulge. He said it was necessary for him to go down after the battle to "tidy up" after the Americans had halted the German attack—at great loss and with no help from Montgomery.

On that morning, as hundreds of C-47s towing gliders passed overhead, I learned someone else was flying in 951 with Major Hosier, our task-force commander. It was so disappointing to be cut out of flying our old plane that I tried to get the schedule changed but I was without success. Colonel Luper got word I was making a nuisance of myself and gave the order for me to be grounded. So on the greatest day of the 8th Air Force, I sat on the ground while 11,000 planes filled the sky.

My tail, along with my wings, was clipped that day, but after we waited a long while for 951 to return, we were finally told 951 had gone down over the target. It was the only four-engined plane shot down that day, although all of the gliders and many of the C-47 tow planes were lost.

Looking ahead to October seemed to give me confidence, as I felt accepted as a better-than-average pilot by the group commanders. Most pilots came to their units with relatively little time in their type of plane. I was above average because of the extra flying time built up by my assignments in the States and, further, by flying many training missions with new crews that came to our group in England. I had gained that "money in the bank" experience and had received a few compliments from squadron commanders and one, especially, from Colonel Luper, the group commander. He was a stickler for precise formation flying and said he was impressed by my skill; no doubt for that reason I was assigned to fly with new crews to orient them toward group flight techniques.

My career as a pathfinder (radar) and squadron lead pilot had been discussed and I had agreed to return for a second tour of duty after my leave. My new bombardier and navigator had already been selected. This meant promotion to the rank of major should I be fortunate enough to complete the second tour, and it meant having an opportunity to work with the top lead navigators and bombardiers.

Events in late October were to delay my promotion to major for many years and alter my lifestyle forever.

Flack barrage on the way to the target. On the bomb run it sometimes seemed thick enough to walk on—but be careful where you step.

1944 October 7, Politz Mission

When recalling events of many years ago, the memory dims with regard to small details but the major experiences and happenings remain quite clear for those involved. Members of the aircrews of the 457th Bomb Group leading the task force in the assault on Politz will never forget the violence that took place just before the end of the bomb run. My crew had been trained in radar-bombing techniques and had several hundred hours extra flying time in the B-17, but we were all too often required to fly in a non-lead position. Usually we led the high squadron, but on October 7 my plane was leading the high flight in the lead squadron, a position that turned out to be best for observing the sequence of events for that mission.

Politz was located in Peenemunde, the center of Germany's nuclear and rocket research in East Prussia, south of the Baltic Sea. The installation stretched for 70 miles, with most facilities underground and protected by smoke screens. Oil storage and refineries essential to the center's operation were located at Politz, just to the southwest. On October 6, we were unable to see through the dense smoke at the complex, so we attacked Stargard, just to the west of our target. This meant another mission on the seventh, to carry out our assignment. The Germans prepared, as they correctly anticipated our return, by rushing hundreds more anti-aircraft guns to the area overnight by fast trains.

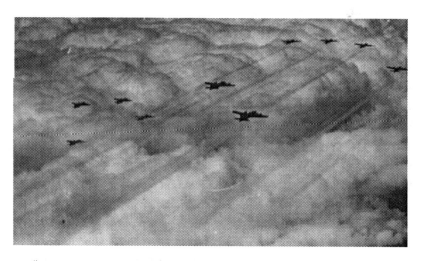

457th Bomb Group over the North Sea leaving light contrails.

Several problems troubled me during this period of our operations. My navigator-bombardier-radar operator 1st Lt. Earl Beyler was removed from my crew and was away at school. He was greatly missed, not only because of his skills with the equipment but because he was an all-around crew-confidence builder. He had been with us for nearly a year, and his extensive training was invaluable. The problem that bothered me most, though, was an operational technique that should have been adopted to improve our bombing accuracy and cut losses as well. It was simply a method of spacing the squadrons and groups by increasing the speed on the bomb run whenever we were briefed to bomb in trail. Normal approaches to a target were made in the same formation used to travel to and from the target; simply closing in the three squadrons was the only change for the bomb run.

Going into "trail" required the high squadron to drop back to follow the lead squadron while the low squadron had to slow down until it could be positioned at the rear of the group. By the time all three squadrons were in trail, the next group behind most often had run out of space. My suggestion had been to stretch out the groups in the bomber stream, giving them more time and space to get into trail. This would have avoided the piling up and over-running by the following aircraft as they attempted to space themselves going into trail at the beginning of the bomb run. This quite often led to formations ending up abreast of each other after the turn at the IP, due to the fact it was very difficult to avoid stalling because of reducing power and speed in order to assume the conformation and spacing.

At Politz, this problem was compounded by a very strong headwind as we turned at the IP to start the bomb run. The lead group was slowed by the approximately 80-mile-per-hour headwind, causing each succeeding formation to pile up behind it. In some cases, groups and squadrons had to scatter because there was no airspace behind the lead group. The succeeding groups were overrunning those ahead. As a result, we experienced an exceedingly long bomb run and a poorly organized positioning of the aircraft to achieve a decent bomb pattern. In addition to the headwind and consolidating of aircraft as they approached the bomb release point, the anti-aircraft defenses had time to put exceptionally accurate fire directly into the lead group.

During my interrogation at the Dulag in Frankfort at the end of October, a Luftwaffe officer commented on the Politz raid. He said that because of our failure on October 6 more guns were rushed to the area by high-speed trains, as the Germans anticipated our return. They also expected a larger-force attack on the nuclear research center in the area. As a result, the volume of anti-aircraft fire amounted to overkill, enough for four times the number of aircraft. This same officer remarked that their newer, more sophisticated gun batteries had indeed monitored our radar emission's with considerable success.

My crew worked very well together, keeping me informed of what was happening around us. T/Sgt. Tunstall of Worcester, Massachusetts was on his ninety-second mission. S/Sgt Maynard Judson, on his twenty-seventh mission, occupied the tail-gun position and had sharp eyes as well as the huge binoculars that were issued to us before leaving the States. These were duly collected from each crew on arrival in the U.K., causing some to suspect a scheme for profit. However, one of our crew managed to "collect" a set, and Judson used them quite effectively. None of us had ever seen such powerful binoculars. It was an option in my crew for the ball-turret gunner to roll up and open his hatch during the bomb run, as no enemy fighters ventured into the barrage of their own anti-aircraft fire. However, S/Sgt Van Tine usually preferred to observe the bomb drop as well as watching for any of our own planes that might drift under us and be struck by our bombs. He kept up a running commentary on the scene below and around us. T/Sgt Howard Lang, in the top turret, had a good view above, and it paid off one time when a stricken plane veered directly over us with its bomb-bay doors open. His timely warning gave me a chance to move away before they salvoed their bomb load.

Another policy we adhered to was for the bombardier to keep locked onto the target even if we were expected to drop on the smoke marker of the lead plane. In the event the lead plane was disabled, we had a better chance of hitting the target. After carrying a heavy load, burning all that fuel and endangering the lives of so many men, missing the target was extremely draining emotionally. For a frugal Vermonter like myself, coming from a rural area and remembering the Great Depression, wasted effort and resources was an abomination.

It was also my observation that much of the inaccuracy was due to the full use of the autopilot in conjunction with the bombsight. Turbulence could and often did cause the nose of the lead plane to pitch up, which resulted in a slight change of airspeed as a plane tends to "wallow" in the nose-up configuration—especially with a heavy load at higher altitudes. A lag in the response of the auto pilot all too often caused bombs to fall into orchards, fields and occasionally into residential areas. Not a good use of our resources. Our solution was to leave out the elevator controls of the autopilot to achieve more accurate speed control manually. This also resulted in fewer power changes, saved fuel and increased accuracy.

As we approached the target, the intense flack was concentrated on our lead group. We had never experienced such massive defensive fire. The lead squadron practically disappeared into the black cloud of smoke from the exploding shells.

Capt. Alfred Fischer in the lead plane with Col. Luper aboard, as task force commander, (the 457th was leading the 94th wing) was struck almost immediately and the number three engine began to burn while the plane slowed and began to roll to the right. As it lost speed, the lead plane drifted directly under us in the formation. We passed the stricken plane about 50 feet above the left wingtip. Within seconds, the men started bailing out. Van Tine and Judson both reported a parachute on fire and what appeared to be someone with his parachute leg straps unfastened slipping through the harness. At least three crewmen opened their chutes prematurely. Within about 30 seconds, the burning plane was directly below us and falling back rapidly. We were concerned the rest of the planes in the formation might drop onto Fischer's plane. He appeared to still be in his seat.

Several planes dropped their bombs when the deputy lead was knocked out of the formation and salvoed its load. To avoid this premature release of bombs, I had instructed our bombardier to always stay locked onto the target rather than dropping on the smoke marker of lead planes that might be damaged. If the lead planes were on fire, usually they got rid of their bombs and left the formation resulting in the following planes to release theirs in error.

The day before, at Stargard, our newly assigned bombardier, Flight Officer Robert Maitland, adhered to this practice, but at Politz, Charles Osborn stated years later that he (Osborn) was flying as "togglier" and dropped on the deputy lead's smoke bomb.

Van Tine and Judson reported on the severely damaged planes leaving formation and also that bombs would likely fall short. Meanwhile, the savage, intense anti-aircraft fire still enveloped the formation.

As we left the drop zone, an electrical failure prevented the bombardier from closing the bomb-bay doors. It was essential to clean up the plane aerodynamically as soon as possible as it was nearly a thousand miles back to base. So, our waist gunner S/Sgt. Charles Osborn came forward to assist Lang in the bomb bay to close our bomb-bay doors manually. This was a risk, as we anticipated a possible fighter attack after leaving the target area, requiring every man to be at his gun position if possible.

The scattered condition of our formation would have been inviting to the enemy, but we saw no German aircraft in the air. It was logical for us to assume the lead for the return flight, so navigator Lt. Sam Plestine, another new crew member, began his task, which he carried out very well.

It was my intention to open up space to relieve the congestion of aircraft over the target, but based on Judson's observations we maintained our customary speed so as not to leave damaged aircraft behind. By employing a technique of flying in a series of "S's," we were able to let each plane catch up to us. Van Tine reported about this time that the lead plane (Fischer's) had crashed in Stettin Bay. He saw no explosion up until this time but did observe pieces flying off the plane as it spiraled down to the bay a few miles to the west. Two chutes were seen going into the bay as well. All those who abandoned the plane did so in less than 30 seconds.

As we were leaving the Baltic Sea, there seemed to be some very large flying boats on the water. Calling Judson's attention to them, he was able to see, with his oversized binoculars, three six-engined flying boats apparently at anchor. It was up to Lt. Sam Cashman, the copilot, and T/Sgt. William Thomas with his radio magic to call for some of our escort fighters to investigate. Later, from about 100 miles away, Judson could see three fires burning on the water.

We led the formation across Denmark, managing to avoid the flack from Flensburg on our right and Kiel on our left. At my request, Plestine was working on a change of the route back to Glatton, as we realized the planned course was much longer since it would have taken us far to the north to Scotland. He advised me we could save about 25 minutes by altering the route directly to base. However, while he worked out the final navigation, we needed to hold a constant heading, which carried us slightly to the north of the track due to a lessening of the wind over the North Sea. Saving 25 minutes enabled those crews with damage or wounded men aboard to make it to base. Many were very low on fuel. Once on our new track, Sam Cashman reported we would pass close to the air/sea rescue boats, as they were on station considerably south of the original course. First Lt. Earnest Salzar probably appreciated ditching his out-of-fuel Fortress between two of those boats rather than splashing into the cold North Sea elsewhere. Salzar made a "textbook" ditching, although to me it seemed better than textbook. All the crew was saved, and the airplane did not sink; in fact, it had to be sunk a few days later, as it posed a hazard to navigation.

My plane had only minor damage, but Clayton Bejot dragged a dead engine back to base and only 4 of the 48 B-17s that left that morning returned without damage or casualties. All in all, the 17 planes lost, 106 damaged, 17 men wounded and 171 missing in action was a high price to pay for the little effect the 94th Combat Wing had on the synthetic oil plant at Politz. It was always my opinion that results could have been much improved by spacing out the aircraft for the bomb run. That, of course, was 20-20 hindsight.

There was a Wing critique the following day, attended by Wing Commander General Lacy and several West Pointers from headquarters. Considerable criticism was directed at me by the "operate-by-the-book" West Pointers for changing the route from the planned scheme to return by way of Scotland to my decision to shorten the trip by heading directly to base. When I had an opportunity to ask my accusers why they had routed us so far north, thereby lengthening our time in the air, they informed me it was not up to me to change their plans but to follow the mission briefing to the letter. Inasmuch as my group was leading the entire task force, it was all the more my duty not to deviate from the instructions of the mission briefing, they responded. They interrupted my explanation as I was describing how the tailwinds we were able to take advantage of were the only reason some of the crippled B-17s made it back at all.

They were interrupted by General Lacy who finally stood up and ended the proceedings by announcing he would have done the same thing had he been in my position. He chided my detractors for heaping the blame on me for the failure of the mission and said I should be recommended for the Silver Star. Needless to say, the West Pointers (most of them from Wing Headquarters, not from the 457th) didn't push his recommendation, nor did they make life easier for me in the 457th. "We won the war in spite of those West Pointers" was a remark we sometimes heard but, truthfully, the training at West Point was valuable especially for other branches of the service.

In retrospect, Politz should have been—and hopefully was—an expensive lesson for future operations. My crew had little time to benefit from the lessons learned, as we took our unceremonious departure from the 457th on the mission of October 25 and had the distinction of having the only plane actually lost on that day's operation. One other aircraft went down but landed behind Allied lines.

It never ceases to amaze me how so many people made themselves available, with total commitment to the war effort. The aircrews were unique because those of us in that age bracket participated in an effort never before seen and never to be seen again. Thousands of planes and tens of thousands of men in the air at one time over the continent of Europe was almost unreal and terrifying to anyone on the ground. The aircrews relied on the support people on the ground and will never forget their dedication to their responsibilities. People like Clayton Bejot, Clarence Schuchmann and myself climbed down from our Farmalls and John Deere tractors to climb into B-17's. We came from all walks of life and, for the most part, did the best we could. There were worse missions than Politz, but it stands out for us and will never fade from our memories.

The evening after the Politz debacle, we were all feeling the loss of our downed crewmen. Some turned to a few extra drinks to take the edge off while others lapsed into silence, focusing on their own thoughts. For me, following the stressful debriefing at Wing the day after, I felt the need of By's companionship, and as usual she was aware the 457th had been through some kind of ordeal. Some way, perhaps through her wartime work, word filtered through about happenings the general public wasn't supposed to know about. Without awkward expressions of sympathy, By steered our talk to pleasant things as we danced to our favorite Glenn Miller melodies. The brush of her hair against my cheek, the haunting fragrance of her perfume and the closeness of her melted away the remorse I had felt so heavily for the past two days.

We left early as she had a "surprise". Her cousin Beryl had been going with a young New Zealand airman full of exuberance, a gunner on an RAF Lancaster, and they were celebrating his twentieth birthday with a little party. We had sweet cider and sandwiches, along with the laughter the young man generated with his stories and Kiwi accent. It was apparent he had taken more of a liking to By than to his date. I had an apprehensive feeling about him that bothered me, so it didn't surprise me to learn he was shot down over Brunswick a few nights later. At times we do sense impending danger.

Six months later, we saw and recognized each other through the barbed wire fence at Mooseburg and had a chance to visit. Finally, he said, "You are going back to see By, aren't you? Do you think you might marry her?" He didn't speak of Beryl, and when I told him I had no plans for marriage, he responded, "You will make a most frightful ass of yourself if you don't, a most dreadful ass of yourself." Our conversation made it clear I was not the only one attracted to By.

By and I dated a few more times and spent quiet time at her gracious aunt's house, where I was invited to dinner once or twice. When there was a party at the base, By would come down and quite a few guys better looking than I would cut in on the dance floor. By turned out to be popular with my comrades, and she appreciated her visits to Glatton.

It would only be fair to relate following events that best described By's character. After my injury on the Cologne mission, she convinced me we could dance with my arm in a sling and we did. A few days later when she rode her bike the 12 miles from Peterborough to bring me some plums and grapes, I decided to show her I could ride my bike with one arm as well. Making a turn on the old north road in front of the base, I stalled out and began to roll backwards down off the shoulder of the road into the ditch. "You already caught my attention once when you fell down the stairs, you didn't have to perform this trick," she quipped after again checking to see if I had injured myself.

Sadly, this was to be our last meeting. We had a date for the evening of October 25, but I stood her up when we failed to return from that mission.

On the twenty-sixth, By was at work but probably wondering what had happened, so she called the chaplain at Glatton. She had met him and had told him she had started taking instruc-

tions in the Catholic Church; the chaplain had told me on the
morning of our departure on our last mission of her plans to
leave the Anglican Church. They would not put her call through
to him, so By left work and rode her bike to Glatton. There she
found the chaplain holding a requiem mass for me because the
other crews in the formation had reported only two chutes before my B-17 exploded. She went under the assumption I had
survived anyhow and soon was in contact with the Red Cross.
Without waiting for confirmation of my status she started writing
a letter each day to the Swiss Red Cross to be forwarded to me if
and when my name showed up on the list of prisoners.

Unfortunately, no mail reached me in prison camp, and her
letters were sent back to me over a year later. In 1946, I received
three bags of the letters from Switzerland.

Each letter was numbered, up to #154, but I was never able to
read more than about 30 of them before they were accidentally
destroyed. One reason for my reading so few was that she had
coded messages by an ingenious method that slowed me down.
By had two styles of handwriting: a type of finishing-school script
and normal lettering. After about the fifteenth letter, I noticed
sporadic differences in the writing. Every once in a while, a normal letter stood out in the script handwriting. Not a single
phrase had been blacked out by the censors, but she had included many bits of news I was able to bring up by writing the
odd letters down until they revealed messages that would have
been of great interest during the bleak days in prison.

One message was not coded but passed the censors without a
black mark. She managed to tell me the families at home knew
which of my crewmen had survived. In one letter, she wrote:
"The winter was not kind to my roses. The second one from the
front of the garden died as well as the fifth, the others came
through except for that last one by the gate. The third one from
the front, my favorite, should be in full bloom by early summer."
Of course, the second from the front would be my navigator, the
fifth, my faithful engineer and the last one "by the gate" would
have to be the tail gunner. Writing of the third rose was her way

of conveying her confidence that I would be well and free by early summer.

In our exchange of letters in the summer of '45, I mentioned not receiving any mail in prison although she told me she had sent a letter every day. Both of us accepted they were lost forever in the hectic last months of the war. It would cause me an everlasting sadness for not realizing the effort and clever thoughtfulness she had put into all those wonderful letters. Not knowing at the time they would appear a year later prevented me from expressing my full gratitude. By the time I learned their value and content, we had ended our relationship and gone our separate ways. So much for a wartime romance.

Missions that fall were frequent and varied. Oil and industrial targets took us to Kassel, Osnabruck, Mannheim, Merseburg, Hamm, Liepzig, Ludwigshafen, Berlin, Munster, Weimar, Kiel and many other parts of the Continent. Losses declined from fighter attacks due to acute fuel shortages and the protection of our increasing numbers of new P-51s, but as the Nazis withdrew into Germany, their thousands of anti-aircraft batteries became concentrated. This led to more intense barrages brought to bear on the attacking Allied bombers with not only huge numbers being shot down, but aircraft returning with substantial damage and more and more casualties being brought back in need of medical treatment. The workload of the ground crews repairing our B-17s was compounded, and the hospitals had their hands full as well. Many wounded crewmen were evacuated to the States for long hospital stays. The higher attrition rate was offset to a degree by an increased flow of replacements both of planes and personnel, but the losses of well-trained, experienced crews and machines added to the appalling cost of our operations.

1944 October 14, Mission to Cologne

Air reconnaissance over Germany in early October showed a huge buildup of thousands of tanks, trucks and heavy weapons in the streets of Cologne. This intelligence was ominous news to the ground forces racing toward the German border not only due to the threat of a strong counter-attack but also because the city of Cologne and its civilian population were being used to shield these huge stores of material. The decision was made to warn the people that these supplies would be destroyed along with the city unless the German military removed them from the city streets. Leaflets were dropped and warnings were sent by every means in an effort to spare the loss of life that would result from the bombings.

The 8th Air Force commanders and British Bomber Command were forced to make a dreaded decision. The Allied air forces were to bomb day and night for four days until the war material and the city were destroyed. We hoped the civilians had evacuated, as the great stores of fuel and munitions in the city added to the inferno caused by our bombs. Only the blackened twin spires of Cologne Cathedral were still standing after the prolonged blitz. The German military had to bear the responsibility for the disaster.

My crew flew only the first day of the four-day destruction of the city due to a piece of shrapnel that blew through the side of the plane and into my upper arm. An unusual sequence of events saved my arm and my life as well. Partway through the bomb run, turbulence from planes ahead caused me to turn the control wheel to the right to level the plane. A burst of flack went off just to our left front. My left arm was raised just enough to be in line with the trajectory of the shrapnel. As a result, my arm was free to move when the small projectile knocked it up and away from the wheel. If my hand had not been on the wheel, my arm would have been held against my side and probably been broken as it could not have "given," as it were.

Our fairly new flack suits were open at the sides under the armpits, providing protection only to the frontal area of the body. If I had had to correct the attitude of the plane by turning the wheel to the left, my arm would not have been hit, but the shrapnel would have gone through the open side of the flack suit and probably penetrated deep into my body. If the plane had not needed any correction, my left arm would have been in a position to protect my body but would have suffered much greater damage. As a result, the injury proved to be minor compared to the serious wounds many crewmen had suffered.

The redhot piece of metal came through the side of the plane just under the side window and was about the size and shape of a section of tangerine. My copilot Sam Cashman, always the joker, pushed his mike button and said, "Hah! You flinched!" As the bombs were almost ready to drop, it was a matter of just steadying the plane for a few seconds before having Sam take over while I assessed the damage to the left wing and engines. It was obvious my condition was not serious, but the hot metal burned painfully. The shrapnel had entered my upper arm on the underside, slid around the bone and lodged in the bicep. Sam soon looked over at me after I told him to take control for a while and asked if that was blood coming out of my sleeve. "No, just some of that catsup we put on those awful powdered eggs this morning."

As we were leading the high squadron, positioned just to the right and above the lead squadron, it was awkward for Sam to see well enough from the right seat, so I flew with my right arm while Sam manipulated the throttles and whatever else was required. Once over the Channel, I moved my squadron off to one side so Sam could relieve me. The number 2 engine had been running rough and finally began to smoke and shake, so we elected to shut it down. Fortunately, no one else was injured and none of our other planes were lost.

After a four-hour flight back to base, I was taken to a nearby hospital in Cambridge, where the piece of shrapnel was removed from my arm. The nurse I'd asked to call my girlfriend forgot to do so, leaving me in a poor bargaining position for the next date. By left the next day to visit her parents at their farm out in the country, thinking I had stood her up. But we were able to get together a few more times before I was to stand her up again.

There was one more unusual happening near the beginning of the mission. On October 14 a cold, wet fog was on the ground at Glatton. Everything was dripping wet, and in the early morning darkness it was easy to become disoriented just going to the next building. At briefing, the weathermen reluctantly told us the thick weather extended to 26,000 feet over East Anglia so our assembly altitude would be at 27,000 feet. To get thousands of planes up through over five miles of thick weather required precise piloting on the part of air crews and a very complex organizing within the 8th Bomber command to orchestrate the departure of the air fleet from dozens of airfields—without collisions if possible. The control of this traffic was a massive undertaking.

The procedure, basically, was to have all planes climb to 13,500 feet (in this case), one half the distance to the assembly altitude. At this point, a right turn would be executed to return over each group's field. This maneuver was facilitated by homing in on a radio beacon at home base. Theoretically, all should arrive in proper sequence over the home field at the assembly altitude, the space in the clear above the cloud tops. Unfortunately, there were occasional collisions that usually were fatal to both crews due to the huge explosion of all the fuel and bombs. When I was at Alconbury at the end of June, there was a collision during assembly in extremely bad weather. The flash of the explosion lit up the clouds, but we could see nothing until parts of the planes started falling out of the clouds onto the airfield.

The success of this method depended on the most precise adherence to a procedure entailing identical airspeed, a constant heading of 30 degrees, and adhering to a rate of climb of 500 feet a minute. This was followed by a "standard rate turn" at the halfway point of the climb where we took up a reciprocal heading of 210 degrees. Planes from each group were spaced 30 seconds apart, and the location of each field determined the distance between the flight paths.

In other words, planes from Alconbury were seven miles behind us while those from Polebrook paralleled our course four miles to our left. Any deviation from these fixed flight paths could place two planes in the same airspace. If a plane lost an engine on the climb, the pilot had two choices. He could use more power from the other three engines to maintain his speed and rate of climb in hope of reaching the clear air at 27,000 feet before another engine failed, or he could break off and fly away from the assembly area, hoping there would not be another plane maneuvering in the murky clouds.

It is impossible to fly blind in weather for any length of time without an airspeed indicator. On this morning as we started our 180-degree turn, at 13,500 feet, my airspeed indicator went down to zero. The pitot tubes had frozen, blocking off the flow of air. A quick check showed us the heater switches were on, and after a search by the engineer in the cramped space under the pilot's compartment, we learned the fuse had blown and there were no replacements. By interpolating information from the other instruments and adding power periodically, I managed to maintain our rate of climb. We entered the thinner air as we climbed, and the throttles eventually hit the stops, at which point we advanced our turbo superchargers to maintain power.

We broke out on top in the vicinity of the first planes that were circling the homer beacon, but realizing I could not lead a squadron without knowing my airspeed, I flew off to the south and away from the clusters of planes. To abort the mission would lead to consequences on the ground, but to fly a heavily loaded B-17 through weather and land with any degree of safety without an airspeed indicator would be an awesome endeavor. However, luck was with us. About 60 miles south, toward London, was a bowl-shaped depression in the clouds, so, gambling that the temperature (and moisture) would be in our favor, I dove down into the depression. At the very bottom, about 7,000 feet, the temperature reached the freezing mark, and after we circled for a time, the airspeed indicator flickered and slowly came up. Now the problem was to climb back up, at great expense of fuel and time in hopes of catching the 457th Group. It was also necessary to avoid any clouds, as a bit of moisture would freeze us up again.

The point of departure for the bomber stream from the U.K. was at Great Yarmouth on the coast of East Anglia. Our task was to intercept our 457th and take over the lead of the high squadron before it was beyond our reach. A group of 36 planes passed the departure point every 30 seconds—about one-and-a-half miles apart. After identifying our group, we had to join the formation by intercepting it at the proper angle. Our navigator had to figure out a course that would put us abreast of our own group. We had to arrive at a point over the North Sea where our group would be at precisely the same time. Arriving too early, we would not be able to fly a circle, as that would take too long and they would be past our point of interception. Arriving too late might mean never catching up, as we could not expend the extra fuel.

Our navigator did a magnificent piece of work, and we intercepted our group perfectly, but my deputy had assumed the lead and didn't want to give it up. Of course, there was radio silence, so after numerous hand signals (all ignored), I pulled up in front of him and squeezed him out. If I had aborted the mission, there would have been much paperwork, but it wouldn't have been just my arm that was in a sling.

Aborting a mission in the 457th could get another part of your anatomy in a sling.

Colonel Luper never wanted to accept an abort, and anyone who did one was in for a humiliating experience and might have one or two missions added to his tour. On one occasion, a pilot elected to abort a mission because his ball-turret gunner had been caught between his steel entry door and the ring gear that allowed the turret to revolve. Before he had time to get fully into his position, the turret started to revolve, forcing his face against the ring gear. His face was being torn off by the gears. The two waist gunners quickly held the turret and kept it from turning, using a machine gun barrel, until power could be cut off. The pilot returned to base because the crew determined the injured man would bleed to death if they continued on the long 10-hour mission. In addition, there was no way to give the man oxygen with his cheeks torn off.

Luper met the plane in his jeep as it rolled to a stop and proceeded to chew out the pilot, who was preoccupied with getting his crewman on his way to a hospital. The crew of an aborted mission had its photograph taken on landing, and there was much paperwork to fill out. According to the colonel, a pilot should check out his plane so thoroughly before takeoff that there could be no chance of any systems failing. Luper told him he should have parachuted the man out to be taken care of by whoever found him. This was the most absurd statement we ever heard from the colonel. Common sense would say the man might not be found in time—if ever. He could have landed in the swamps or in water and, at any rate; he might have bled to death even if someone did find him out in the country.

Had it been me, as soon as the colonel stopped for breath, I would have swung the plane around, taken off and tagged onto a group somewhere over the North Sea to complete the mission. I never did find out what happened to the young man, but it must have taken years to reconstruct his face[5].

Problems with military correctness, protocol and politics naturally affected me adversely because of my very unmilitary stance. Our group had wonderful and dedicated leaders, but there were some individuals who resented my having more flying time to my credit and especially took offense to my flying missions with other groups.

More than once, I was threatened with charges of being AWOL, (absent without leave) when I volunteered to fly radar planes with other groups. As soon as I learned I was standing down—not flying with the 457th—I made myself available, as it seemed a way to get sufficient missions to complete my tour sooner. Some of my crew had been flying with other crews before the rest of us arrived at Glatton, so they had a head start on me. Even though I duly signed out and had tentative permission from the group commander to be absent when not scheduled to fly, there was considerable harassment from my detractors.

---

[5] On October 25, an unusual incident took place. One of the ground personnel, for reasons unknown, stowed away on a plane that was departing on a mission. The pilot reported it and was advised to continue with the mission and supply the man with an oxygen mask and flying clothes, as each plane carried a large bag with spare items. As the plane reached 19,000 feet, the stowaway jettisoned the waist door and jumped out without a parachute.

After I was shot down, some of my records were not forwarded back to the States, and although carefully itemized by friends, my personal effects were never seen again. Someone was lax in his duties or deliberately left parts of my records out. My footlocker holding my uniforms, many photos, letters, mementos along with my quite-expensive bicycle had added up to the sum total of my worldly possessions.

1944 October 25, The Longest Mission

On October 24, 1944, I went off DNIF (duty not involving flying) back on to flight status after ten days of recuperation from the shrapnel wound in my upper arm, a memento of the mission to Cologne on October 14.

Relaxing and writing letters until almost midnight, I had just decided to get some rest when a jeep pulled up to the door and a very polite sergeant said, "You are on alert to fly tomorrow's mission, if you feel up to it." This was not the usual procedure, but I appreciated the concern for my physical condition. We were all aware that the group was very short of crews due to heavy losses in recent raids. I felt "up to it."

Breakfast, as I remember, was terrible—worse than awful! The powdered eggs and catsup had a slight petroleum taste. I was never one to complain but thought it OK to bring it to the cook's attention. In the same light-hearted manner (for one o'clock in the morning), he promised me pancakes and real Vermont maple syrup "next time."

But there was not to be a next time for me at Glatton Station.

After getting my gear ready and removing the names of some of my crew members from the schedule (one of them, Tech Sergeant Tunstall, had flown 84 missions), I went to the final briefing. It looked like a fairly routine mission, a strike at the port of Hamburg.

Aircraft No. 42-97951, the one assigned to me at Langley Field, Virginia on my twenty-first birthday (what a present!), had had 16 hour's ferry time and 4 hour's shake-down when we left for the United Kingdom via Gander, Newfoundland to Holyhead, Wales. It was a beautiful radar-equipped pathfinder plane with all the latest gadgets installed. My navigator-bombardier-radar operator and best friend Lt. Earl Beyeler checked out the performance of the equipment and the flying qualities with me, and we were as pleased as if we had a lifetime title to No. 951. However, once we arrived overseas, everyone else wanted it as well and I was nearly court martialed for refusing to give it up at each base where I landed. Generals and colonels all insisted they needed the pathfinder-equipped aircraft, as they were fairly new and scarce at the time.

My crew and I were well-trained in radar techniques and had orders to proceed to the 457th Bomb Group station to which we were assigned. It was a real letdown to report to Glatton without our new, super-equipped B-17, but it was reassigned to the 457th in early August. On September 17, 1944, No. 951 was shot down in the invasion of Holland, with Major Hozier flying as task-force commander with another pilot. Eleven thousand aircraft took part in the day's operation, and because I had argued to fly my own plane the Group commander had, in effect, grounded me for the day, so I had to stand down during the largest air operation since "D" day. However, I lived to fly again.

The aircraft assigned to us on October 25 was 42-97899. I conducted the pre-flight inspection with my flight engineer T/Sgt Howard Lang and the ground-crew chief as well as the communications and armament people until we were satisfied with the condition of the plane. It was in excellent shape, nearly new, so we took off and climbed up through 23,000 feet of fog and weather to assembly altitude, where I assumed my position in the formation as leader of the high squadron.

As we approached the island of Helgoland, just north of the German coast, we turned right, according to the briefed route that would take us along the east side of the Weser River estuary. We saw the usual flack coming up from Helgoland, letting us know the enemy was awake, but it was too far away to bother us.

Our penetration of enemy territory was through reported light defenses over a cloud cover—according to weather forecasts—at about 2,200 feet. This cloud cover obscured the coastline, and when I observed the first anti-aircraft fire from the mainland, it appeared to be eight to ten miles ahead and dead level with the groups flying in front of us but considerably to the right of our flight path. Another four bursts of heavy caliber fire appeared dead ahead of our aircraft, and as I was flying to the right of and somewhat higher than the lead squadron led by Capt. Bill Doherty, I moved the squadron slightly to the left to avoid subsequent fire.

Meanwhile we were conducting an oxygen check. I had advised the crew there was flack at our level at 12 o'clock. "Check your flack suits and oxygen and acknowledge, please." Just as the tail-gunner, S/Sgt. Maynard Judson acknowledged, three bursts of flack appeared immediately in front of us and the fourth burst struck between the No. 3 and No. 4 engines, blowing a large hole in the leading edge of the right wing approximately three feet by six feet and back into the wing as far as the main spar.

A small fire with a peculiar blue-green flame started in the No. 4 engine. We expended our fire extinguisher on the fire with very little effect. I found I had no control over the two starboard engines, with No. 4 revving to the red line and No. 3 shaking violently in the engine supports. The engineer called out, "The whole right wing is on fire." And indeed, the fuel tanks were burning so intensely that we could see the internal structure of the wing glowing red. No. 3 engine was bending down, and vibration soon tore it loose from the mounts.

Realizing there was no way to save the aircraft, I called my deputy leader and asked him to move the squadron above and to the left of us to avoid any of my crew striking the other planes in the squadron as they bailed out. I had just hit the bail-out bell and told the crew to leave the aircraft when the No. 3 engine and right landing gear fell away. Pieces of metal from the debris struck S/Sgt. Osborn, cutting his face as he bailed out the waist door.

Hoping everyone had left the airplane, I attempted to turn out of the formation, but the maneuver turned into a roll and a horizontal spiral due to No. 4 engine running wild and uncontrollable. I pushed No. 1 to full throttle in an attempt to balance No. 4; No. 2 had shut down.

Lack of oxygen was beginning to blur my vision. I no longer had any control of the plane and was attempting to leave my seat when the plane went into a steep climb. This caused heat from the fire in the bomb bay to rise into the cockpit, and although there was no fire around me the heat was becoming unbearable. The paint on the instrument panel was already blistering, and I thought it was all over, for sure.

When the aircraft reached a vertical nose-up attitude, all power stopped abruptly. The plane started falling tail first. Then it exploded—violently.

Approximately two-and-one-half minutes had elapsed since we were hit by the burst of anti-aircraft fire. It was generally agreed that a B-17 would explode in about 40 seconds after being on fire.

I lost consciousness from the concussion but had the sensation of being ejected out the right side of the cockpit and remember feeling the intense cold.

After falling about two miles, I came to my senses. My immediate concern was the condition of my parachute; I anticipated that it might have caught fire or been damaged in the explosion. Reaching around to examine the backpack, I was greatly relieved that although my leather jacket and flight suit were badly torn, the chute seemed to be intact. There was a light coating of ice on me, no doubt caused by the sudden change from the intense heat to the minus 50 degrees below 0 outside. The layer of ice began to fly off in the wind my fast fall was generating. I was bleeding from several cuts and could hear absolutely nothing.

Some people have the misconception a person falling from great heights would "be dead before hitting the ground." The sensation of falling lasts only during the time a body is accelerating. After that it is a feeling of being supported by a strong rush of air. I had missed that initial feeling of falling because of my momentary loss of consciousness.

I was falling "like a log"—on my back, without spinning or tumbling—and, looking about, I could see both the east and west coasts of Denmark on my left and the Zeider Zee and Friesian Islands in Holland stretching out to the western horizon on my right. Because the plane had no forward motion when it exploded, the debris was falling with and around me.

The entire tail-section of the plane was tumbling slowly, due to its comparative light weight for its size, about a mile higher. The bright yellow eight-man life raft had inflated and was floating down another half a mile above the tail-section.

Directly above was the left wing, with both engines and the bomb bay still attached to it. The bombs, which had not been armed, were still in the bomb bay. They were completely exposed and formed a pivot around which the wing was spinning quite rapidly, much like a maple seed spiraling down on its own wing.

The control cables, with the bell cranks still attached, were whirling around outside the 200-foot circle transcribed by the wing and would have created another obstacle for my parachute if I opened it. There were also other pieces of the plane that could damage the chute if it was open. The main part of the right wing was falling about a half mile away, still burning, and leaving a long trail of oily, dark smoke.

Remembering we had been briefed that the cloud layer over the coast was at about 2,000 feet, I decided to roll over and look at it, to help judge my altitude and determine how much time I had remaining to safely open my chute. Up to this point, I had had nearly complete control, but in turning over there was some unpleasant tumbling and I had difficulty breathing in the wind rushing past. I was, however, able to see the cloud layer and felt I would have a little more time to give the spinning wing a chance to drift off to one side or the other so my parachute could pass through without becoming entangled in the control cables or other debris.

Somehow, I had managed to monitor the time but had mistakenly calculated my time to reach the ground at about two-and-a-half minutes although it actually took less than two minutes.

The wing was at this time less than 200 feet above me when, suddenly, I passed through the cloud layer and could see tree branches and a dark brown landscape. I pulled the ripcord with the feeling it was too late, but it functioned perfectly and I struck the ground almost immediately.

The parachute was a backpack that I had worn all the time in the plane. It had a 28-foot canopy, in contrast to a chest type that had to be buckled on when needed and was only 24 feet in diameter. The extra width of my chute, no doubt, saved my life by slowing me down quickly so close to the ground.

Although it was instantaneous, I felt the sequence of events as I hit the ground feet first with tremendous force. My shoulders struck my knees, dislocating both shoulders. My face hit the ground, causing a severe and permanent neck injury, while the jolt of the impact did considerable damage to all my joints and caused some internal injuries.

The wing with the bomb bay still attached landed some 200 feet away and was burning quite intensely as fuel drained down out of the wing, which was tilted at an angle against some trees. Other debris was still falling into the three-acre clearing in a woods where trees had been cut and left lying on the ground. The tail section of the plane floated down with an oscillating motion and landed in the upper parts of some pine trees several minutes later.

Usually when a large plane exploded, the debris would be scattered over a five- to six-mile path on the ground, due to the forward momentum of the plane and its contents. In my case, the plane had no forward speed as it was falling tail first when it disintegrated, causing the parts of the plane, me and the body of Howard Lang, the engineer, to land in a small area. Had I successfully opened the chute at a few thousand feet, it would have carried me perhaps miles away from the crash site.

The impact stunned me for a time, but the heat from the fire and the realization the bombs could go off when they got hot enough motivated me to begin the painful process of getting out of the parachute harness with two dislocated shoulders. My back pained me so much I believed it was broken, but it was due to damage to several vertebrate. Somehow, I crawled out and was sliding and rolling toward a little wood road nearby, when I saw a body lying face down in a small space between parts of the wreckage. It was Lang. He had not opened his parachute, possibly due to injuries from shrapnel or not having cleared the plane when it exploded.

After identifying him, I continued my awkward travel away from the burning aircraft, and upon reaching the little wood road completely exhausted, I used my feet to push myself across the roadway into a shallow ditch on the other side. The intense pain triggered my memory enough that I realized there was morphine in my survival kit. With difficulty, I opened the surret and gave myself a shot. The bombs went off perhaps 10 minutes later, uprooting and knocking over trees. I was unable to breathe for a time, because the blast created tremendous pressure followed by a vacuum as it pushed and rolled me through the underbrush. I experienced excruciating pain in my lungs and stomach. When air rushed back into the vacuum, it dragged me back through the underbrush but, thankfully, enabled me to breath again.

As I slowly recovered from this second explosion of the day, my hearing returned in my right ear, although I was experiencing a severe headache and considerable distress from my other injuries. Two boys, about 16 years of age, were making their way toward me, one with black hair and the other blond. The blond boy reached me first and tried to shake hands with me. By this time my shoulders, elbows and knees were badly swollen and very painful. Shaking hands was not what I needed at that time.

"I'm a Dutchman," he said in fair English. I knew we were not in Holland, but I asked him anyway, "Is this Holland?" The black-haired boy, probably a member of the Hitler Youth, answered arrogantly, "Nein! das ist Deutschland!"

On a hill about three-quarters of a mile away, was a hospital, a convalescent home for burn victims from Hamburg. There was an inspection party there that day, and some of them had watched the pieces of the airplane falling into the wood through the overcast. They had not seen my parachute as it had opened at tree-top level, and from experience they had learned not to approach shot-down bombers until the bombs had exploded or until they were fairly certain there were no bombs aboard.

A tall, very homely man in some type of uniform, probably Home Guard, approached me down the old wood road, slowing down as he struggled to get a large pistol out of its holster. He held the gun ahead of him and came up very close to me until the barrel of the gun was in my face. The man was shaking, obviously quite frightened, and I expected he would pull the trigger either by accident or by intention. "Pistol! Pistol!" he shouted with a trembling chin. I rarely carried my .45 and also advised my crew not to do so. If one crew member shot either a civilian or one of the military it would mean the death sentence for the rest of us. When he was satisfied I was unarmed, he uncocked his gun.

A party of about 20 people started down the hill after the bombs went off. The first people to reach me called me names and yanked me to a sitting position in the road, kicked me repeatedly and when they had knocked me over, stomped on me. Some of them shouted with sarcasm and anger, "Liberator! Terrorflieger! Gangster bastard!" while others kept asking, "Anglis? Anglis?" A woman pushing her bike close by said, "Don't tell them you are English, even if you are, or they will hang you." An old man with a long club struck me in the nose just as some of the military arrived and drove off the civilians at gunpoint. I do not remember the trip up the hill because of the hard blow to the nose, but I do remember my arrival there.

The Burgomeister punched me in the face and rifled my pockets as they searched me. They left me in the switchboard office, sitting on the floor where four or five girls were working while the guards looked in at me through the open door every few minutes. They could see I wasn't up to escaping!

One girl cleaned the blood from my face, and another one gave me tea. She hid the cup in a drawer when an officer came in to return my billfold and rosary, which the Burgomeister had taken. Two medics finally put my shoulders back in place after a struggle and excruciating pain. They put a tight band around my upper arms to hold the shoulders in place.

Finally, after I got them to understand what I needed, two guards took me to a bathroom, where I required assistance because of my painful shoulders. It was then I discovered my hard landing had caused a rectal prolapse, a rather bloody sight that sent one of the guards scurrying away to get the medics again. Another, more painful, procedure took place while the guards, both very young, looked on wide eyed as the two medics struggled with the biggest case of hemorrhoids they had ever seen. I don't really think they tried to be unnecessarily harsh, but it was not a thing I would ever want to go through again.

This was followed by a perfunctory interrogation by an officer who explained how we were shot down by a new gun battery that monitored the emissions from our radar and synchronized the guns to lock on to a lead plane and fire when the range was optimal. The lead plane showed up as a clear blip on the radar screen. Now I knew why lead pilots drew straws or flipped a card to see who would lead the next day's mission.

How I wished there were a way to let them know about this new system. A telephone call back to England would have saved lives, but I didn't have the dime—or fenning, whatever they used . We knew they could read our radar emissions, but it was news to me that they had been able to tie into the aiming and firing of the guns.

They told me my crew members had come down about 20 miles away and would be brought to the hospital. They arrived there in a large open car at about dusk. They had been captured by farmers, one of whom had two sons in a prison camp in the United States, so they were well treated and not badly injured. We were all taken to a jail several miles away on a flat-bed truck. None of us felt welcome at that hospital that cared for the burn victims of our target for the day.

I knew Lang was dead, and an officer told me the tail gunner's body (Sgt. Judson) had been removed from the tail section, which had landed in the treetops several minutes after the main part of the wreckage had come down. He had apparently been killed by shrapnel. The fate of Lt. Plestine, the navigator, was unclear, but one of the guards later asked me if he was the one with "the ring," saying he had been killed. Plestine had always worn a Jewish ring, in spite of repeated warnings as to what might happen if he were captured. Later comments by guards led me to believe he was killed by civilians a few miles from the crash site. In my case, had the military not intervened, I'm certain I wouldn't have survived the worst beating of my life.

My condition left me too weak that evening to give my crew a "pep talk" on surviving what lay ahead of them. Some of them had been with me for nearly a year, and I had love and admiration for all of them. I fervently wished their fate could have been avoided and their families spared the anguish they were about to experience.

Nevertheless, all who survived the shooting down also survived the prison camps, even though the enlisted men worked under inhumane conditions and endured a long march in winter under much worse conditions than the rest of us.

It was very difficult for me to climb up onto the flat-bed truck they were using to transport us. My back, right knee and swollen joints restricted my movements, but the guards provided incentives. Two armed guards rode with us while a third sat up front with the driver. There were no sideboards on the truck and just a light layer of old straw that did little more for us than blow into our faces. We wondered how the driver kept the old truck on the road in the darkness without lights of any kind. After about a half hour, we arrived at a local jail—a dimly lit two-story building where they separated us, with much guttural shouting and shoving in the dark.

My room, on the second floor, was about six feet by nine, with a high ceiling and no furniture. There was a platform on one side for a bunk that had no mattress, only a thin, ragged blanket. Near the ceiling was a small window. The door had a peephole so the guards could check on the occupant. An electric heater was attached to a wall. A pail was placed near the door, completing the facilities.

I lay on the bunk, shivering, until the heater came on and stayed on for about 20 minutes, making the small room uncomfortably hot. Then it clicked off, and soon it was very cold again. This went on all night while I took an assessment of my condition.

My nose was so badly smashed from the old man's club that I couldn't breathe except through my mouth, a painful process because I wasn't used to it, and my throat was raw due to breathing in some of the superheated air in the plane just before the explosion.

All my joints were swollen and my back gave me no relief regardless of any position I tried to assume. With my painful shoulders and neck, it was impossible to sleep. The on-and-off heat seemed to be a contrived means of adding to discomfort and worried me that it might cause pneumonia. While the heater was on, I tried to keep on top of the blanket, and when it began to get cold again I tried to keep it on top of me. A pillow of some kind would have helped position my neck better, but there would be no pillow for me for many months.

1944 October 26, Missing in Action

By noon the next day, hunger set in. It had been some 32 hours since I'd had any food or anything to drink except the bit of tea the girl in the office had offered me. Finally, a guard brought another pail; this one held a container of tea and another one of barley soup. He took the other pail out, and although it was somewhat repulsive to have tea and soup delivered in the toilet bucket (in separate containers, thank heaven), the soup tasted delicious to me and the tepid tea was welcome.

Soon after dark, with much loud talk and noise, we were assembled together and stood outside for some time, waiting for another truck, which delivered us to the outskirts of the city of Bremerhaven. As we marched toward the railway station, an angry crowd surrounded us and demanded the guards turn us over to them. They were very noisy and frightened our four guards until they leveled their guns at the crowd and tried to out-shout them. They finally moved us into the station, where other civilians threatened us but were restrained with the help of local police. It was understandable the people should hate us because of the bombings they had endured for five years, but they didn't seem to comprehend the suffering of people in other countries bombed by Germany. It made no difference to them that they had started the war with overwhelmingly violent tactics against civilians in every country they invaded.

A short time later, an air-raid warning sounded, and everyone moved to shelter under the station although no bombs fell nearby. One of my men saw a man who looked like a doctor, well dressed and carrying a black case. One of the guards went to him at our request and brought him back. He was a French doctor, a prisoner of the Germans for four years, but because his family was in Paris they sent him to new assignments without escort as he knew they could retaliate against his family if he tried to escape.

He taped up my body to give support to my back and made a makeshift collar for my neck and a harness for my shoulders out of materials he sent a guard to fetch. A superficial cut on my scalp and across my right eye and cheekbone required only perfunctory attention, but he did leave me with some pills and something for my rectal injury. When he had finished with me and a quick check of my crewmembers, he wrote a letter for me to give to someone down the road requesting further treatment.

He had to leave abruptly to catch his train, and although a German civilian interpreted for us, no one got his name—a circumstance that bothered me ever after. This man was a wonderful human being, living under great stress and deserving of some recognition for his timely aid to me. The letter, written in French, was torn up and thrown into the wastebasket during my interrogation.

The train taking us to Frankfort, to the interrogation center Dulag Luft, was made up of old coaches, but they were clean and our car had only my crew and two guards—one of them quite young—about 16 years old. He was eager to talk about the U.S. with his very limited English, and he drew pictures of planes with their speeds, range and armament. It surprised me to see how much he knew about planes and the U.S. He even drew a fairly accurate map of the country on the steamy window of the car.

Progress was slow down the Rhine valley as it was necessary to monitor Allied air activities and either avoid cities or race through them while no air raids were reported in the vicinity.

At Frankfort, they transferred us to an old trolley car and, after much counting of the six of us, we were marched to the Dulag. With the usual shouting and shoving, they placed us in separate cells much like the jail we had been in first. Mine was a small room with a bunk, the same type of high-up window, peephole door and a ragged blanket on a worn-out burlap mattress containing a small amount of old straw and probably thousands of lice. It was 24 hours before anything happened—more barley soup, some hard black bread and tea. One trip to the bathroom a day was allowed, with an old man with an even older rifle watching us. Solitary confinement when you are in pain and have no idea what was coming next is not something one gets used to right away. Trying to move about for a bit of exercise tired me quickly, but it was impossible to sleep more than short periods due to the discomfort of aches and pains. To pass the time, I decided to review my life; all 21 years used up about half an hour.

1944 October 28, Interrogation

The second day, a rough-looking soldier pounded on the door with his rifle butt before unlocking it to take me for the first round of interrogation. In an office behind a large desk with many papers displayed, was a Luftwaffe captain who introduced himself as Ernst Hauptmann.

I had only given my name and rank, but he proceeded to tell me all about myself—where I trained in the States, the date we arrived in Wales, my bomb group and information about my friends. He told me Colonel Luper, my commanding officer, had a 1940 Buick sedan at the base at Glatton. When he asked me what significance 341 Keystone Street had for me (By's address), I wondered if my surprise registered in my expression.

I was standing—in my torn shirt and bloody pants, nose plugged with dried blood, joints still swollen—in front of the immaculately dressed officer.

Trying not to be surprised or expressing any sign of disbelief, I was amazed to hear so many accurate details. Finally, he asked me if I cared to know if my friend Ellsworth had survived his shoot-down. When he had no answer from me, he opened a folder and laid out several files with the names of acquaintances printed in large letters on the cover. One of them already had my name on it.

His tactic changed after a half hour with no acknowledgements from me. He slammed the files down and yelled, "I can only assume you are not First Lieutenant John Angier since you don't know any of these men and don't know what bomb group you are from. That leaves us no alternative but to consider you a spy or a saboteur." With that, he motioned to the guard to take me out—for all I knew, to execute me as a spy.

Two days later, I was taken back to a silent officer who had two apples, a pack of American cigarettes and two cigars on his desk. Without a word, he peeled one apple and ate it very slowly while staring intently at me as I stood in great discomfort—still breathing through my mouth. He took no note of my humiliating appearance but proceeded to slice the ends off of the cigar before lighting it and tilting back in his chair to enjoy it. There was no way I was going to tell him I was a nonsmoker. Suddenly he tipped his chair back down and shouted this was my last chance to identify myself. He shoved a document with Red Cross printed across the top toward me and ordered me to read it. It had all the information about my crew and the 457th Group and assurance that the Red Cross had to have me sign it in order to identify me and get word to my family of my circumstances. Hauptmann was furious when I refused to sign it. He ap-

proached to within inches of my face, shouting loudly and spray-
ing saliva and the odor of cigar smoke on me while he threatened
all kinds of bad things that would happen to me.

This went on for days, but one morning he provided me with
a chair and offered me a cigarette while he pulled down a map of
Hamburg to show me where his house "had been," even hinting
he had lost his family as well. Then I asked questions about my
dead crewmen: where were they buried, what caused their deaths
and any information about them I could take and keep with me.
He began to bargain, offering to trade information I desired in
exchange for my signature on the "Red Cross" paper.

That night, in my isolation, many thoughts went through my
mind. It didn't seem likely they would keep me here indefinitely;
if I signed the paper, however, I might be penalized when and if I
returned home. "Name, rank and serial number only" had been
drilled into us in case of capture.

My interrogator still threatened me with the spy thing and
had asked me about Major Rod Francis, who had been shot
down in France, made his way back by way of Spain and received
special permission to fly again[6]. Francis and Chuck Yeager were
the only two I know of to resume flying over the Continent after
evading capture. Anyone who had worked with or been helped
by the French underground would face terrible consequences if
captured, as the Germans used any means to get names of underground members. They employed torture that could get any
human being to talk.

"We are waiting for him and will extract much information
from him before he dies as a spy," warned Hauptmann, in an
effort to make me cooperate.

They had thrown away the letter from the French doctor that
explained what medical attention should be given me, and had

---

[6] In April of 1945, Major Francis was shot down again over Berlin but nursed
his B-17 eastward toward the Russian lines. His crew was captured, but at
that stage of the war, with the Nazis in full retreat, prisoners were practically
abandoned. Francis and his crew were liberated by the Russians and eventually made their way back to England.

left me in the lice-infested cell with very little food. Of course, none of us expected treatment that even German civilians were denied, nor did we anticipate a country-club environment as captured Allied airmen. All this, I reasoned, was their way of trying to get me to sign: keep me in the most uncomfortable circumstances and hope to glean a bit more information. Even inconsequential additions to their files could be added together to reveal overlooked items and substantiate remarks by other POWs.

After studying the document next morning, I concluded there was nothing in it he had not already shown me from his files. Also, he had a draft of a letter for me concerning my crew members. While I hesitated, he asked me what our target had been that day. "It was where the bombs fell," I answered. We shook hands, and on his word as an officer that he was to have the letter for me next morning, I signed the paper.

Next morning, a different officer was in the office. He exploded when I asked for the letter. "I am in charge now, and there will be no letter!" he shouted. "I want my letter or that paper I signed given back to me," I said, adding, "I should have known better than to trust a German officer." Realizing I had been had, I made the mistake of bringing up the "officer's word is his bond" rule and vented the feelings that had been building up in me during the past nine days of playing their games. Before I finished expressing what I thought of German military courtesy, the bull-necked, fat, mean man from the Stone Age signaled the two guards, who slammed me onto the floor and began to roll me up in the filthy carpet filled with sand and other refuse that had been tracked in.

With my arms pinned against my sides, wrapped tightly in the carpet, with no air, as the ends of the material folded down on each end, I began to gasp and struggled to breathe. All I managed was to inhale sand, dirt and the taste of the carbolic acid they had used to disinfect the carpet. My nose was still plugged up, my eyes filled with dirt, and the taste of the disinfectant and sand in my mouth made the ordeal worse than anything I had ever experienced. I desperately wanted to get a hand up to cover my mouth, but my arms were held to my sides too tightly.

As I felt the lack of oxygen causing me to get weaker and weaker, I wished only for it to end. And it did end for me when I passed out.

Regaining my senses, somewhat, as the guards dragged me down the steps into the cold air, I couldn't get my breath until one of the men kicked me in the ribs. For a time, it was impossible to get up as I lay on the thin layer of snow, hoping my breathing would get back to normal.

That afternoon, about 40 prisoners were marched to the trolley car and carried to a train that was to take us to Wetzler, a city down the Rhine River—an overnight trip. At the station, a frantic crowd attacked us and pushed us, with our guards, into an alcove-like area. They were the most belligerent we had encountered, and as more and more people joined them our few guards became very agitated and seemed about ready to give in. Then a high-ranking officer in the SS uniform interfered, and with much swearing and shouting he drove them back away from us and ordered us into the train while the angry crowd pounded on the windows in their frustration.

The Dulag at Wetzler was a distribution point, where it was determined to which prison we would be sent. There was plenty of food from Red Cross parcels, and British prisoners cooked two good, warm meals for us while we were there. I found a place to wash and cleaned up my shirt and pants, drying them over a heater in one room. I was still in my torn shirt, with no jacket or sweater to keep the chill off. My leather jacket and flight suit had been confiscated shortly after I was captured. Fortunately, we were each issued a fiber, briefcase-type container about 14 by 5 by 22 inches in size that contained a toothbrush and paste, a needle, a bit of thread, soap, cigarettes and a few small tins of food.

In addition, a huge wool GI overcoat, a blanket, English gloves, a good heavy undershirt, a scarf and a wool knit cap soldiers wore under their helmets were issued to us. This was all handed out, courtesy of the Red Cross. This was the first incident to give us hope that we would survive the coming winter and was greatly appreciated.

Wetzler was the center for optical works research and manufacture, situated on a high hill looking out over hills and picturesque country. The prison was pretty much under control of the Red Cross and Swiss Allied protectors. The food and supplies given us there was surprising to me and a great comfort as well. A delousing team worked 24 hours a day but could not rid us of all the lice we carried.

Anyone who had a twin brother in prison, it seemed, would be sent elsewhere. But I was fortunate in being put in a group with acquaintances that included my copilot Sam Cashman.

The train carrying us to Stalag Luft III in Poland was made up of a few regular passenger cars but pulled by the same type of locomotive with the shrill, screeching whistle that was unnerving and seemed to portend a bleak future. It was an ominous sound. At the station, an officer requested we give our word not to escape en route and asked if anyone objected. Certainly I was in no condition to escape, and many others were in the same state. However, one "new" prisoner raised his hand. "Any others?" the German major asked. The objector was hustled out of sight, and we heard a shot. Most of us believed it was a trick—that he was a plant—as none of us had seen him before, and we hoped it was just for emphasis.

Our journey took us through the midsection of the country, passing through the outskirts of Berlin. We saw appalling destruction, with many people wandering about aimlessly while hundreds of workers cleared rubble, mended phone lines and leveled pavement. Other cities were badly damaged, as were bridges and one power-plant dam.

On the farms, work was being done almost entirely by older women, all wearing dresses out in the fields. We saw several teams plowing with a horse and a cow hitched together. Many fields were still being harvested of potatoes, turnips and other root crops that were piled into "clamps," long slope-sided piles covered with straw as storage for the winter. These were opened as needed at one end and covered again to prevent freezing. At a stop about midnight of the second day, some guards got out and brought back sandwiches of black bread and some kind of sausage that they passed around. We were given very little water and, of course, no beer at all.

The straight-backed, hard seats in the cars became very uncomfortable and pained my back and shoulders. It was cool inside, but our wonderful overcoats and gloves made it tolerable. My nose had become unplugged of dried blood shortly after the rug incident, which was a great relief, although it was still a mess, as I found when I looked into a mirror in the bathroom at Wetzler.

My eyes were still a little black from that blow to the nose, but we were not headed toward a beauty pageant. As we traveled eastward, we grew apprehensive about our destination; in fact, Sam Cashman said, "If we go much farther, we'll be at the Russian front."

That was something to think about, as there were posters trying to recruit us to join the fight against communism since we would end up fighting them sooner or later anyway. This recruiting campaign was kept up until the last days of the war, offering bonuses, plenty of food, warm uniforms and many other incentives. The recruiters even offered work on farms, living with families in a healthy environment. It sounded ludicrous to most of us at first, but the feeling grew that Stalin would be worse than Hitler.

At one stop, four or five guards took six of us to a type of diner in the station while the tracks ahead were being repaired. During the six-hour layover, our young guards called some relatives and friends, who came down and were quite civil toward us. We didn't know if we were in Germany or Poland, but the civilians in that small city seemed to have a different attitude than other civilians we'd met. We were allowed to eat there, but they had brought us along to carry the food back to the others in the cars. I certainly welcomed the opportunity to stretch and walk around. This group of guards appeared quite casual after some we had earlier.

Early one morning we saw the sign for Sagan and remembered from our briefings that a large POW camp was located there. Whenever we attacked a target near a prison, we studied aerial photos of it and made sure we knew its exact location. On our way out of town, we passed a meat market, where many sausages and other meats were hanging in the windows. They looked pretty good to us. Approaching the main gate of Stalag Luft III, we crossed a desolate area where trees had been cut but the stumps were still there. The level, flat plain was surrounded by pine trees, leaving clear areas around the camp for observation, I suppose, but it also provided fields of fire from the guard towers. The towers, placed at intervals along a high (12-foot) double barbed-wire fence, gave the place a formidable looking, impregnable appearance.

Once inside the double gates, we were processed, searched, given a metal tag with our prisoner-of-war number and assigned to a room in one of the barracks called blocks. Each room held 12 men organized into a "combine" to live together, support each other and manage our food rations, consisting of Red Cross parcels and irregular issues of German food referred to as "Goon" rations. "Goons" or "Krauts" had become the terminology for any of the German military, but I felt uncomfortable using those references, mainly because the Luftwaffe operated the camp and it became obvious members of the Luftwaffe were much different from the Wehrmacht (German army). We were told that very few of the Luftwaffe officers were Nazi party members.

We found the Hollywood portraiture of the Nazi officers to be quite accurate, but some of us wondered if perhaps they had seen American movies and were trying to live up to the world's view of them. They strutted about in their shiny leather boots, pistols and daggers attached to belts, with many decorative appointments on the meticulous uniforms. It made us wonder how they could spare so many officers from the fighting fronts, as they appeared everywhere.

They were extremely arrogant and rude as they shouldered people aside and never spoke quietly, but shouted at everyone. The world was their oyster, and they did as they pleased. The black uniforms of the dreaded SS frightened civilians and military alike whenever they were present.

To be fair, most of us had to admit the Luftwaffe went to considerable effort to follow the Geneva Convention in providing food, shelter and humane treatment. This was very difficult with the country waging war on two fronts and experiencing huge losses to transportation and supplies due to our bombers and fighters. The records show 13,000,000 prisoners were held by the Nazis at one time, requiring great expenditures of manpower to control. Usually, half of the Russian prisoners were dead on arrival in the cattle-car trains that carried them for days without food or water. The plan was to use these prisoners to work in the war industry, but because of harsh treatment, most of the Russians were unfit to work after riding up to a thousand miles in those terrible railroad cars. This was another case of Germany's failure to follow through on a plan because of their cruelty. The Americans were the most fortunate of all.

The six compounds within the camp were divided among American, British, French, Polish, ANZACs (Australian and New Zealanders) and several other nationalities. These were all Air Force flying officers except for one Naval officer captured in 1939 while flying as an observer with the RAF. The sole black officer with us created some perplexing problems for the "pure Aryan race" as to where to house him. Some of the Southern animosity became apparent, much to our dismay, but the fine black pilot finally shared a room with the chaplain and two majors.

The name of the camp was Stalag (prison) Luft (air) number three. The prison was built exclusively for Allied airmen. Kreigsgefangenen was German for prisoner of war, so we called ourselves "Kriegies."

The American and British compounds were very well organized, along the lines of regular military structure consisting of Supply, Operations, Security and Intelligence (G2). Departments were further broken down to tunnels, logistics, rations, escape plans and other duties. Our senior American officer was the commander and held regular staff meetings with his other officers resulting in a fairly smooth-running camp. The staff worked closely with our captors as regards to food deliveries, limited medical efforts, discipline and other activities.

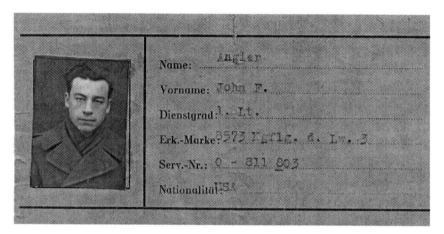

My Kriegie ID Card

1944 Nov and Dec, Behind the Barbed Wire

My new roommates always interrogated each new Kriegie to insure that he wasn't a German "plant." With my limited knowledge of sports (the first quiz), I said, "Ask me anything but that. You know, a plant would be schooled and up-to-date on sports." Fortunately, a few acquaintances came forward to properly identify me. The routines were explained, and the intense security required for the tactical operations such as tunnel digging, "ferret" watching and undercover schemes for outwitting the Goons had to be rigorously emphasized.

Ferrets were small, older German soldiers, victims of malnutrition after World War I, who crawled under our buildings or into the attics while we were out being counted, to remain hidden and listen to our conversations when we returned. Most ferrets had been tamed by being paid in cigarettes for services such as bringing in a bit of wire or some small tool.

Once one of them had been paid, he could be pressured into more serious duties because they were monitored from the time they entered the gate and a record of their activities kept by teams of Kriegies. If critical items such as a pair of wire cutters or a radio tube were needed, there could be no refusal, even though this would have dire consequences for the ferret if he were caught bringing in such forbidden items. It could mean his being sent to the Russian front, the worst punishment for an older man. Each ferret knew we only had to turn in his record of accomplishments and what he had been paid if he refused a request. I didn't hear of one of them being reported.

The commandant of Luft III was a 62-year-old veteran of World War I—a fine Luftwaffe officer who worked closely with our staff and did the best he could under difficult conditions. He showed his sporting side by handing out less punishment for a returned escapee who had been free longer or traveled farther than some poor devil who was caught nearby. The maximum, he felt, was two weeks solitary in the "cooler."

After the "Great Escape," which took place at this camp, this officer complained bitterly to Berlin when the escapees were executed on recapture. Hitler ordered him to Berlin, and nothing more was heard from him, but rumors spread that he, too, was executed. Shortly after this, the SS was put in charge of all the Allied airmen camps, and finally Hitler ordered the execution of all American and British airmen. The German High Command generals refused to carry out the order, and more of Germany's best officers were hanged. Fortunately, Hitler's second and third such orders were likewise put off.

Many remarkable and dedicated men with diverse skills were incarcerated and put their ingenuity to work performing many tasks. The tunnel committees managed to build thousands of yards of tunnels that served as more than escape routes. When men did escape, prisoners from another compound would go through the tunnels to be counted in their place to buy time before an alarm went out. Communication between compounds was facilitated by the tunnels—an operation that required a number of Kriegies to watch for the approach of guards while the tunnel openings were in use. Access to tunnels was through such places as under stoves in kitchens, where the concrete base had been cut out. Special lifting devices allowed two men to lift a stove and put it back quickly even if there was a fire going at the time.

To provide ventilation to the tunnels, bellows had to be fabricated and operated continuously while there was anyone working down there.

"Scroungers" had liberated coils of wire and electric light fixtures and bulbs from workmen who could be distracted by a gift of a cigarette. This was to provide sufficient lighting for the work in the tunnel. A set of wooden tracks carried small carts loaded with excavated dirt to be brought back to the shaft for disposal. Because our captors could listen for sounds of digging down to 25 feet, a Scottish engineer had put the depth of the tunnels to 30 feet. This required expenditure of enormous amounts of energy to haul dirt up the shafts and carry it outside without detection.

Much of the dirt was spread on a perimeter track that circled the inside of the barbed wire fences, and much more was deposited under the sloping floor of the theater. Small tubular bags were fashioned to fit inside pant legs so men walking the perimeter track for exercise could jiggle a string and allow the dirt to be spread where other walkers scuffed it in.

The theater was built by the Kriegies out of scrap material, much of it scrounged by the local pastor in Sagan, who contributed greatly to our welfare. He acquired musical instruments and other paraphernalia to produce plays and musicals. But the greatest use of the theater was to dispose of dirt from the tunnels. It was built with a steep sloping floor to permit bags of dirt to be dumped during the entertainment. Each seat had a small door fitted into the backrest that could be opened to pour the sand down.

The tunnel people pressed would-be entertainers to put on more shows to help get rid of the mountains of dirt. Actually the tunnels were located in a layer of sand that was very dangerous, as a small leak could soon block off escape. There was always great pressure to find wood to shore up the tunnels, wood that was stolen from under the floors of all the buildings. Hardly a room was left with a sub-flooring. In some cases, plaster had to be used on the walls and ceilings of the tunnels. Ferrets sometimes used water hoses to flood the tunnels, a practice that often caused the sandy tunnel walls to collapse.

The stumps surrounding the prison we had seen when we arrived were a source of fuel for our use. Teams of able-bodied men would be taken out to dig up the stumps and cut them into firewood. The trees were continually cut farther back from the fences, making tunneling to the shelter of the woods a much greater chore. The staff occasionally sent out a man or two for reconnaissance and information. They might be gone a day or possibly a week or more. These men were selected carefully for their nonchalance and ingenuity and without exception were longtime prisoners, usually British.

After the tragic results of the Great Escape, from which only three men made it to freedom, rules for escape attempts were tightened—to require a period of training, a need to go and profiling for suitable characteristics. Nonchalance was a plus for an escapee as well as the ability to move about unobtrusively. A knowledge of German gained the most points, but a keen memory was an absolute necessity as no written addresses or instructions for the fragile German underground were allowed.

Among our people were skilled forgers and photo people who provided passports, IDs and counterfeit money as well as billfolds containing ticket stubs, bus transfers, ration coupons and other items to help an escapee pass for a normal citizen.

All of this painstaking work had to be performed in greatest secrecy and under the security provided by other Kriegies. Uniforms were altered to look like civilian clothes but could be changed back. Some of the more daring escaped in German uniforms made up with remarkable accuracy. To be caught in enemy uniform could mean death.

Many escapes and subsequent evasion were highly ingenious and showed great imagination. For example, one man found a wheelbarrow, equipped it with a shovel and broom to wheel along posing as a worker. He slept where night found him, avoided contact with people and occasionally, when observed, shoveled items into the wheelbarrow, pretending to work. He made it nearly to the Swiss border when a gendarme thought he walked too fast for a European and arrested him.

Another escapee liberated a cow and led her down the road for weeks. He had milk to drink and companionship, and he fit into the rural scene. He was stopped at the border, where his papers checked out OK, but he had led the cow too far and had no ownership or importation documents. On his return to prison, he was accused of becoming too fond of the cow.

The many activities of the well-organized camp—twice daily count (called appell) on the parade ground—helped to keep our minds off our troubles. Nevertheless, reality did set in, especially at night, when sleep came hard or not at all due to aches and pains, hard uncomfortable bunks and the never-ending hunger. We realized we were under the complete control of disciplined men who took orders from a madman. Months and years of our lives could slip away without our being able to enjoy the normal pursuits of free people. Our medical problems were compounded as time went by without proper care, and we put up with unfamiliar shortages of things we had taken for granted. The lack of a nail clipper, scissors and other sorely needed articles and the shortage of toilet paper were especially hard to endure. Fingernails and toenails were a problem and led to our painfully hacking them off with old, worn-out razor blades, causing many painful cuts. We owned nothing of our own.

For all we knew, the war could go on for years. The end was inevitable, but *how* would it end—in violence from the frustrated, vindictive Nazis bent on revenge—or a simple surrender and handing over of prisoners?

Several slogans went around the compounds, expressing opinions as to when the war would end: "Home alive in '45". "Out of this fix by '46." "Golden Gate in '48." "Social Security in Red Cross parcels?" "Our grandchildren won't know us when we get home." Kriegie cartoons appeared, showing General Ike riding a horse. "Ike's ass is in the saddle and look at him ride" was the caption on some, while others were less optimistic. The Battle of the Bulge was very depressing for all of us, and our hearts went out to our soldiers in their courageous attempt to halt the German offensive. While German propaganda made it sound like a great victory for them, the few bits of news that came through our radio from London BBC was more encouraging, though it made us realize great sacrifices had taken place to halt the Nazis' last counterattack.

Getting used to the routine took a lot of my time, and I could feel the effects of expending so much energy. When it seemed reasonable to get into my crude bunk to spend most of the day, I took time to rest and take stock of my condition, which grew more serious as the cold winter set in. My headaches and earaches continued to plague me, the result of being in such close proximity to our bomb load when it exploded. What had seemed like a blister deep in my throat caused a change in my voice and a soreness that persisted for about three months. It finally occurred to me that just before the plane blew up the pilot's compartment had become superheated, and as I struggled to get out while the plane was in a vertical position, I was unable to hold my breath. Without the oxygen mask on, a gulp of the intense hot air had burned my throat. But with the immediate disintegration of the right side of the bomber and my being blown out into the minus-50-degree thin air, I thought no more of that damage until some time later.

One ear had super-sensitive hearing that made shrill or reverberating sounds very annoying while the other was much less able to hear normal levels of sound. My nose healed slowly but left me with considerable irritation, occasional blockage of the air passages and a more nasal tone to my voice. The structural damage to my neck, shoulders and back caused great discomfort whether I was walking or trying to rest.

Fortunately, I had suffered no compound fractures, but X-rays many months later showed several hair-line fractures. I couldn't assume any position without feeling pain in all my joints. Climbing into the top bunk was a major effort, but even after I got into a horizontal position, the wide-spaced bed slats and thin straw mattress brought little relief. Pinhead-sized bits of shrapnel eventually surfaced from my right forearm and the back of my hand. Internal injuries to my stomach from concussion when the bombs exploded and the effects of the rectal prolapse that occurred on my hard landing subsided slowly over the first three months. However, the arduous march that was to come in late January caused a relapse of these problems.

Nights were long and cold. Sagan is nearly as far north as Quebec City, so nights were long and days short in the dead of winter. Each room had quite large casement windows that were kept open after dark, but the fresh air this provided was more beneficial than the discomfort of the cold. This may have reduced the incidence of colds and pneumonia—as long as the Red Cross parcels arrived with their nutritive essentials.

Periodically, a guard and his dog would pass close enough by the window that we could see his breath and hear him puffing as he made his way through the snow. A few times, the dog stood up with his paws on the window sill, sniffing and looking about the room. Every few minutes, the search light from a guard tower would sweep past, making sure no Kriegie was outside, bent on escape.

When the Allies drove the Germans back, the Nazi propaganda minister Joseph Geobels would tell the people, "Our brave forces took up new defensive positions on the east side of the river (the Rhine) and inflicted tremendous losses to the aggressors." The Germans never mentioned retreat.

Meanwhile, the Russians were advancing toward Germany on all fronts. As Stalin's armies approached Warsaw, the Jews in the ghettos rose up with a vengeance after their years of miserable existence. They thought it would help the Russians if they created enough diversion in the city, but the Russians held their positions within sight of Warsaw and allowed the Jewish resistance to fail, with terrible consequences. The Poles helped the Russians, rather than the Russians giving aid to the Poles in their tragic uprising.

We were in constant danger of the strange whims of our captors. Outdoors, we knew the armed guards in the towers watched our every move and if anyone stepped over the 50-foot warning wire in front of the main fences, he was shot. One enlisted man, an orderly for senior officers, was shot and killed in the doorway of a cookhouse. The Goons would come in at any hour, usually just after midnight shouting and yelling, "Get out! Rouse! Everybody out now!" This meant for us to assemble on the parade ground as for appell, with little chance to dress properly.

Our bunks and belongings were trashed, every container opened and examined while we stood—sometimes for hours—to be counted over and over. Some of these raids culminated in photo-ID matching that could take more than half a day as clerks with thick glasses compared photos to the faces of disheveled men standing before them. Questions were often raised because appearances changed in the months since the photos had been taken shortly after arriving at Luft III.

They always looked for radios and occasionally found one, but most radios—our link to the outside world—were well hidden. We were also required to turn in an empty tin can for each one that came in a Red Cross parcel, and for every can unaccounted for, a bed slat was taken. This was a severe punishment as there was only a minimum of slats left. Many of us obtained pieces of barbed wire, removed the barbs, and stretched the wires across our bunks in lieu of a wooden slat. All available cans had been made into pans and kettles for cooking as we were issued only a bowl, a cup, a fork and a spoon. We learned that the spoons were made from the aluminum of shot-down Allied planes. Each barracks had a kitchen in the center, with a stove, sink and cooking kettles that were shared by all the rooms in the building on a rotation basis. This was mainly for the German or "Kraut", rations that came in sporadically and depended on a supply of fuel, which was in the form of a small amount of coal or pieces of the stumps the Kriegie work parties dug up.

There were individuals among us who deserve great credit for taking the edge off prison life. Those who went out into the wintry wind to dig stumps for fuel made tremendous sacrifices but, of course, had to be in better condition than most of us. We had artists, playwrights, actors, musicians and tireless organizers who put on entertainment with very little to work with. The Catholic priest in Sagan worked tirelessly to scrounge musical instruments, props and stage clothing and was successful in assembling many books for a library through the Red Cross. Our senior officers pried concessions from the German commanders to allow Kriegies to attend affairs after curfew and helped explain that rehearsal activities were necessary. Of course, any excuse to use the rickety theater to get rid of the dirt from the tunnels was a great help to the tunnel engineers.

Many of us suspected one compound of the camp was receiving special privileges in the way of food rationing, showers and more lenient treatment. Many of these prisoners had been incarcerated for a longer period of time than the rest of us. This compound held more high-ranking officers who later, after the war, confirmed our suspicions when they wrote in a matter-of-fact manner of hot showers and meals served by orderlies. They wrote of foods that not only had variety but were in much greater quantity than the rest of us had. Prisoners in that compound enjoyed more entertainment and appeared to have more free time for other activities. Some medical treatment was also available there as well. As we set out on the march, some of them had sleds loaded with much more food, blankets and other paraphernalia than they could have carried. Perhaps their prison seniority entitled them to certain advantages.

"D" bars were a marvelous concoction of hard-pressed chocolate and some fruit and became the most coveted and most expensive possession a POW could hope to own. They were extremely durable, were almost impossible to bite into because of their hardness, kept very well and provided great energy. Some enterprising individuals started a "store" where anyone with a good supply of cigarettes could buy a "D" bar. The price went from 3 packs for one bar to an astounding 50 packs near the end of our stay in Stalag Luft III. We never learned where they obtained their stock of bars to sell. The fact that food supplies arrived in this compound to be distributed to the rest of the camp may have been a factor. I had traded about 10 packs toward a bar, but the inflation kept ahead of me, resulting in the loss of my cigarettes as they could not be redeemed. A colonel in this compound declared in his memoirs he took only 18 "D" bars from his stock as we left the camp to begin our march. He told me on the march that he would miss the lively bridge games with other senior officers. We had no such largess and privileges in our compound and had only one shower over a six-month period.

The two senior officers I knew who accepted no concessions or privileges from the Germans were Colonels Goodrich and Alkire. Several other officers worked hard for the welfare of all the POWs and shared all the hardships with us. To read some of the post-war accounts would lead one to believe the prisoners in this compound spent their entire incarceration in an endless series of plays, musicals and sports. There is no doubt but what they had a longer tenure in Stalag Luft III and had accumulated many parcels from home and sports equipment from the Red Cross.

But in our West Compound, the newest, very few parcels were delivered and mail was sporadic. I received none of the parcels and no mail that friends and relatives sent to me. My compound may have been targeted as more troublesome because of the constant pressure we kept on the German staff as well as intense training and equipping of prospective escapees. The extra attention and manpower expended to watch our activities helped to drain our captor's resources.

At Christmas time, all the combines saved Red Cross parcel foods for a big "bash." (combines were organizational groups of POWs, usually 12 in number to support each other and ration the food as it came in) These extra items together with a special Christmas Red Cross parcel provided a very enjoyable holiday banquet. Each man had a small portion of canned turkey, Spam, cranberries and other goodies and made it a day to remember. The Catholic and Protestant chaplains held almost non-stop services from Christmas Eve until noon on Christmas Day. It was a change from the usual day-to-day existence.

A strange, happy coincidence occurred at this time. My boyhood friend Jim Bouvier and I were in separate areas of the camp, but we managed to visit occasionally. In each Christmas Red Cross parcel there were photos of many parts of the U.S. such as New York City, Golden Gate bridge, Niagara Falls and many other scenes of our beloved and sorely missed country. The photos were handed out indiscriminately to each man. To my surprise, mine was an aerial photo of Lincoln, Vermont a few miles from my hometown. It was taken from an airplane by George Lathrop, a sportsman, motorcycle cop and for a time, owner of one of the first cumbersome, primitive aerial cameras. I hurried over to show it to Jim, as we both knew George well and the scene of Lincoln was no more than two miles from Jim's home. To our astonishment, we both had the same picture and as far as we could find out these were the only two. It was an amazing coincidence and gave us both the feeling it was something that was meant to be.

Sooner or later, the Russians would reach our location, and the Germans had to make decisions: leave us as they retreated, march us out of the camps to points farther west or as speculations circulated, annihilate us by one means or another.

One version of the latter scenario was for them to take our clothes away and drive us out of the camp to freeze. None of these scenarios appealed to us, so we started a program of exercise and began to lay aside bits of food from our meager supplies that could be carried with us. Our senior officers required us to walk the perimeter track daily and do whatever we could to gain strength to be as fit as possible for whatever was to come.

Plans to resist attempts to do away with us were developed as a last resort. Almost everyone preferred to avoid being liberated by the Russians in the dead of winter, as our "ally" would not be likely to provide transportation or food. As it turned out, those who escaped on the subsequent march were given a rifle, taken by the shoulders, turned around toward Germany and given a shove. The escaped prisoners were not allowed to ride the empty trains going back east for more supplies, nor were they given food or shelter. It was only scattered Polish farms that provided any sustenance. Only a handful ever reached a port in Russia (Odessa) where they might get transported toward home. One man from Vermont told me he didn't arrive in the States until August of 1945.

1945 January, The Long, Cold March

Finally, we could hear the Russian artillery off to the south-east toward Breslau and could see the flashes on the skyline. On the evening of January 26th, 1945, the guards noisily crashed through our barracks, shouting for us to be ready to march in an hour.

There was some irony and some morbid humor in the imme-diate turmoil. On that very day, I was finally able to draw the book "Mien Kampf" from the library. The thick book, Hitler's bible, offered a way to pass a chunk of time during the uneasy, dreary winter days. In the English compound, the Kriegies, many of them four- and five-year incumbents of German prisons, were highly indignant as they claimed, "But we are just about to have tea!" We had all contrived some sort of pack to carry our food and belongings; the most popular was just a blanket tied at each end to sling over the shoulder.

There was pandemonium as people scrambled to get ready in an hour. At about nine o'clock, it was announced that each man would be issued a Red Cross parcel if we proceeded by blocks to the assembly point of departure. Most of us filled our big GI overcoat pockets with tins of food and whatever we could get our hands on. The boxes of Red Cross parcels were too awkward to carry, so we emptied them and carried the contents in pockets or packs. My "briefcase," issued at the Dulag in Wetzler, came in handy as I proposed to pull it along over the snow by tying a piece of cord around my waist to one end of the case. I cut the hard covers and back off the copy of *Mein Kampf* so I could remove pads of about 100 pages each to pack in my case for toilet paper. My blanket was available to tie up over my head for added protection from the cold. I had traded some cigarettes for the bottom half of a new mattress cover made of a quite heavy, durable cotton. It was clean and made a bag to carry over my shoulder with a few lightweight items that wouldn't fit into the case. Later on it proved to be a godsend, as I used it to cover my head and upper body while resting in the hay and chaff of the barns we slept in as well as later giving me protection from the dirt and insects that filtered down in the miserable prison at Mooseberg. All in all, I felt as prepared for a march as our limited resources permitted.

It was midnight before the gates swung open and 11,000 of us started our march in a snowstorm. POWs from seven or eight Stalags to the east of Stalag Luft III were on the move, preparing to march or had already left for prisons in Germany. Some 40,000 men were being moved west by the Germans, using thousands of their troops to escort us. It seemed ridiculous for them to spare so much manpower at a time when the Allies were closing in from all sides. We could only surmise we were to be used as pawns to counter the Allied "unconditional surrender" terms. We had been briefed by our senior officers as well as the German staff on the conditions of the move. The likelihood of successful escape was practically nil, considering the lack of sources for food and the severe weather.

We were given to understand that guards would fire at anyone trying to leave the column and that our captors would endeavor to get us safely to another camp in Germany (Stalag VII A in Mooseberg, Bavaria for my group), but they could guarantee nothing due to the limited manpower they could provide and the instability of the front lines. The 400 or more infirmed or crippled POWs had to be left at the prison with the hope the Russians would look after them. Enough food in accumulated Red Cross parcels might last them a month. We never learned of their fate.

On the roads of western Poland, the 40,000 prisoners who were being evacuated to the west ahead of the advancing Russians were separated by times of departure and the distance between groups. We never saw any in our immediate area, but from high ground we could see our column stretching out for many miles. We were in danger of attack by the Mongolian cavalry as well as aircraft of the Axis or the Allies. We were vulnerable to mistaken identity by military forces that would shoot at anything or anyone that moved—or didn't move. It wasn't a very good time to be touring Poland or Eastern Germany.

The guards were mostly old men, some partially disabled, declared too far gone to fight in the regular army and, as it turned out, not well enough for the rigors of a march in winter. Most of them had dogs on a chain that pulled them along on the shoulders of the road. Each man carried a rifle, and some younger, stronger guards stationed at intervals carried submachine guns that they occasionally fired over our heads to keep us subdued. The first shots were fired into the air to alert the guards to get off the shoulders of the road; we were told to lie flat on the roadway as they fired over us for several minutes.

Before morning, the snowfall increased as we walked directly into the wind four abreast on the narrow road. Practically everyone had tied a blanket over his head and shoulders, leaving just enough of an opening to see through. About every hour we halted to rest. The old guards would collapse on the snow, and at times the dogs would drag the old men along for a bit. We shook the snow from our blankets and rested on the hard-packed snow, but it was very difficult to get moving again as we all stiffened up from the cold.

My small case slipped along easily on the snow, but some of the men had to spend the rest period rearranging their packs. Some had loaded up with the excess food distributed just before leaving the camp. I saw a large round chunk of solid honey in the ditch, along with loaves of the accursed black bread and other food that was now just too much of a burden, food that a day before was carefully rationed.

As we struggled on, men began to fall back, shoes wet from the snow froze, making each step painful. At dusk, my group entered a small deserted village and rested in and between buildings out of the wind. No food was issued and no fires permitted, so we ate, if anything, the cold and frozen rations we carried. It was with great difficulty that we and the guards set out before daylight, plagued mostly by fatigue and frozen shoes.

The snow had stopped, but it was overcast and a cold biting wind still blew out of the north. We began to see refugees trying to escape the Russians, some with scrawny horses pulling sleds or wagons piled with what possessions the people thought they could manage. Some tried to push baby carriages or pulled small sleds. Old people and small children rode on the horse-drawn vehicles. Many had burned their houses and barns, killed the pigs and cows and dumped outhouses down the wells to leave nothing of value for the Russians. The roadsides were littered with cast-off furniture, clothes, farm tools, dead horses and broken-down wagons. Our guards beat the refugees to get them out of the road for us to pass, but by this time, our escorts began to drop their rifles and some fell helpless in the snow.

By mid-afternoon, the sky had cleared. Because of the danger of being strafed or spotted by either Russian or German planes, it was decided that we should halt in a village. It was a very small hamlet, with houses resembling plain boxes placed close together. The houses appeared empty at first, just bare rooms, no people. The guards formed a ring around the area to confine us. I staggered into the hallway of a house to get out of the cold, and a door opened where a half dozen people were huddled in one room. There was no furniture in the house and, of course, no heat. The people were terrified, not knowing what to expect, but a young woman who spoke some English whispered, "American prisoners!" They seemed relieved, even though we were still under control of the Germans. They wanted us to stay with them until the Russians arrived. These were Polish citizens who had no desire to escape to Germany. The refugees on the roads apparently were German citizens who had moved into Poland after Hitler invaded that country in 1939. The outlook was depressingly bleak for all of them.

Our rest was short because as soon as it was dark we were moved out to march at night to avoid being seen in daylight. Around midnight, we could hear yelling and wild sounds. It was a troop of mounted Mongolians, racing over the hills and fields to our right. Everyone hit the ground, as these advance forces sent ahead of the regular Russian forces to strike fear into the residents were extremely wild and dangerous. They were provided support with 1932 Model B Ford trucks that carried food, ammunition and vodka from point to point while the Mongols rode their horses cross-country. They had been told those golden-haired German women were theirs when they found them and to show no mercy. Needless to say, by the time the main Russian forces moved in, the people had already been subdued.

Our next rest stop was in a cluster of farms with barns containing hay and straw that we could bed down in. We burrowed into the hay and took off our shoes to thaw them out. I pulled my cotton mattress bag over my head and slept warm and dry for the first time during the march. As I had two pair of socks, I wore one and carried the other pair inside my shirt so I would have a dry pair at each stop. It was necessary to sleep with our shoes under us to thaw them out during the rest period. A guard stumbled over my legs in the dark and when I pulled off my bag (mattress cover) he indicated he would like to trade a half bottle of schnapps for a cigarette. Deal. One sip was enough for me, but my bunk mates, or hay mates, emptied the bottle in no time. I took the bottle back to carry water in if we ever passed a supply that looked clean.

We marched all that night and into the next day before a halt was called while the Germans negotiated with the owner of a large estate for food and barns to rest in. They moved us into the large front yard of a gigantic mansion while the owner had food prepared. We formed into concentric circles where we waited for an hour or two before the farm workers began to carry out large tubs of thick barley soup, the first warm food we had had in days. By dark, all the men had been fed and given warm water, as what little we carried had frozen. I placed my schnapps bottle, with its convenient wire bail that locked the cap on securely, inside my shirt. There were barns enough to accommodate most all of us, and we rested much better with the warm food in our bellies.

The next stop was in a small hamlet with a church with only 300 pews, but 2,800 cold Kriegies managed to get inside. I looked in and saw the last ones to enter walking on top of the others, trying to find a place to lie down or sit, so I settled for a dilapidated shed that was filled to overflowing as well. There were two officers, a colonel and the only general in German custody, who slept on the altar of the church. Colonel Spivey was not rated for flight-crew duty, but as a gunnery officer fresh from the States he wrangled a ride on a mission to "study the performance of our aerial gunners in combat." The plane was damaged four hours into the mission, and the pilot crash-landed in a Dutch field.

General Vanaman was offered privileges and partial freedom in Berlin but ended up in Stalag Luft III. He was older than the other senior officers, but his reasons for flying a mission were never explained. He was not in condition for the march and frequently had to be helped to keep up. The last I saw of him, he was riding on one of the wagons that were commandeered to pick up men who had fallen and couldn't get up. Before the march was over, these two officers were taken to Berlin, fed, wined and entertained by no less than Field Marshal Hermann Goering, head of the Luftwaffe. Vanaman was in Paris and Spivey was back in the States while we were still in Mooseberg. It was my opinion that Goering was trying to use these two officers to negotiate certain conditions of a surrender to the Americans.

We progressed down the same road used by Napoleon on his retreat from Moscow and passed a monument set close to the road, marking the spot where the Russians turned back when there wasn't enough of the French army left to pursue. It was in the dead of winter when Napoleon rode past there in his sleigh, leaving nearly a million men in the snows of Russia.

Our route had been winding generally northwest, ostensibly to reach Cottbus on the German side of the Oder River. Our guards took a wrong turn that eventually led us in a semicircle up around Cottbus, through Gorlitz and then toward Spremberg, but our final segment of this part of the march brought us to Moskau. We were led north, west, then south in a great loop for nothing and had lost most of our people due to the blundering.

This wandering added many miles and days to our march, resulting in our missing a rendezvous with a promised truck convoy bringing us food and replacements for our escort. Then began the worst ordeal most of us had ever experienced or imagined. The cold persisted, wearing us down, but we marched all day through barren back country. Occasionally, we passed units of the German army digging in for the expected Russian attack. There were a few scattered foxholes prepared, but tanks had been driven into holes dug by slave-labor battalions and buried except for their gun turrets, which were exposed.

We surmised these tanks were out of fuel and could not maneuver but would provide effective firepower. We saw other tanks, camouflaged, that most likely would be ready to move when needed. The tank crews seemed well clothed for the severe weather, but more than half of the troops could not have been more than 16 years old. All of them appeared very somber; they were on the east bank of the Oder and so were expendable. Once we crossed the river, heavy guns were in place in what looked like a major defensive line.

Shortly after dark in this worst night of the trek, a young enlisted man from Island Pond, Vermont began to hallucinate. He saw a cabin on a hill about a quarter of a mile from the road and decided it was his mother's house and she was baking pies. He lunged off the road and started for the house. The guards began shouting and tried to get in position to fire at him. One of our senior officers called out in German to the guards to hold their fire, that he would take care of the situation. Amazingly, there was no shooting, but the colonel was having a hard time trying to hold the man back until finally he slugged the boy and carried him back to the column. There was almost complete silence during the entire event. Although I had seen the enlisted man working in the Stalag, and the incident took place practically in front of me, I didn't learn his name until many years later.

Our old worn-out guards were falling down, some threw their guns away, and they were demoralized because their replacements had not arrived. As the night wore on, more and more Kriegies began to fall down and could not be awakened because of the cold and their weakened condition.

Stronger men helped others until there was no one left with the strength to help anyone else. I felt my brain getting numb while my body was chilled to the point where there seemed but one relief: SLEEP. It seemed a superhuman effort to put one foot ahead of the other, and my vision started to fail.

I tried to concentrate on surviving at all cost because I was too young to die, was still innocent and had too many plans for the future. In spite of my efforts to keep awake, I finally fell asleep walking, taking steps unconsciously as I leaned forward farther and farther until I landed face down on the hard-packed snow with my arms at my sides. A huge guard dog yanked his master off his feet as he lunged for me. The impact woke me, but I had no strength to get up or to pull my arms up from my sides until the dog put his nose against my ear and seemed to speak in German, "Rouse! Rouse!" meaning get up, go, hurry! The adrenaline began to flow enough to get me onto my knees, but my head was still bowed low. I needed to sleep! The dog didn't bite me but kept banging his nose against my head and growling. Two Kriegies came up behind me and helped me to my feet, and as they trudged on, I felt a bit of energy, enough to put one foot ahead of the other. That was the only thing left to do, put one foot ahead of the other, stay awake. And so the hours passed.

The inviting picture of a soft, warm bed was registered vividly in my mind. Nothing else mattered except for me to collapse into that warm softness, to finally sleep. A person can tolerate intense cold and fatigue for a long period if he knows he will eventually reach a place of warmth, some shelter to rest and thaw out. There was no assurance that any of the thousands of us would find escape from our ordeal in this hostile country with enemies in front and untrustworthy "Allies" close behind us. That warm bed was months away. My clothes, after being wet with snow, had frozen stiff. It would be months before I would feel the luxury of clean, comfortable clothes.

Our body temperatures had become so low we no longer felt the cold except for our eyes and cheekbones—the only exposed parts. Men staggered and weaved from side to side, sometimes getting over onto the shoulder of the road where the snow had not been packed down. The horses pulling the wagons carrying the men who had fallen, collapsed from cold, hunger and exhaustion. Replacement animals were taken from barns along the way, but most of these had not been well fed to begin with. Some of our comrades who had fallen rolled into the ditches and were partially covered with snow. They could not be awakened. Very few German guards were still with us, and most of them had shed their weapons, helmets and other equipment they had been carrying. The dogs plodded on alone, dragging their chains, heads down and probably suffering greatly from hunger and fatigue.

Other groups of prisoners, under better leadership, had taken more direct routes and reached Germany days ahead of us. On our second day out, I could see from a hilltop the dark lines of men stretching many miles to our rear and out of sight ahead of our column as well, but just at dusk of this last terrible night, from a rise in the road, I could see from the front to the rear of the line of march. Even though the interval between the ranks of marchers had lengthened, the total distance from front to rear was less than half what it was starting out from Sagan, an indication that many men were missing.

Just before daylight, we reached a paved road and entered a more open area. It was easier walking on the pavement but some men just lay down, unable to take another step. We had been 24 hours on the march in the penetrating cold since our last rest. Word was passed back that a city lay just three kilometers down the road. Food and shelter would be provided, and we would be allowed to rest for a few days. Men lucid enough to comprehend urged the others onto their feet, and the march resumed.

1945 February
Boxcars—Another Test of Endurance

We entered the city of Moskau. The first large buildings made up a huge pottery factory and foundry complex with smoke or steam coming from tall smokestacks, indicating a place of warmth. French slave laborers ran the mills and kept the fires and boilers going night and day. As soon as arrangements were made, the worn-out, desperate men began to file into the very warm—actually hot—multi-storied factory. I made my way up to the third floor on my hands and knees, traveling over a thick layer of sandy grit from the grinding and polishing of the pottery and similar products. The clay dust had, no doubt, never been cleaned from the loose plank floors.

The heat was almost unbearable at first, but I managed to get my heavy coat off and pulled my wonderful cotton sack over my head to keep out the dust. The plank floors had three or four inches of the gritty stuff, but we couldn't brush it off because it would have fallen on men getting settled below us. There were no walls, only timbers that supported the roof and the floors we occupied so we had to be careful not to roll off our high platforms. I took the last sip of water from my bottle and went to sleep feeling brain dead.

By mid-afternoon, most of us awoke, probably because of hunger, and organized ourselves into groups to go outside, where the French workers had prepared barley soup and some kind of tea. I took my tin can of soup and supplemented it with a tin of corned beef I'd carried in my coat pocket, eating as I walked around looking for water to fill my bottle. The dust had made us all very thirsty. The weather had warmed considerably; in fact, after another good sleep, we found it was thawing the next morning.

We stayed three days and nights at the pottery factory, resting, tending our frostbitten feet and rearranging our packs. The fourth morning we again formed up and marched out, headed northwest toward Spremburg in better spirits but limping on our blistered feet and wondering what would come next.

The snow was almost gone and, although it was overcast (good protection against the rampaging P-51s), the weather seemed warm for the first two days. More men had to be left at Moskau due to their disabilities but our 12-man combine was nearly intact after much searching for one another.

At Spremburg, 53 kilometers from Moskau, half of our group entrained for Nurnberg while the rest of us marked time near the station until boxcars began to arrive for us. Another cadre of guards took us over and were very brutal, pushing and striking while keeping up their typical cursing, yelling and grunting. In the darkness, they lined up 50 of us at a time in columns on ramps that reached to the boxcar doors. Suddenly we were shoved rapidly into the cars by the guards, pushing with their rifles on both sides and at the rear of each group of men. The small cars filled quickly, so the last men had to be squeezed in with much pounding by the guards so they could shut the doors.

These "40 and 8" cars, actually four-wheeled "goods wagons," had been built for World War I to carry 40 men or 8 horses, and our cars had just carried horses and had not been cleaned. The cars had no windows, the doors were locked, and we had to stand on the semi-frozen horse manure. It seemed unreal that they would actually load human beings into such quarters for we knew not how long a time.

In the total darkness, we organized by counting off and found we had 54 men and no room to sit down. After the most panic-prone of the group calmed down, it was decided that one third of us, by number—mine was 13—would try to get comfortable by sitting or squatting while the other two thirds would stand. I maneuvered to a wall location to steady myself while standing and hopefully to sit against when my turn came.

The locomotive gave off its shrill nerve-wracking whistle, then lurched forward, sending us into a pile one on top of the other. This was to be repeated hundreds of times over the next four days and nights. It took great restraint on each man's part to untangle and submit to having to lean against those standing next to him in the darkness.

Within a half hour, a new problem arose when some of the group had to urinate. Someone volunteered a tin can, which was passed around when needed, although we soon decided to make it a group operation to avoid having to constantly pass the can around. We didn't have "tea time" but rather "pee time". With considerable difficulty, men in one corner of the car managed to press outward a few boards at the floor level to dispose of the contents of the can.

This worked well, if slowly, until the small opening began to freeze. The air was foul due to overcrowding and the aroma given off by the horse manure. We found the layer of manure useful, however, when the inevitable time came that someone had to defecate, which turned out to be not very often. When it did come time for someone, it required considerable moving around to make space, but the layer of horse manure could be used to cover the human feces.

During most of the daylight hours, the locomotive unhooked from the cars to seek a hiding place from the very active fighter planes, leaving us exposed and vulnerable to attack. The one time the train was spotted by the deadly fighters was an experience beyond imagining. Locked in, and with only the old wooden sides of the cars for protection, we were trapped—and terrified. Locomotives were easy targets, and the boilers would blow up, scalding the train crews, but boxcars would usually burn if the pilots had incendiary bullets.

In this instance, the pilot of the first plane broke off his strafing run almost immediately. He probably realized it might be a

POW train. Pilots had been briefed about the many prisoners being transported. The damage was done in the first brief burst of machine gun fire. The eight 50-caliber machine guns had ripped into the forward cars, wounding several, but we knew of only one fatality. Later, some of the men in a car that had an opening to see out reported the two planes came up over a hill, around a bend and saw the train. It was their practice to follow the tracks, looking for targets, but in this far corner of Europe they could not spend much time and still have fuel enough to get back to base, so we were lucky for that. The man who was killed had slung his blanket as a hammock in one corner of the car. No one knew he was dead until blood started dripping down on the men seated below him.

The men in my car were certainly a cooperative group with whom to endure such an ordeal. Most of us scarcely knew the others, but there immediately developed a concern for each other and by necessity, tolerance of those who were the most claustrophobic or in need of support. Many of us began to sleep or catnap while standing. We rarely started to fall down as we stood body against body. Those standing close to the seated or squatting men quite often were thrown onto those poor people. But again, most of the party managed to be civil about it. One man turned out to be someone I had known earlier. He was the captain from Mississippi who had been so mean to the cadets during advanced flight training. None of us forgot his harassment and his attempts to get us thrown out of the cadet program just before graduation. He suffered greatly from claustrophobia from the start, but I didn't recognize his voice right away. At any rate, during the third day, he went berserk and thrashed about the car, throwing himself around, cursing and yelling. It became necessary to subdue him and tie him up, but he continued to moan and whimper until we arrived in Munich where we turned him over to the Germans. We had no way of knowing what became of him, but our senior officers requested he be put under the care of the Red Cross agents.

Someone in the next car was able to see out of a crack enough to read the names of stations and pass our location on to others. The train wound through Chemnitz, Regensburg, across Czechoslovakia, Austria and finally to Munich in Bavaria. The route was much safer than directly across to Munich by way of Dresden, a city crowded with marching POWs, refugees, Gypsies and many recuperating German troops from the Eastern front.

Stalin had put great pressure on the Allies to bomb Dresden to create chaos, disrupt transportation and render the area around the city indefensible to allow the Russians an easier approach to Berlin. Dresden had not been bombed before, and it was in great dismay that commanders ordered the carrying out of one of the most destructive raids of the war in Europe. The RAF and U.S. Army Air Forces each attacked the city twice on February 14th and 15th, 1945, with scarcely any loss of aircraft. Never having been bombed before, the city had meager defenses. The huge tonnage of bombs started fires that developed into a tremendous fire storm that drew winds in from all around at over one hundred miles an hour, causing an estimated quarter million deaths. Dresden was one of the most beautiful cities in Europe, with splendid architectural and artistic centers of interest. The unwilling participants in these raids realized the Allies had made a most tragic blunder.

Mooseberg, Purgatory

On February 8, our train arrived in Munich, where boxcar loads of weak, sick, hungry, thirsty prisoners were allowed to get out to relieve themselves beside the track. Some of the men were so cramped from the close quarters they could not walk, and everyone had some type of sickness.

Dysentery, sleep deprivation, pneumonia-like symptoms, frozen feet from the march and an indescribable weakness had taken its toll.

The bright sunlight after the darkness of the boxcars blinded us. We were not a formidable group, but the Germans took no chances; the guards had rifles and machine guns leveled at the staggering group of totally ineffective men. When the order came to get back into the cars, it was like a death sentence; all hope seemed to vanish as men tried to help each other up to the car doors. How much longer could we survive these conditions and when would we ever reach our destination? It seemed we had reached the limit of our endurance.

To our horror and despair, the doors were closed and locked, but the train remained in place all night. In the early morning, the shrill, irritating shriek of the train whistle signaled our departure for another unknown period of time in the stinking cars. In about two hours, with much jerking and shuddering, the train stopped, and before long the doors slid open amid deafening guttural commands from the new guards who had taken over. We had arrived at Stalag 7-A in Mooseberg—about 14 miles north of Munich.

The guards appeared to make every effort to earn the approval of their superior officers by abusing and browbeating us. Again, many of us could not walk and those who fell were poked and prodded with rifle butts, with the usual yelling and cursing at which most of the German military had become very proficient. Our senior officers, in very poor condition themselves, tried to get those in charge to understand how thirsty, hungry and ill the Americans were and how desperately they needed relief and attention. The Nazi officers turned a deaf ear and gave the impression they wished we had been sent to some other camp as they were already overcrowded and short of food.

After passing through a slow process of identification and being counted, we were issued a share of hard, black German bread that did little to alleviate our hunger. Our new quarters consisted of sheds open at the front, with a scattering of fairly clean straw on the dirt floor. A wooden beam a little over a foot high ran along the front. This obstacle proved to be too much for me to step over, so I rolled over into the straw, pushed my precious pack into a corner and fell asleep next to it. Thirst woke me up about midnight, along with most of the 40-odd other Kriegies in our shed.

We found a guard just outside and asked for "Wasser." He pointed to a group of men around a faucet, filling their containers. We went there and waited our turn. Everyone had become extremely dehydrated during the long train ride, as no water was given us and most of our canteens had frozen during the march from Sagan.

Our small temporary compound had only an overflowing slit trench as a latrine, and it had no protection against the wind. There was no toilet paper anywhere around, and most of us had used up what little we had carried on the march. My pages from "Mein Kampf" came in handy, and those who shared Hitler's book with me showed me respect and gratitude. Fortunately, my bowels had been kind to me during our period in the boxcar. Whenever I traded my ration of Red Cross cigarettes for food, I had insisted on keeping the cigarette package for toilet paper. The inner wrapper was also good paper for drawing or writing on—if one could spare it for that.

I had made notes and drawings of barns and houses on several sheets and managed to preserve them even during the terrible periods of dysentery. It was pitiful to see the victims of this malady trying to cope with the very frequent trips to the slit trench in the cold. It was my opinion that a large number of pneumonia cases were a result of this constant exposure to the wind and cold with such a large part of the anatomy uncovered. For a good part of this time, my visits to the latrine were quite infrequent but a few weeks later it was my turn to endure the awful agony of dysentery.

The second night in the shed, I arose and sat on the beam across the front to stretch my limbs and enjoy the star-filled sky—a beautiful night. About one o'clock, someone approached; he had a slight limp and looked familiar. He put his hand on my shoulder to step inside, and when he spoke I knew it was Col. Luper, our group commander. I had seen his plane shot down at Politz. The survivors had been captured and were incarcerated in a prison some distance from Stalag Luft III. He sat for a while to tell me of his escape attempt from there, his sojourn through southern Germany and finally his recapture. Luper had toured Germany and Bavaria by bike in his youth and could speak the language quite well. He had also taken the course on escape and evasion that was required of every Kriegie before attempting escape and had assembled the papers, money and other identification that might help if he were stopped.

His freedom lasted a few weeks, and because of his nonchalance he was able to get food and board trains without too much scrutiny. As he neared the Swiss border, he may have become overconfident. He entered a café for some sausage and beer, visited with a few men and finally started playing the piano. He had noticed one of the patrons leaving when he started playing a popular American melody that apparently gave him away. As he casually eased out the door, he met the local gendarmes, who took him into custody. Because of his rank, his punishment was very light by ordinary standards.

A few days later, we were transferred to some astoundingly filthy barracks that had the smell of death and had been vacant for some time. We scraped with pieces of glass and swept with crude brush brooms for several days and tried to make the dark, gloomy buildings more tolerable. The prison had held American Air Corps prisoners during World War I, and from 1933 to 1945 the Nazis had used it for political prisoners.

It certainly smelled as if many had died in the building. It was a single-story structure with small windows placed just under the high ceilings. There was a door at each end. The bunks were 12-man affairs; two bunks wide, three high and two long with barely room enough for a person to squeeze between. It was a claustrophobic nightmare because the buildings were nearly 200 feet long and the 500 of us in each one had but two doors to escape through in case of fire, panic or any type of calamity. We were locked in during air raids, adding to the stress.

It was necessary for everyone to make room in the small floor space to allow movement for activities such as visiting the latrine or leaving the barracks. During the day, to pass the time, six men would sit on the bottom bunk facing each other with just space for the 12 knees and 12 feet. The height of the bunks did not permit sitting upright, forcing us into painful and awkward positions. The other six men had no choice but to remain in their upper bunks or stay outdoors. The air, especially at night, was fetid and damp from the moisture given off by so many bodies, and there was constant coughing and groaning. Mattresses made of ancient burlap filled with very old, dirty, vermin-ridden straw were laid over four or five bed slats. The open-sided sheds we occupied on arrival had clean fresh air, at least, and I for one would have welcomed a permanent space on the comfortable straw.

It seemed incredible that even the Nazis would compel other human beings to endure so much filth and discomfort. The lice would have driven most people mad, but we had been subjected to lice for some time; there were just some new species now to contend with. I slept with all my clothes on, including that wonderful GI woolen overcoat, shoes and wool cap. The lice attacked more at night and were literally so thick we could hear them being crushed as we moved about. At one point, we had large predatory rats that moved in until they discovered there was not a scrap of food for them. Whenever one could be caught, he ended up in stew.

The rats would go for the cheek if you were sleeping, as that was the only exposed flesh. One caught my attention in the middle of the night, sniffing his way up my body until I felt his whiskers against my face. I clutched him in my gloved hand and squeezed until he stopped struggling. Yes, someone asked me for it the next morning.

Conditions at Mooseberg continued to decline as more thousands of prisoners of many nationalities were brought in. Food shipments became scarce due to the pounding of all transport systems by both the RAF and U.S. Air Forces. As German forces retreated toward the central core of the country, they removed every edible product they could find in the occupied countries. Cows, pigs, potatoes, grain and other foodstuffs were sent back to the homeland, but much of it was destroyed en route.[7]

---

[7] Over 2,000 POWs and 28 German guards died on the 10-day march.

The civilians and the armies to the east facing the Russians were on starvation rations, even though they had priority on foodstuffs. The greatest problem was the concentration of people in Germany. As the perimeter tightened, millions of slave laborers who kept industry going had to be fed, even if only small amounts of the poorest food. All of the country's military was being forced back into smaller and smaller space, and the resources of the conquered countries Germany had depended on were now denied them.

Nearly 2 million civilians were homeless, the wounded and injured numbered in the hundreds of thousands; 20 million were without utilities. More and more trainloads of sick and wounded soldiers kept arriving from both the eastern and western fronts. The burdens on hospitals and makeshift clinics were overwhelming, as the military and civilian casualties, especially the burn victims of the bombings, required great care. It was beyond the capabilities of the able people to care for the disabled.

The problems the German people had to contend with were overwhelming. The members of the Nazi party had become very bitter and had an apparently uncontrollable hatred for the Americans especially. They had put all their hopes and efforts into Hitler's insane idea that the "master race" would rule the world for a thousand years—only to realize, at last, that they had lost. Millions of the young men of the "master race" were buried on the battlegrounds of 20 countries. The resources of the nation had been expended. They knew the war was lost unless Hitler could get his much-publicized nuclear weapon in time to change the outcome. The preponderance of the population was not in the Nazi party but could do nothing because they were constantly monitored by the party members. If a soldier deserted, his family would suffer; if anyone complained or indicated all was lost, he was likely to be sent to the Russian front or to a labor battalion. Any indiscretion could result in parents or other family members suffering beatings and torture.

People had nowhere to turn. The indoctrination of the "Hitler Youth" through the 1930s led the by-then young adults to inform on parents and older siblings. With all the problems before him, Hitler kept up his relentless genocidal extermination of the Jews and political prisoners until the very day he committed suicide. The SS continued to kill those left in concentration camps even after Hitler died.

The millions of prisoners they had captured in so many campaigns had presented a gigantic challenge regarding what to do with them—or how to dispose of them. In 1941 and 1942, 3,500,000 Russians had surrendered and were expected to become slave laborers, but they proved unmanageable. These men faced punishment at home after the war for surrendering to the Nazis. When the notorious Russian General Andrei Vaslov was captured, he helped to organize the Russian prisoners into a strong army to fight against Stalin. These troops were exploited by Hitler, who sent them underequipped and outnumbered against the best of the Soviet armies, resulting in high casualties.

Vaslov was captured by Patton in May 1945 in Czechoslovakia, who turned him over to Stalin to be tortured and hanged. In my opinion, this was a despicable action on the part of Allied officers.

When Italy surrendered to the Allies in 1944, the German forces still in Italy seized 640,000 of their former Italian Axis partners and treated them so badly more than 30,000 died in captivity in less than a year.

To us prisoners, it appeared we would be the last to expect food, medicine or any chance of freedom. The Allied airmen were especially vulnerable due to the hatred caused by the terrifying bombing attacks and destruction of industries. There were, perhaps, over a million German POWs under Allied control to consider. Hitler was preparing a "redoubt", or fortified hiding place, as a final refuge for the Nazi survivors near his Berchesgarden in the Austrian Alps and planned to use POWs as human shields to defend it. The General Staff wanted the airmen as bargaining chips as they faced the ultimate unconditional surrender mandated by the Allies. Hitler still hoped a nuclear weapon would be available at the last minute to turn the tide, but his generals feared he might use it to blackmail the world; a move that might result in the destruction of civilization. No one knew what form the nuclear device would take—or even if it could be controlled. Many scientists feared a chain reaction would result that might render the world uninhabitable. Our outlook was bleak considering these factors.

Eventually, a considerable number of us were housed near latrines that were an improvement over the windy slit trenches. The "aborts", as they called the latrines, were masonry buildings built mostly above ground, probably to facilitate removal of the thick liquid to be spread on cropland. The design of these structures consisted of a flat concrete floor with numerous holes that opened to a huge pit or basement.

These began to overflow in spite of around-the-clock efforts by farmers with horse-drawn wooden tanks and the few tank trucks left. Many of us elected to stay out of doors to escape the conditions in the barracks, with their danger of disease, giving us yet another situation to deal with. With men sprawled everywhere, the overrun from the aborts would flow silently among them until a considerable number of Kriegies took to sleeping on the roofs. More slit-trench latrines were dug as the aborts could not handle the thousands of people with dysentery. Probably 40,000 to 60,000 suffered from this miserable ailment during February and March. We dreamed of the day when toilet paper would be plentiful and we could have warm bathrooms.

To the Very Edge

My recovery from the march and train trip was slow. The injuries from being shot down began to cause considerable pain, and the terribly uncomfortable bunks, cold and dampness aggravated my condition.

After a long ordeal with dysentery, I developed a severe infection, caused by the rectal-prolapse injury, that forced me to remain outside because of the offensive odor. My combine of 12 Kriegies from our room in Sagan had eventually come together at adjacent bunks and tried to meet outside at least once a day to have our rations together, as there could be no cooking inside with our "Kriegie" burners. It had been my habit to go to my bunk during the day for a rest and to escape the cold, but it became too much to expose my friends to my infection.

By the end of February, I was unable to eat anything but warm liquid, and we had very little of that. After more than a week of severe pain, I developed a fever and began to lose hope of recovering. I thought constantly of good, hot chicken soup. I walked around all of one day with the fever and, finally, at dusk was so weak I simply slid down onto a stone step and leaned back against the wall of a building out of the way.

The fever was burning me up, and my mind began to slip away; I thought death was finally catching up to me after I'd gone through so much stress and discomfort.

It had begun to snow large wet flakes, and my shoes were covered in a short time. The snow came down faster and the evening dragged on. My thoughts were not of family and home or the salvation of my soul, but only that in a few hours it would be all over and the last thing I would see in this world was my shoes being covered with snow. It would be an easy departure except for the headache and fever—just drifting off to sleep to freeze and not wake up in the morning.

Something woke me. There was a fire close by, and the flames were flickering against the building I'd been leaning against, but now I was facing the wall, with the fire behind me. Could it be I'd gone to Hell?

(No, there was still snow on the ground, and it was continuing to snow lightly. A German guard was standing close by in his shiny black boots, so I tapped him on the leg and asked, "Voss iss los?" "Nix iss los!" he snarled.

Suddenly, I was lifted up and turned around, facing the fire, and noticed someone was holding a cup of hot tea or broth to my lips. Several other Kriegies were gathered around the fire, and two large young men in white coveralls were attending us. Fires or lights were "verboten" (forbidden) at night, but because of the heavy snow and cloud cover these men had been given permission to have small fires. They had come from Switzerland in one of the Red Cross trucks that had been provided by the Allies to transport food to the prison camps. They had been allowed to evaluate conditions in the prisons and this particular night had come to Stalag 7-A, to my compound, and had rounded up people like myself to do whatever they could to help us.

They soon were aware that something was seriously wrong with me, and they avoided getting too close. At about two or three in the morning, an older man, probably a doctor, bald and bare-headed in the snow, appeared and talked with the two visitors. He pulled down my pants briefly to examine me and then left while the men put my clothes back together. The doctor returned sometime later and injected a thick, white liquid up into my lower tract. It was very cold but soothing, and he used a large quantity of it, probably a pint at least.

The guards had put the fires out, and the three men left us for the trucks. The doctor gave me a cup of tea and put two or three pills into it before he left. It had stopped snowing and was nearly daylight when two Kriegies helped me to my barracks and into my bunk, where I went to sleep.

The medication had a long time to help me, as it was over a week before I had a bowel movement. The fact I had eaten very little for several weeks and drank practically no water probably caused severe dehydration. The cold water tasted very bad to me. Just a few sips caused me to shiver uncontrollably. Meanwhile, I rested and we made good use of the Red Cross parcels the trucks had brought from Switzerland. It amazed me to realize I would have died without the intervention of the medics when only a few hours before it seemed the only remedy for my condition would require surgery, which was simply not available within a thousand miles. The arrival of the first Red Cross truck in my particular compound—at a rare time when a fire was allowed, on a night when I was most in need—and the arrival of the old doctor with a remedy for my affliction, all added up to a fortunate series of coincidences, really a miracle at the most critical hour for me.

1945 March, Hunger

Since virtually all surface transport had come to a halt, some-thing had to be done to get food to the camps. The Allied powers in Switzerland managed to put a fleet of GI trucks together to bring the Red Cross food in, after alerting the air forces to watch out for white trucks with red crosses on top. These came in quite frequently during March, but feeding 125,000 of us in Stalag 7-A as well as the people in dozens of other prison camps in the area would have required thousands of trucks. Finally, a train was es-corted through from Switzerland with over 40 carloads of food, but the allotment for 7-A was enough for just a few days. The meager supply of German food was unbelievable.

Bits of trash, dirt, spoiled food and even an occasional dead mouse could be seen if one looked, so most of us didn't.

We had turnips, potato peelings, blood sausage, dry salty sau-erkraut, foul-smelling cheese and the usual black bread. The bread had sawdust mixed in with the coarse flour, a fact admitted and confirmed by the Germans.

Each loaf had a date marked on the top, so we knew much of it was nearly a month old. (Later we learned the bread was developed as a staple for civilian food emergencies and could and did last for years.) It didn't spoil and was handled and delivered unwrapped in open trucks that were loaded and unloaded by men who looked as if they hadn't washed their hands in months. Butter was mostly inferior lard mixed with a coal-based product of a process used to obtain gas from coal. This was also confirmed by the Germans, along with the admission that because it caused chronic stomach problems it was no longer issued to their soldiers.

The breakdown of all services in the country became more apparent as the quality and quantity of the food we were given decreased day by day. The potato-peeling soup, blood sausage, turnips and buckets of unidentified ingredients began to arrive frozen, making the rationing of everything much more difficult. More wood had to be split into small short pieces to fuel our "Kriegie burners" in order to thaw out our rations, so we began to systematically remove the posts in the fences that separated our compounds. We cut the posts down to finger-sized bits of wood that could be fed into the burner to produce an intense heat from a handful of wood.

The Kriegie burners were ingenuously contrived by shaping tin cans into a vertical firebox connected to a short flue in the bottom. A drum type of blower turned at high speed by a crank and pulleys that were driven by pieces of shoestring or strips of leather for belts, forced air into the firebox. The guards made no effort to halt this operation (removing fences), as they had stopped segregating us by nationalities as well as dispensing with the tedious chore of appell.

The Red Cross trucks were bringing enough parcels for one-half parcel per man per week; that amounted to one can of Spam for 24 men per day. There were two interludes when the trucks could not get through, and at one period, my group went four days with nothing at all to eat unless we had stashed a piece of that awful bread in a coat pocket.

Hunger led to long discussions of food, and for most of us this helped us carry on. Almost everyone had ideas for some special dish to prepare once our ordeal was over, and lengthy recipes were composed. My good friend Norman Tiefel, of Indiana, would settle down and inform me we would now have a "soda-fountain conversation" for the day, and on another day it would be stews or hot dishes or baked goods. As we ate our meager rations, after closely observing the division of portions, we kept each morsel in our mouths for as long as possible.

Norman had a hair-raising experience when he was shot down in Italy in his B-25. Because of a raging fire in the bomb bay, he had to get out through a small side window so small he had to climb out first then snap his chest-type parachute on. Apparently he failed to get the chute on completely or he struck a part of the plane when he was swept away by the slipstream because he came to in the air, head down, suspended by one ankle caught in the harness. He fell headfirst into a drainage ditch. After a time, Italian civilians pulled him out and he was hospitalized with burns about his head and other injuries. His eyes had been burned so badly that they would water quite frequently, but talking about food caused them to run more freely.

A POW named Wilson periodically made the rounds of the barracks, hypnotizing people who had medical problems, and he quite often had success. Tiefel's turn came, and those of us in the barracks able to get close enough saw the tears stop. It was a few months before the malady started again.

Another man had an arm that was useless and had no strength at all. He was seated in a rickety chair and told to raise his arm while under hypnosis. "Hold it up at a 45-degree angle. It will be as strong as an iron bar, strong enough to support my weight," said Wilson. And indeed it did. Wilson raised himself up off the floor with all his weight on the man's outstretched arm. It was a remarkable demonstration, as were other helpful attempts to relieve pain and discomfort among the prisoners.

Prolonged hunger affected men in many ways, but the constant gnawing and yearning for warm, decent food put everyone in a sober mood as weakness increased day by day and week by week. The need for calories to combat the cold caused great concern as our strength diminished. Everyone had a feeling of abject poverty. We had nothing for personal care, not even a mirror to check out how thin we looked. Our clothes had become rags. Blankets were worn through by the weather and the crude bunks. We had been sentenced to execution three times by a madman and his fanatic supporters. If, indeed, Hitler's scientists succeeded in completing a nuclear weapon before the Allies reached us, the outcome of the war could change in a matter of hours. With freedom only days or weeks away, it was depressing to realize all could be lost at the very end of our efforts to survive.

Quite frequently a man would suddenly fall down and begin to shake uncontrollably. These people had reached the end of endurance and were totally helpless. One of our 12-man combine, Joe Stager, fell down to the floor while talking with us and apparently thought it was all over for him, as he asked us to see that his journals got to his family. He had two books of notes and well-drawn cartoons. We managed to get him up to the "hospital", a brick building for those who could not make it any longer. It was severely overcrowded and a despairing place. But gave shelter, and one of us went to see him every hour with something to eat or sometimes just a cup of warm water. He was still there the morning we were liberated, and while the Luftwaffe were wresting control of the camp from the SS, a machine gun stitched a line of holes in the brick wall, knocking pieces of mortar off the inside wall onto several of the patients. A few of them jumped down and lay on the floor; the first move they had made since being carried into the building. Joe survived and made it home with his narratives and cartoons.

In March, several cold wet storms blew down from the Alps, causing great discomfort especially to those people outdoors. Three or four of us would pool our blankets to put over us as we sat back to back in a circle during the night. If it became too wet and cold, we could always squeeze into the barracks, but few of us could tolerate the foul air and close quarters. The overflowing aborts became even more unbearable as the wagons were delayed, crowding their way through the throngs of POWs. Our senior officers constantly pleaded with the German SS, who now controlled the camp, for some kind of relief. In the last week of March, large white tents were being put up in a field for more shelter. The tents probably came from Switzerland at the behest of the Allies.

1945 April, Hope Building

On April 1, Easter Sunday, I was moved into the tents and had a space about seven feet by two feet all to myself. The day before, I had washed myself and my clothes, shaved with my last razor blade and had my hair cut with a friend's dull scissors. The water had come from pools that surrounded the tent area after a heavy rain. My greatest concern was that my wool shirt and pants would shrink too much to put on, but I found that I had shrunk, too. I had kept my wool shirt in my "briefcase" to conserve it for a day like this. Usually my heavy undershirt was the garment of choice. It felt good to be cleaner, and we attended Mass between two buildings, with at least 2,000 of us in the congregation. Just before the consecration, we heard a tremendous roar and whistle as a P-51 flew over us at less than 100 feet above the ground. Everyone hit the dirt as it was such a surprise, and there was no sound until it flashed over our heads. The chaplain said "Praise the Lord and the P-51s!" It was a signal of encouragement and gave our morale a boost.

Near mid-April, we began to have visitors, as the group of POWs from Sagan who had been held in Nurnberg was sent down the autobahn to Mooseberg. I was near the fence when my friend Jim Bouvier (from Bristol, Vermont) came into view. We agreed to meet as soon as possible at the same location along the fence separating us. Jim had worn out the soles of his shoes and then his socks on the trek down from Nurnberg. He had no underwear, toilet paper, cigarettes or anything that could be called a necessity in our situation. I had worn summer and winter underwear on my last mission, so I gave him my cutoff long johns, a pack of Red Cross cigarettes and a pair of socks since I had two pair, and I found him a piece of toilet paper. "Just like a Vermonter" he said, "always has the first dollar he ever earned."

The next time we met, I was outdoors in a snowstorm, trying to use up my group's last bit of flour. With only a small tin pan over my Kriegie burner, it was a losing game. Jim, always the humorist, remarked, "This is the first time I ever saw anyone trying to make a pancake outdoors in a snowstorm in a tin can." About then, a Mongolian came up close to me and demanded by sign language that I trade my good wool GI coat for his ragged filthy coat. He emphasized his desire by brandishing a long, wicked-looking knife. There were hundreds of Kriegies around us, and soon a few started a scuffle that allowed me to melt into the crowd. It was a near disaster as the Mongolians (Russian prisoners) were extremely dangerous. This one had escaped from the Russian compound and mingled with the other prisoners, who were no longer confined to compounds. The population of Mooseberg had reached 130,000 prisoners of many nationalities, and it was getting impossible to move without touching someone.

On April 18, my group, the 457th, attacked the marshalling yards near the small hamlet of Freising, about five or six miles from our camp. It was a clear, sunny day, and it seemed as if the formations with their bomb-bay doors open were right over us. They were probably two or three miles east of our location, but at five miles high it looked closer. We had no idea which groups were participating in the attack just down the road from us at that time.

We watched one plane go down. Only years later did I learn it was the last 457th crew lost to enemy action. The pilot's name was Lt. Thistle. The plane was on fire, and some of the crew jumped right away while the plane turned left (away from us) and salvoed their bombs. We were relieved they didn't turn right toward us to get rid of their lethal load.

The sight of our bombers was heartening to us but a bit frightening as well. The long plumes of the smoke bombs dropped by the several lead planes to signal the rest of the formations to drop their loads marked the target and created an awesome, spider-like diagram.

As wave after wave of B-17s dropped their loads, the smoke markers fused into a weird, gigantic flower pattern at the targets and joined with the smoke of the fires on the ground. The bombers were leaving no contrails, but the fighter escorts a few thousand feet above them scribed long, curved white trails as they patrolled for enemy fighters that never appeared. Without the telltale contrails, we could not have seen the P-51s at that great altitude. It was a spectacular display, but the ground shook under our feet and the concussions vibrated through our bodies. The sound of the exploding anti-aircraft shells and the familiar hum of the B-17s reverberated through the sky.

The Luftwaffe began flying its ME-262 jet fighters more frequently and at lower altitudes near the end of April, and we began to see new types of American planes practically skimming the ground—a sign of close support operations for the tank and infantry units approaching our area.

One of the new types of planes had a unique profile; we later learned it was dubbed a "Black Widow." It was a highly sophisticated plane with much radar, remote-firing gun turrets and the ability to fly close to the ground even at night. As more and more medium bombers appeared, flying low, we knew the Allied ground forces were close by.

Our senior officers sent two men through the fence to Switzerland on a mission to contact the Allies and alert them to the fact we had documents from Heinrich Himmler, the head of the SS, ordering that "all Allied airmen must be destroyed before recapture."

One of our best POW intelligence workers had made a daring visit to the headquarters of the prison commandant and actually brought out the order, so within hours the two were dispatched to alert the Allies that time was running out. The mission was successful, but within a few days we could hear the tanks growling and firing just to the west of us. Meanwhile, the Luftwaffe from a nearby air base had approached the SS controllers of Stalag 7-A with an offer to take over the camp.

Freedom

On the morning of April 29, a P-51 flew over the camp at low altitude and did a roll that was a prearranged signal to expect the Americans to reach us during the day. We could observe the Germans pulling back their tanks to a line even with the prison. The guards were nervous and carried their gas masks with the flap open, ready for use, while the dogs were already fitted with gas masks. The SS plan was to open lethal gas lines throughout the camp, followed by setting fire to gasoline lines, to burn the place with everyone in it.

Soon the Luftwaffe appeared and began to forcibly take control, and at this point the guards began to leave their posts and go over the fence, some of them throwing their rifles away. The SS was resisting with firearms, and the Luftwaffe returned fire. In the melee, a few POWs were wounded by stray rounds, but most of us kept down close to the ground. Before noon, the Luftwaffe had control, and as the German tanks drew back behind us, the Americans came in sight in hot pursuit, leaving us in no-man's land with shells flying in both directions overhead.

I returned to my tent, and we decided to eat the last of some bread and a bit of jam. I spread the jam from a prone position, as I thought it prudent to keep my head down low. I moved outside the tent briefly and could see the shells from the mobile guns flying overhead, flashing in the sun.

Much as I wanted to see history made, I thought it better to lay low and wait—no need to be killed at the last hour.

About noon, the first vehicle, a half-track, broke through the main gate amidst the cheers of tens of thousands of prisoners. Within minutes, the hated swastika came down and the stars and stripes went up the flagpole to more cheering. It was an emotional experience, seeing our flag again.

Tanks halted on each side of the camp and fired relentlessly at the retreating Germans. One half-track drove around the interior of the camp with a big captain in a raincoat yelling, "Where's McCraken?" McCraken was lying head to head with me in the tent, waiting for the activity to settle down. His brother was the big captain looking for him, and it didn't take long before he had scooped up his 80-pound sibling and soon was throwing oranges and cans of rations from his vehicle to the cheering Kriegies.

In mid-afternoon, the troops began to arrive. They were in a rage because the day before they had reached Dachau, a concentration camp just down the road from us. These men were fighting mad after seeing firsthand what had been done to human beings in that place. The next day younger, newly trained replacement troops arrived; they were in shock, incoherent and out of their minds because of what they had been exposed to. We knew what was happening but never guessed it was on such a scale or that inmates were still being killed the day our troops reached the concentration camps. We had heard of conditions there from a man who had been imprisoned for political beliefs for six years. He had finally escaped and posed as an Allied serviceman to get refuge in our prison. He had survived because he had been put to work handling the bodies from the gas chamber to the crematoriums.

A group of American airmen spent three months in Buchenwald, an extermination camp near Dachau, before their plight was discovered by the Red Cross inspectors. These people filled us in on what was happening.

There were reports of vivisection performed on prisoners who were immobilized on operating tables without anesthesia, unable to scream or call out because their vocal cords had been cut in order to not distract the surgeons. Even as the Allied troops entered the prisons, victims were found still on the tables, giving evidence that the "doctors" had just left.

It seemed incredible that people could be found to do such fiendish tortures, let alone carry on to the last few minutes. Most of the poor victims could not be saved. Many had had organs removed, and meticulous records kept by the perpetrators indicated that organs had been removed from one victim and exchanged with those of another. Sections of skulls had been removed to allow direct study of the brain and how it reacted to various stimuli.

General Eisenhower was so appalled by what was found in Dachau, as well as in other concentration camps, that he ordered civilians to walk through the prisons between the rows of corpses piled high on each side of the paths. He wanted no excuses that "it didn't happen" or "we didn't know about this." The people who walked through that part of Hell on Earth, even those who fainted from the sights and smells, certainly knew from that day on and would never forget it as long as they lived. Some of us saw photographs that were developed a few days after we were liberated, and some Kriegies went to see the camp at Dachau for themselves. I had no urge to visit such a place after viewing the photographs, nor did I feel up to traveling even that short distance.

The day we were liberated, field kitchens were set up and soon beautiful white bread was being distributed. We were sure it was angel-food cake, even after tasting it. The proper authorities soon collected the remaining SS and took the Luftwaffe people into custody, with considerable numbers of favorable reports from our senior officers. We all hoped they would be treated well, because in effect, they had saved us from likely annihilation.

Security was tight, as the Germans had taken up defensive positions about four miles behind us and within artillery range. We ex-prisoners were not allowed to leave camp for the first few days for this reason, and the Americans were likely to shoot anything that moved. Three light bombers were launched one night to bomb the camp at low level but failed to reach us. One was shot down, one crashed, and the third turned back. Sporadic gunfire kept us uneasy and prevented sleep, but it was comforting to have so much protection around us.

Stories went around that General Patton was in the camp, and our senior officers met with him to discuss the critical shortages of food and medicine for the 130,000 of us. But Patton said he had a war to win and was headed for Austria before the Russians got there.

He was gone—pearl-handled revolvers, shiny helmet and all— bouncing away in his jeep. "No trucks to spare for POWs. Don't you know there's a war on?" He left the tidying-up for others far behind the lines, so everyone was on short rations again. A few trucks soon arrived with food, but they could not evacuate us because the roads out were still within German artillery range.

On my first day out, I hooked up with a friend who had liberated a small pickup truck that ran on gas generated by a trash-burning stove in the back. We had seen these little three-wheeled trucks made of plywood on our trips across Germany, apparently war-time vehicles made of nonessential materials. We viewed the destroyed bridge over the river now guarded by two MPs at each end. The Army had built a temporary bridge beside it, but civilians were not allowed to use it; they had to climb the twisted superstructure of the old one to cross the river. One of the two towers in Mooseburg that we had seen from the camp had been hit by tank guns to take out a sniper, and the upper floors held tons of paper money from the 1920s. We were up to our knees in 100,000,000 and 500,000,000 mark notes that Kriegies gathered up in baskets and boxes to cook with. Everywhere, we saw liberated chickens, pigs and handy gadgets the men picked up, but it seemed wrong to me to take these things, as they belonged to civilians who had suffered for nearly six years under Hitler.

My friend and I saw a woman and a little boy of about six going from a barn toward the house carrying a white flag on a stick. There was a white sheet hanging from an upstairs window as well. We decided to try to buy some eggs, as we hadn't seen one since leaving the States. By sign language, we thought we had made our point, but the woman went into the hen house and brought out a hen. We finally bought six eggs for a pack of cigarettes, an extravagant price after trading across the fence, but even at that, she was reluctant to take pay. I had a small package of Red Cross coffee for the woman and one of cocoa, which I gave to the boy along with some bars of sugar. We went into the house to show them how to fix the cocoa with warm milk and politely declined an offer of black bread. The woman didn't know how to use the instant coffee and seemed amazed and pleased not to have to percolate it. They showed us photos of three young men I assumed were older brothers away in the service, a photo of a priest and a man obviously the father.

With many signs and more tears, the woman explained her husband had been away working for a long time, no doubt in a labor battalion. The good Christian people of Bavaria received harsh treatment from Nazi party members. As we left, the little boy gravely shook hands and his mother—still crying—gave us each a light hug. We hoped our visit left them with a favorable impression of Americans in spite of our appearance in rags. It was a sad encounter as it seemed we had triggered memories of the rest of the family long away from home. They probably had no idea if they would ever see their loved ones again.

1945 May, VE Day, France

On May 6, 1945, the military decided to move us out, as Patton finally got the word to send every truck in the area to our relief. Within a day, hundreds of trucks began converging on Mooseburg, and we were packed in randomly with standing room only for the long ride to Ingolstadt on the Danube River. The autobahn the trucks used for part of the trip had many bridges and overpasses destroyed as the Germans retreated, causing the drivers to negotiate some steep temporary roads down to places where they could safely cross the rivers or valleys. There were many burned-out vehicles, both friendly and enemy along the roads.

At Ingolstadt, we were quartered in an ancient round fort, three stories high with a large courtyard on the ground level in the center, with ramps leading to the upper floors. More than likely when the fort was built, hundreds of years before, horses were taken up the ramps, as some spaces looked like stables. The rooms were filled with gear for mountain or ski troops as well as some frogman equipment. Some very small outboard motors, weighing perhaps no more than eight or ten pounds, looked tempting to carry with us, but I had enough to carry with just my old Red Cross pack.

I slept in a room filled with flags and had at least two feet of swastikas on my bunk for a mattress. I took only a bayonet, a fork and spoon, a canteen and some letters and papers—in German, of course. I still have them now.

The old fort was adjacent to an airfield with hangars filled with unusual types of planes, some in experimental stages. I was most interested in a four-engine jet bomber and a sleek jet fighter plane that looked as if it had been flown, probably in a test flight for research. The aircraft industry continued testing planes until its facilities were overrun in late April. Several German pilots attempted to land planes at the field but were shot down or driven away. Some one- or two-place planes were loaded with four or five men trying to surrender to the Americans. The anti-aircraft people took no chances with thousands of newly liberated prisoners on the field.

One British Mosquito bomber with three crewmen aboard flew over and fired flares, hoping to land, but was shot down with only one survivor. It was said the flares they fired off for identification were of the wrong color for the day; it was a sad and somber happening.

The next morning, May 8, quite a number of gooney birds (C-47s) had arrived to evacuate us. They were filled with five-gallon cans of gasoline that had to be unloaded. The cans were too heavy for me to handle, but I did slide some along the floor to the men in the doorways. As we filed in, all I thought of was someone fool enough to light up a smoke, as the plane reeked of gasoline fumes. Rather than send empty planes for us, they very prudently loaded them with the much-needed fuel for the front lines. As we got under way, the pilots warned us of the dangerous fumes, and most of us were vigilant. We didn't want to come this far to be incinerated. We made sure the windows were kept open all the way.

The pilots were real good guys, but they looked too young and had nice clean uniforms on. We had been fumigated with a potent bug-killing powder as we approached the plane for boarding, a process that caused almost as much itching as the lice we had carried with us. Our route took us over many of the destroyed cities and towns, with a loop up around Cologne, where only the two blackened towers of the cathedral were standing.

When we approached the Rhine River, I asked the pilots if I might fly the plane out of Germany, across Luxemburg and into France. They accommodated me and it was a wonderful experience, a fitting farewell to the Third Reich.

Upon arrival at Rheims, we boarded the large open trailer trucks again and saw the roads lined with cheering French people giving us the "V" for victory sign and shouting, "Le Jour V!" They were delirious with joy at the news the war was over. I was in a group deposited in a small grassy field within sight of the big cathedral and close to the area where the surrender was being worked out.

We could see much coming and going of high-ranking officers and civilian diplomats from many countries. We had again been deloused with the awful powder, down our necks, up our pant legs and under our shirts. Right away, we had a quick lunch of Spam sandwiches, followed by a partial payment of 4,000 francs, one half of which was enough to buy a shirt, pants, underwear, socks, toothbrush and a razor with blades. By this time it was getting dark, and after finding a tent to sleep in later on, I joined a queue for a shower.

The long line moved slowly as hundreds of dirty ex-Kriegies scrubbed under the warm water of their first shower in months. From nine o'clock in the evening until two o'clock the next afternoon, 17 hours, I waited and hoped they wouldn't run out of hot water. The troops manning the operation kept the heaters going 24 hours a day. I took my time in the pure luxury of soap and hot water then, afterwards, slid into clean clothes free of lice and bad odors. My old pants, purchased just before graduation from cadet training, were buried under a shrub in the yard. The shrub had died by the next morning, or at least so I've related ever after.

I washed my GI wool shirt thoroughly and had it deloused again, as I wanted to take it home. It came through very well, but it hadn't been worn all the time in the prison camps as it was more comfortable to wear my heavy undershirt.

After a short sleep, I paid a visit to the grand cathedral of Rheims, where I gave my heartfelt thanks for my deliverance and promised to never ask for anything for myself again as reparation for my survival.

We got under way by truck again to Camp Lucky Strike, on the French coast near the town of Fecamp, several miles east of the port of Le Havre. Our rescuers provided each of us with a narrow, hard canvas Army cot, a clean blanket and five meals a day, supplemented with thick eggnog kept in huge tubs with a long-handled communal dipper handily hung on the edge of the tub out under the trees. We ate under a canvas shelter with a dirt floor, standing up at a shelf, but no one complained. It was a marvel that so much planning had gone into providing for the tens of thousands of us. The medical problems were dealt with as best they could. A pipeline of food had been set up, necessary supplies were stockpiled, mountains of paperwork was done to sort out bonafide ex-prisoners from the nationals attempting to get out of Europe, and organizations were set up to deal with sticky problems for some once they returned to their families. Some men would return with great expectations of taking up with wife and children, to begin life anew. Many would discover the wife had gone off with or married someone else. The scope of the operation was enormous, and great credit was due to the planners.

The sprawling camp was on a high bluff overlooking the beach still not cleared of mines and other ordinance. Only one or two well-marked paths led down to the English Channel, and they were too narrow to accommodate more than a few dozen of us at a time. I was satisfied to sit on the clean grass and look across to the White Cliffs of Dover, reminiscing of my months in beautiful England. Mixed memories of the pleasant interludes as well as the unpleasant happenings of our operations came back, but the wonderful days of spring—and peace at last—made the location ideal for recuperation. It was easy to gain a pound a day on the five meals and the peaceful environment. We were the survivors of the most savage air battles the world had ever seen and had come through unpleasant and arduous trials while under the complete control of madmen. For myself, the fact I still had all my limbs and eyesight, albeit some painful injuries, was a blessing to be very thankful for.

I had four fillings in my teeth when we were shot down, and they loosened up to cause me some distress during my incarceration. Two fillings fell out at Mooseburg, so when they announced that a dentist would be in camp I joined the queue. A big Frenchman arrived with a dentist's chair on a wagon and set up shop under the trees, but as no one stepped up for treatment I foolishly took my seat in the chair. Bad move.

The old Frenchman had a foot-powered drill with a bit that hadn't been sharpened since World War I. No painkillers back then, so it was excruciatingly painful as he routed out the four teeth and prepared for the fillings. All through the torture, he kept up a cheerful running commentary in French, with much waving of hands and gestures to emphasize whatever he was talking about. I think even his horse winced whenever he hit a nerve. My fingerprints probably stayed on the arms of his chair for a long time.

Le Havre was an interesting city, with half of it down near the docks and the other half 500 feet above. There was a moving, covered stairway (an escalator) built of wood that carried people up and down the long, steep slope. Fairly tight security was maintained at the camp to help keep track of all of us since we were all back under control of the U.S. Army, but a good number took off for Paris to see the sights. I tired too easily for such a long bus ride, and I didn't want to miss out on a trip back to the States. I bought sweet cherries, other fruit and pastries at the plentiful markets in the city to offset the meals I missed at camp while exploring the area.

At one farm, the family insisted on our touring the farmstead, showing off with great pride the manure pile just inside the entrance to the compound. The house was about 700 years old, with a huge iron gate that opened from the street to a courtyard with buildings on all sides. We were ushered into the kitchen at about two in the afternoon, to eat a meal that was well prepared and tasty. The men—the father and, I believe, his brother and full-grown son—ate with their hats on, while a girl was completing butter-making in the same room. Just as we finished eating, thank goodness, she poured the buttermilk into a trough that ran directly into a pig pen just outside the kitchen where the pigs woke up and noisily fought over the delicacy.

The time passed, and we felt we should get back to camp, but the family brought in some cognac they claimed to have kept buried in the garden during the occupation. I took one sip, and that was enough because, although it was very good, it was much too strong for me. The other two joined in the family's celebration of peace and their visiting American guests until after dark, so it was easy to accept an invitation to stay the night. The brother and his son left to go home, and we had a room that was sparse but clean. We left after a fine breakfast, and they were delighted when we pooled our cigarettes to leave for them. Our Red Cross cigarettes would still buy anything in Europe, so I accepted the GI smokes we were issued at camp, as well, and used them to trade.

The critically wounded and those suffering from other ailments were air-evacuated to the States or to England for hospitalization as soon as possible. Others left for medical treatment by ship as space became available, while people in my category waited, put on weight and enjoyed the chance to recuperate in the delightful spring weather. The sea air was invigorating and very beneficial after the fetid, smelly air in the barracks at Mooseburg and the awful stench of the boxcars. We were all anxious to get home, but I didn't begrudge a day at Lucky Strike.

1945 June, Heading Home

Word finally came to prepare for our trip back to the States. On June 6, we began to assemble near the docks at Le Havre, where our ship would soon dock. While there, we witnessed a revolting incident. Some black servicemen were unloading a "duck", an amphibious vehicle ferrying supplies from a ship to shore. One of the workers, a large black man, lost his footing and plunged from the craft into the water close to the water-level dock.

The white officer supervising the work watched as the man sank into the water. Just as he resurfaced but before he could get a breath of air, the officer placed his foot on the man's head and shoved him down again, remarking in a southern drawl, "Look at that nigger blow bubbles." Instantly, some of the ex-POWs grabbed him while others retrieved the nearly drowned victim and rendered assistance. Someone called for the MPs, who called someone from the provost marshal's office to come and take the officer into custody. We all hoped he would be punished severely for his callous treatment of a fellow human being.

Our ship was a brand new cargo/passenger vessel with a Vermont captain who had lost his last ship in a hurricane a few months earlier. Captain Dunton had served in World War I and retired to Vermont to operate a mink farm but was called back to duty in the Merchant Marine. One other Vermonter was on board, ex-POW Carl Hedin of Westfield, Vermont. All the passengers were liberated POWs.

We watched the shores of France fade from view with some profound memories and were thrilled to see the White Cliffs of Dover slide by as we made our way to Southampton. The harbor pilot came aboard before dark, and we spent a restful night. No one was allowed off the ship unless he signed a statement of intent to marry an English girl, and much as I would have liked to see By, I didn't feel ready for a commitment to marriage.

The next day, we left with a convoy and passed Land's End at dusk in a light rain. The next morning was bright and sunny, and because Captain Dunton wanted to get us home in a hurry we had left the cumbersome convoy behind. A cursory exploration of the ship was first, followed by an invitation to the bridge, for Carl and me, then later to the captain's quarters, where we were served ginger ale and jelly roll each afternoon from then on.

It was a treat to be guests of the captain by virtue of being Vermonters. Our customary five meals a day and tubs of eggnog were continued all the way to New York. Officers had comfortable bunks in the upper-deck cabins, but enlisted men had the usual abominable hammocks slung four or five deep down in the hold. I managed two visits down there and nearly became seasick myself, as that was the lot of those poor fellows.

There was but one day with a little rain and bigger waves but mostly just sunny days to relax and enjoy my first ocean voyage. The third day, I was on the bridge watching the crew on duty and studying the intricate auto pilot that was clicking the wheel back and forth to keep us on course. The captain was conferring with a crew member when I noticed a ship making up on the horizon. I looked again in a few minutes and was startled to see the gap closing between us. I interrupted the captain, saying, "It's none of my business—" There was no need to say more, because he saw the ship coming very close and started shouting commands. I could look right down the center line of the oncoming ship as the helmsman shut off the auto pilot and spun the wheel to turn right.

The other ship passed not more than 50 feet on our left, and it could be its crew never saw us, but their deck rail was lined with very young men probably going over for occupation duty in Germany. They yelled and cheered as if it were a great lark. We could have thrown an orange over to them, we were that close. If we had collided head-on in the middle of the ocean, it is possible no one would ever have known what happened to the two ships and the people on board.

The captain thanked me and complimented me on my good eyesight, but it was really a conditioned habit of observing everything around me as an act of self-preservation, a holdover from the stress of being behind the barbed wire as well as the need for vigilance while flying formation in combat.

Adjustments

On the morning of the fifth day out, we were wrapped in dense fog just south of Long Island. The captain had invited Carl Hedin and me up to the bridge to observe the arrival in New York harbor. We crept along very slowly, watching the radar for other ships and sounding the fog horn frequently. By mid-morning, we entered a bowl-shaped area of sunshine. The fog obscured the surface of the water and everything around us, but dead ahead, in the bright sunlight, with its base in the fog was the Statue of Liberty.

It was my twenty-second birthday.

The captain had just congratulated me; then, pointing forward, he said, "There is a sight you will remember as long as you live." It was an emotional event, and after a moment of silence, everyone on board began to cheer. The providential view probably meant more to our shipload of ex-POWs returning safely from the combat zone with our part of the war behind us than most people could imagine.

Liberty's torch was a bright, shiny, dazzling gold. Within minutes, the fog cleared away and we picked up speed to make our way to the docks on the west side of Manhattan Island. Several tugboats and fireboats came alongside with music playing, girls dancing and fire hoses throwing up great streams of water. The captain pointed out his wife's apartment near the top of a tall building as we eased into a slip next to where the scuttled French luxury liner "Normandie", had lain on its side since 1940.

Captain Dunton was certainly very gracious to us, and I never forgot him. On our way to Florida, in 1947, my wife Madeleine and I stopped at a store a few miles from our farm in Middlebury. To our surprise, we found Captain Dunton had bought the store and lived on a little farm nearby. He later started a dairy operation, as he and his wife had a foster son who lived with them, and they ran a successful farm for a number of years. He used to come to our farm to hunt every fall, and when I stopped to see him one day, his foster son said, "If you want to see him alive you have to do it now." I stopped at the hospital, but he was just barely awake and died that night at about 90 years of age.

We had had our last breakfast early in the morning aboard ship, the tubs of eggnog were put away, and there were no plans for the second, third, fourth or fifth meals we had been accustomed to. By mid-afternoon, we boarded a launch and traveled up the Hudson River, a beautiful sight on the eleventh of June. We disembarked at Nyack for more delousing, showers, haircuts if we wished, and finally near midnight entered a large banquet hall with tables loaded with every kind of food we could imagine. We stared at the seemingly endless tables of steak, ham, pork, seafood, salads and desserts, all beautifully displayed. After being cautious for six weeks about overeating and then not having eaten for the past 18 hours, most of us "pigged out." It was wonderful, but I lost my appetite and the ability to digest solid food for the rest of the summer.

The next day, June 12, after a good rest, some of us boarded buses to Camp Devens for processing. I signed waivers regarding my condition and was placed on leave until notified to report to a hospital for examination. Being at the top of the alphabet, I was rushed through in an hour, enabling me to catch a bus home the same day.

I arrived at New Haven before midnight, and my aunt and uncle were waiting for me as I had called from Rutland about an hour earlier.

On the bus, I met my first acquaintance, Norma Betts—a schoolmate who lived a few miles from our home. Her folks had no phone, so my uncle offered to drive her home as we couldn't leave her in the dark at the tiny bus stop with no one around. It put a burden on my uncle, as he was tired from being up late and he preferred not to drive at night. The extra time and travel may have taken the edge off our reunion, and perhaps this was what was needed as we eased into conversation quite smoothly. I felt very poor, as my only possession was the battered Red Cross case I had managed to retain through all the happenings of the past several months.

The next morning, it was obvious something had changed, as we lingered over a late breakfast and no one started for the barn across the road to do chores. Nothing was said about it, but I sensed that my uncle was disturbed about something. My brother Lawrence, who had stayed with them while I was gone, broke the news later that forenoon in private. The cows and farm machinery had been auctioned off in early March. While my dear uncle was in the hospital and before he came home, his brother John, a real-estate broker had convinced him and my aunt that they should sell the farm. They didn't really expect Uncle Byron to recover, but over his protests about how he had told me he would keep the farm for me, they brought the papers to the hospital for him to sign, and ownership of the farm was transferred to a neighbor.

About a day later, the letter I had written in November from Stalag Luft III, arrived and gave them hope for my eventual return.

But the deed was done. The farm was gone and my uncle was devastated. I tried to ease his mind by saying it was not a big disappointment to me. It was a greater burden for my uncle than for me, although it was a hard pill to swallow as I'd planned on taking over the farm I was so familiar with. However, if the farm had been available to me, it would have been impossible for me to take over immediately because I was still in the service and my physical condition precluded any strenuous activity for a few months.

I visited my friend Jim Bouvier in Bristol soon after arriving home. Jim had been shot down April 29, 1944 and liberated one year later on April 29, 1945. He came home a few days ahead of me, and we went to the soda fountain at the drug store for ice cream in many forms and in great quantities. I became reacquainted with his sister Barbara at the first dance I attended and spent some pleasant times with her that summer.

My brother Frank had acquired a Model A Ford convertible and took me to see our parents who were living in Keene, New Hampshire with my sister Rena and her family. They had been taken down there from their old home when they both became unable to carry on.

Neighbors had been keeping a considerate watch over them. One morning they could see no smoke from the chimney so they went down and found my father unable to keep the fire going or even to feed his horse. Brother Carl came home about then on furlough from Italy, so he and Rena took our parents to her home in Keene by ambulance. It appeared my father had had a mild stroke that incapacitated him and prevented him from taking care of himself or my mother—who was still an invalid. After spending some time with the family, Frank and I continued our ride around the beautiful early summer countryside, visiting friends and family members.

I was required to attend a fact-finding inquest in Washington, D.C. regarding treatment of prisoners by the Germans. Most of us attending agreed the only improper handling of POWs was by the SS and Nazi party members, while the rank and file with few exceptions just did the best they could under orders. My trip to D.C. coincided with stops at two military hospitals for checkups and recommendations for treatment of my injuries. At Mitchell field, Long Island, they insisted on fusing my neck and back, but I declined and have felt comfortable with this decision ever since.

1945 July, August and September

A second trip to D.C. to check the whereabouts of my records and to sightsee was a pleasant diversion—or seemed to be—as I started out. As I was changing trains in New York, there was a great commotion in the streets and many fire and emergency vehicles all around. Someone said a plane had hit the Empire State Building, and through the fog we could actually see smoke coming out of the top-floor windows. As my train reached Baltimore, paper boys came through with an extra edition about the crash.

I was surprised to learn the pilot was Lt. Col. William Smith, former operations officer with the 457th. He had been promoted to major the day I was shot down and left for home, on leave. On his return to the U.K. he was appointed deputy commander of the Group, and just as hostilities ceased in Europe he was promoted to lieutenant colonel. He flew with the C.O. of the 457th, Col. Rogner, to South Dakota to arrange for the transfer of the group from England to the States.

Lt. Colonel William Smith

His wife had just had a baby, so he borrowed a B-25 twin-engine bomber he had never flown before and flew to Boston, dropping off

Rogner in Newark, New Jersey to visit his family. He had only one day at home before taking off in bad weather for the return trip. He was accompanied by the airplane's crew chief who had come along to look after the B-25, and a hitchhiking sailor they picked up in Boston.

In the light rain and low ceiling, Smith apparently misjudged his position as he flew over La Guardia Field at low altitude, trying to maintain contact with the ground. His unfamiliarity with the B-25, no doubt, contributed to the incidents that led him into the canyons of Manhattan. He struck the skyscraper in a vertical bank, which indicated he had seen it and was desperately attempting to turn away, with the result that the fuselage struck one floor while the two engines crashed through the floors above and below. The three floors erupted in flames, incinerating the three men in the plane and ten girls working for the Catholic Relief Organization on one of the floors. One engine passed completely through the building, and the other one fell down an elevator shaft.

One of the best accounts of the Empire State Building episode, titled "The Sky Is Falling," was written by an eyewitness. The author was about nine years old at the time and was walking near the building with his father when they heard the roar of the plane and the subsequent explosion.

On the sixth of August 1945, I was on a train between Baltimore and New York when it was announced that an atomic bomb had been dropped on Hiroshima, Japan. This meant the end of six years of war around the world. What a blessing it was that the United States perfected the bomb before Hitler's scientists were able to bring it all together. I've often thought that perhaps a few of those German scientists might have intentionally delayed progress on nuclear devices to deny the Nazis the advantage that could have turned the tide of war and changed the future of the world into one of hopeless existence. God was certainly on our side.

Few people realize how close the Nazis came to developing a nuclear weapon or what kind of world we would live in had Hitler prevailed and used that weapon to blackmail the Allies.

Werner von Braun, the leading German rocket scientist who came to work for the United States after the war, said if the workers at Peenemunde, the nuclear research and development center, had had another six weeks to two months of uninterrupted work they probably would have succeeded. It was only the very costly strikes carried out on those facilities by the 8th Air Force that prevented the worst nightmare in history from taking place.

Before   *After*

Hitler would have wreaked horrible vengeance on the rest of the world, and if he supplied a few bombs to his Axis partner, Japan—Hawaii and our West Coast cities would have been destroyed. Germany and Japan would not have rebuilt our country as we did theirs if the war had ended differently. Actually, no one really knew what would happen when someone triggered the first nuclear explosion. It could have resulted in an uncontrolled reaction impossible to contain.

Nearly all ex-POWs were sent for rest and recuperation (R&R) to summer resorts around the country, for at least a week of being waited on and catered to. I chose Atlantic City over Miami not only because it was hot in Florida in September but because the New Jersey shore was closer to home. With so many activities going on, it was hard to choose what to do next.

Celebrating weight gain to 135 pounds with Rollin Brown in July

The Miss America pageant was going on in front of our hotel, but it didn't interest me at the time. Trying my hand at golf—I believe Gretchen Hedin talked me into it—caused a great deal of pain in my shoulders. As soon as the club hit the ball, it seemed like a powerful electric shock went through my shoulders, nearly causing me to let go of the club. That confined my golf to gentle putting. The swimming was very nice, but there was a strong undertow in the afternoons, a strong current running parallel to the beach.

1945 October, Settling In

This was the first time I really relaxed since the interlude on the coast of France, so I took advantage of the opportunity to rest and meditate. Unconsciously, I had been having a difficult time relating to people, especially loved ones, and although I appreciated the help and attention from everyone, it was impossible for me to show gratitude. My sleep was sporadic, and nights were filled with remorse for my comrades who were lost and especially my three crewmen who died.

Thoughts of what I might have done to save them turned over and over in my mind. Did my drilling into them how not to open their parachutes too soon to avoid anoxia or freezing on the way down cause Lang to delay too long? Was I remiss by not digging into their minds as to how they were standing up under the rigors of combat? Years later, one of the survivors told me Sam Plestine, the navigator, and Maynard Judson, tail gunner, had told the others they would not jump from the plane if it went down. Thoughts like these haunted me for months, leading me to look for a farm to keep me totally engrossed.

Nothing excited me, no loud noise close by made me jump, no one could startle me, and I felt compelled to keep on the move. My aunt tried to make good meals for me, but all that summer my appetite was such that I could only eat ice cream or soup. Steak or any other heavy food just didn't agree with me. She must have been very disappointed for all her efforts. I allowed my uncle to let me use his nearly worn-out car so often it was shameful. Walking through the cemetery where I had pushed a lawn mower a thousand miles, I came upon the grave of a classmate who had drowned while in the service in 1943. It was beyond my ability to visit his parents. Two pilots from Bristol were killed after the war ended, their families requested my services as a pallbearer, and I accepted reluctantly. My behavior at times was as baffling to me as it must have been to others, but it was many months before I realized my inability to relate must have been a heavy burden to the ones I loved most.

Some years later, I learned how adrenalin decomposes into a chemical called adrenochrome. This substance can cause a schizophrenic type of disorder in people lacking certain essential vitamins and nutrients in their systems. I had certainly produced an abundance of adrenalin during the past year of combat and incarceration and during March of 1945, when I was unable to eat anything due to the infection of the lower tract.

As I was not eating a balanced diet during the summer of 1945, my system no doubt lacked the right chemicals. Studies by Dr. Abram Hoffer and Dr. Humphrey Osmond in the 1950s indicated large amounts of niacin seemed to correct this imbalance caused by the decomposition of adrenalin, with improved mental stability resulting. Of course, all the pioneering work of Hoffer and Osmond came years too late for me.

After looking around at farms in various parts of Vermont, I was drawn to a beautiful farm near Middlebury that my uncle thought would appeal to me. We paid a visit, but the price of $30,000 seemed too much for me, even though I had saved most of my money in the service. My uncle offered to help me with part of the $10,000 down payment. Several cattle dealers and speculators were trying to buy the farm from the elderly couple who had lived there all their married life—44 years. They didn't want to take less money from the speculators, so I agreed to buy it for the price they were asking. The "loan arranger" at the bank said the rule was one-third down and payment by 40 percent of the milk check each month.

After taking care of all the details, I left for Westover Field in Connecticut to be separated from the military on October 31. The people in charge rushed us through in short order, and I elected to remain in the Officer's Reserve Corps.

I took a bus home that night and took over the farm the next morning.

I soon discovered I was not ready for such arduous work as my back, neck and shoulders were very painful. The barn, built in 1901, was beautiful and very well constructed, but it was somewhat awkward to work in due to the floor plan. I decided that after the next war I would take a whole year off before going to work.

It was many years before I realized that first farm was a bargain. Thirty thousand dollars bought 400 acres, 88 head of cattle, four registered Percheron horses, all the machinery, an outstanding barn and outbuildings, a four-stall garage and shop, a blacksmith shop and a beautiful 18-room house. All this plus barns and silos full of feed. Of course, at the time it was comparable to other properties.

Beginning with the purchase of the farm, a long series of events over the next several years caused me disillusion and depression. My faith in people eroded as I was exposed to injustices from bankers, predatory businessmen and others trying to take advantage of me. The bank holding my mortgage never informed me there were other types of loans with lower down payments and certainly with less than 40 percent of gross income in monthly payments.

Nevertheless, I paid off my obligations, improved the farm and raised the income to four times what it was when I took over. Much of this was done by feeding the cows liberally and milking three times a day.

This first year's success backfired at income-tax time, when two IRS men came to question my return. They wouldn't accept my check stubs showing all my expenses and were very arrogant, suggesting I couldn't have earned all that money from the farm alone and asking where I got the down payment. I paid the extra tax to avoid wasting time with them.

I suspected the attorney who prepared my tax return had reported me to the IRS because he couldn't believe I had reduced my mortgage so much in one year. I didn't argue by saying I was single, didn't buy a car and worked my tail off while not spending any money on myself. The fact that I saved almost every dollar while in the service was one reason I was able to buy a farm. Another outcome was a sharp reduction in the small disability pension I had been awarded. The Veterans Administration reduced my claim from 75 percent to 20 percent, even though the law stated there was not to be any exchange of income information among the IRS, employers and the VA. The argument was that, inasmuch as I was able to work effectively enough to make a profit, my condition was not that bad. How did they know how much I made?

My physical condition was my greatest concern, as I soon discovered the heavy farm work was too much for me. It had been my theory that vigorous exercise would rebuild my body, but it only proved that I had needed more months of recuperation.

I'd always had a principle that anyone working on a farm shouldn't have to do any work his employer wouldn't also do. I now think this was nonsense. We milked and fed the cows early in the morning, had breakfast and immediately started the most demanding chore of all: cleaning the barn by hand. It entailed loading the spreader from a deep gutter, followed by taking the three loads to the fields with the horses. Climbing up on the seat all sweaty and driving to the far end of the farm to unload in the cold wind was brutal, but I preferred to do this myself. Manure had not been spread on the farthest fields for many years, and I wanted it done right, but the most important reason for assuming this chore was to avoid mistreatment of the horses.

My hired man, who came with the farm, was a good worker and had a good disposition, but like many farm owners and workers, he lacked compassion for work animals. The attitude of the horses and their willingness to work improved soon after I took over. Their harnesses had not been adjusted for years, they had not been groomed often and had been fed the hay left over from in front of the cows. The floors of their stalls were worn rough, and nail heads protruded from the planks. It was evident they had not been provided bedding to rest better after working. I talked to them softly and handled the reins gently, and they responded by being less nervous and better workers.

One of my first major purchases on the farm was a field chopper I hoped would save a lot of hard manual labor in harvesting the crops. It had been tested in the "West" I was told, and it was reported to function flawlessly.

But the machine continually broke down from the first day. Finally the local business people who sold it called in the factory representative, who observed it operating. When it began to plug and wind up with hay, he yelled for me to speed up and keep going. The machine disintegrated, sending pieces of metal in all directions. The factory rep, who had hidden behind a pile of hay until things quieted down, declared the expensive machine a failure and said he would return it to the people who sold it to me. I had paid them for it on delivery, but it took over a year to get my money back and I was forced to go to their place and load a new tractor on a truck and put it to work on my farm. There seemed to be opportunists everywhere for people to take advantage of me and try to separate me from my hard-earned money. All this trouble from people I trusted was a great disappointment.

An example of the poor treatment of ex-servicemen after the war ended struck home when I entered a country store while the storeowner was holding forth with some of the locals. A few of his listeners had been draft dodgers, and he himself had capitalized on wartime conditions at home. For my benefit, he began to tell the others how veterans thought the world owed them a living and expected all kinds of benefits at taxpayers' expense. Moving up close to look him directly in the eye, I waited for him to finish before giving him a humiliating lecture on what a waste it was that hundreds of thousands of brave young men had to die for the likes of him. Jim Bouvier had a better answer for a bureaucrat who refused to sell him a special tag for his car. After listening to a persuasive argument, he told Jim, "Well I guess you've paid your dues." "No, mister! I paid YOUR dues," was Jim's reply.

The events following the end of the war in Europe proved a heavy emotional burden for me. While still in France, we witnessed the forced return of Russian prisoners of war back to their homeland. Stalin had decreed there were to be no surrenders, so all returned service men under German control faced years of detention in forced labor camps in Siberia. Many attempted suicide, but the Allies loaded them into trains by force because the world leaders had given in to Stalin's demands. On a much larger scale, turning the Balkan countries and Eastern Europe over to the communists was a bitter blow.

Poland had suffered under the German and Russian occupations for six years, only to be handed over to endure another 50 years of exploitation. The feeling of many of us was that the Allies should disavow the terms worked out by Roosevelt, Churchill and Stalin. Roosevelt was dying, Churchill was weary of war, and

Stalin was triumphant, but the millions of people left behind the "Iron Curtain" were hopelessly condemned to a dismal existence.

My question was, "What if the line drawn between the free world and the slave states of communism had been drawn through the mid-section of Vermont or along the Mississippi River? How would we feel"? These inhuman acts coming after the formation of the United Nations was incomprehensible and grieved me during those times and for the rest of my life.

1946, Madeleine, the Ultimate Reward

The psychological difficulties I encountered trying to adjust were compounded by my physical disabilities, which I denied at first but came to realize were something I'd have to live with. Everything seemed to point to my needing to get into a less arduous livelihood than farming, but the thought of working indoors or at some repetitive function was alien to how I wanted to spend my life. The Air Force told me my flying days were behind me. The Veteran's Administration predicted I would be in a wheelchair within two years if I continued the hard labor on the farm. The future looked bleak until an event caused me to pull things together in a way that might let me continue being a farmer and also cope with my physical problems.

Seeley Reynolds and his lovely wife Anne had a prosperous farm near mine and invited me to dinner and to attend a farm show in Barre with them. My bachelor status dictated never turning down a good home-cooked meal, and the trip to the show gave me my first day off since taking over the farm.

My social life was nil—no dates, no dances, no car and no time for any of these activities. One evening after a long day's work, I fell asleep in my chair and was awakened by someone bumping my knees. It was Rollin Brown, my former roommate from Randolph, and he announced we were going to a dance. I protested, but he insisted and luckily for me we went off to the Washington's Birthday dance.

Anne Reynolds was the only person I knew as I looked around. She right away told me there were some nice girls I should meet, and she introduced me to a very pretty girl, her two sisters and a girl friend.

Madeleine Bourdon was the only one I saw clearly, and we danced a few times before I left early with Rollin.

I don't think she believed I had a farm because a few days later she and two sisters walked up to the sugar house on my farm. There was quite a crowd in the small building, checking out the first run of sap. My visiting uncle, my brother-in-law, my brother, my hired man and, of course, the former owner of the farm, who had come to get some of the first-run syrup, all made for very close quarters in the steam-filled shack. All the men saw the three pretty girls approaching across the field and wondered what they were up to. With difficulty, I was able to get everyone's name straight for introductions but had a hard time watching the evaporator and keeping my mind off Madeleine. I was not successful in the latter.

In the next several months, we dated only rarely as I had my hands full on the farm and was milking three times a day. My work schedule—from 3:15 in the morning until 9:00 at night—didn't leave much time for socializing. Madeleine's mother spoke very little English at the time but managed to get the point across that her daughter would not be allowed to date a perfect stranger. I managed to convince her I wasn't perfect.

There were differences in our backgrounds, and because of her sheltered life in contrast to my exposure to considerable violence and a part of history, we thought in different dimensions.

After a short stay in the hospital, I realized I needed a break from hard work and a change of scene, as my back, neck and shoulders prevented me from working effectively. My plan was to turn over the operation of the farm to my brother to help him get a start; profits for several months would likely be favorable enough for him to set aside a grubstake to go out on his own.

Meanwhile, this would free me up to travel and hopefully mend emotional as well as physical wounds. It would be a lonely journey, and the thought frequently crossed my mind that it would be nice if Madeleine could accompany me. In some mysterious way, this beautiful, devout, innocent 19-year-old girl was talked into running off with a traveling man. A marriage had to be arranged first, of course, and it was—a very quiet yet enjoyable ceremony.

We were married on January 4th, 1947 and have been together ever since.

We meandered down through New York, Pennsylvania and Washington D.C., visiting friends of mine along the way. After a leisurely tour of the capital and Mount Vernon, we entered a whole different world—the Deep South, with different foods and, at times, barely adequate accommodations. We attended Mass in a private home in Georgia. Once we were in Florida, it was familiar places and people, more like home as there were many Vermonters wintering there. After a swing around the state, we followed the Gulf around to Mexico and interesting points in the Southwest, again visiting old and newer friends.

Lawrence Goodman, nephew to "Uncle Sam" of my boyhood days, and his wife very graciously kept us at their home for several days and showed us the Los Angeles area.

The Golden Gate Bridge, Fisherman's Wharf, Muir Woods, Chinatown and Alcatraz (at a distance) rounded out our stay in California, so after more than two months on the road we headed up through Donner Pass with tire chains on. Reno welcomed us, but we pushed on to Salt Lake City, across the rangelands of Wyoming to Cheyenne after stopping for Mass in Rawlins. In Illinois, we visited the parents and family of my engineer Howard Lang, who lost his life when we were shot down, as well as Norman Tiefel, my roommate in prison camps.

The trip rejuvenated me in many ways, so I was eager to get back to work but with a less strenuous agenda. I have to say, Madeleine contributed much to my well being on our return and we started our married life on the farm immediately.

Madeleine has so many talents that make our marriage work. Her common sense and business acumen are wonderful gifts. And after overcoming shyness and a reluctance to meeting strangers and celebrities, she became adept at handling most situations. She has met governors, presidential cabinet members and nationally known people, leaving them impressed with her charming demure and good looks. No matter what she wears, she looks elegant and presents a genuine friendliness.

It is an amazing stroke of good fortune for me to have a wife and companion who makes my life rewarding in many ways. As a mother to our five sons: John, Michael, Phillip, Pierre and Thomas, she exhibited her greatest skills as wife, mother, homemaker, teacher and example for all of us to follow. It's one thing to have children but quite another to raise them, headed in the right direction, trained to take care of themselves and to treat older people respectfully. Madeleine accomplished all this and more. The proof is the extent to which our sons go to show concern for their parents, other family members and people they encounter in their lives.

Her gentleness, her faith, her sensitivity and her understanding have only been fine-tuned as the years passed, and I'm the recipient of most of her giving of herself. The only complaint I can conjure up is how she beats me so often at cards—and it's easy to forgive her for that.

1954-1968, Vermont
National Guard, a Second Chance

A few years after returning from World War II, I felt the need to fly again as therapy for my mental, physical and spiritual well being. The sight of the German ME 262 jet fighters I had observed over Europe had left me with a desire to experience this new type of propulsion and performance.

This was a considerable challenge inasmuch as the Air Force had told me my flying days were over due to my injuries. However, the Vermont Air National Guard was scheduled to convert to all-weather jet interceptors, so with this added incentive I soon lied my way through the flight surgeon's office with a medical waiver and was back in uniform and on flight status.

This did wonders for my state of mind but not too much for the residual effects of combat and POW camps. To fly again and to have a little extra income as well as a slim chance of getting a long-overdue promotion helped take the edge off the rigors of trying to make a living while putting up with my physical disabilities. The Pentagon never did give me my medical clearance, so there was no need to look forward to retirement benefits.

J.F. Angier, with T-33, Vermont Air National Guard, Burlington, VT 1955

Flying jets turned out to be a fairly easy transition even though it had been ten years since I'd flown any type of military aircraft. The Vermont Air Guard had a stable of F-94Cs, a few T-33s, two twin-engine B-25s, a twin Beechcraft C-45, two T-6s and a "gooney bird". "Gooney" was the endearing nickname for the Douglas DC-3 transport labeled C-47 by the military. The T-6s were the most used single-engined trainer many cadets flew during their last phase of training. This was a plane that made real pilots out of novices; once anyone learned to fly it well, he could fly almost any well-built plane. As I went to twin-engine school, I missed out on flying the T-6, but that was what I used to start my

Air Guard familiarization flights. It was not a problem, so I moved up to the twin-engine planes until one day they told me to strap on my first jet. Climbing down from tractors and up into a T-33 was a real transition after my ten-year hiatus.

Some people said flying jets was a replacement for sex. For me, I would go as far as saying it might be almost a parallel. Gone was the nuisance of torque that tried to turn the airplane rather than the propeller, gone were the myriad controls and gadgets of the reciprocating power plants, and the smooth swish of the slipstream replaced the constant roar pilots had put up with for over 50 years. The stick and throttle were the essential controls once in the air.

Before leaving the ground, however, there were certain prerequisites that needed close attention, and you needed to have your thought processes in focus. No daydreaming here, no leaping off in the wild blue yonder to see what would happen next. The takeoff and climb had to be carefully planned as well as having some purpose for going. Fuel management and navigation were critical chores to be monitored constantly, and the thirsty jet engines reminded me of how expensive an operation each flight was. I all too often felt I was paying for the fuel myself as I used it—an expensive hobby, given my lifelong practice of frugality.

The Cold War was on, and most of us felt there would be a need for our skills and experience, but it was a revelation to me to learn that the Air Guard flew more hours, flew more missions and had a higher percentage of planes operational than the Air Force across the field from us at the Burlington Airport. Added to this was the fact nearly every Guardsman had combat flying time, while the Air Force people had very few with combat experience. We all held a job or ran a business, which made our status all the more outstanding. I felt I was in the company of a dedicated, proficient and well-oriented group of professionals.

A flight simulator that allowed the operator to experience flying the F-94 without leaving the ground aided in transitional training as well as giving excellent instrument proficiency. This machine let us go through entire missions, encountering emergencies and changes in weather and making approaches and landings at strange fields in safety—a real confidence builder.

I practiced our instrument letdowns and approaches many times in this device. In weather—let's say clouds up to 20,000 feet—the procedure was to slow down and drop landing gear and flaps as we homed in on a radio beacon just to the north of the field. On passing the beacon, which gave off an audible signal, we dropped wheels and flaps and our dive board, a large door-like panel under the belly, to allow a very steep descent.

All this drag created air resistance to allow us to make a penetration of very short duration, less than two minutes to lose four or five miles of altitude. It also created considerable buffeting, making control more of a challenge. We maintained a heading of 30 degrees to about half our starting altitude, then turned northwest, aiming for another beacon located on Grand Isle, all the while maintaining sufficient flying speed and a constant rate of descent. Turning toward the field, we lined up with two more beacons, an outer marker and a middle marker, while keeping a rate of descent that brought us down a glide path to the end of the runway—an exercise in concentration, for sure.

On one such approach, I was flying on instruments while Col. Robert Goyette was observing in the front seat. We entered a bowl-shaped opening in the clouds. Just as we reached the homer beacon where I was to start our penetration, I heard Goyette draw in his breath. We had "live" microphones between the two seats to communicate quickly and more easily than using buttons or switches. I glanced out in time to see a huge Air Force transport sliding past, to disappear in the clouds. Goyette said we were so close to the big intruder he could have counted the rivets on the fuselage as it passed at right angles to our flight path. The crew had not called the Burlington tower to report its presence, and the plane continued on its journey without any response to repeated requests to identify who they were. We were seconds away from a major collision.

Colonel Goyette was a highly skilled pilot, took his participation in the Guard seriously and was very popular. Shortly after this incident, a plane he was piloting experienced a partial power failure and engine fire. Rather than eject, leaving the plane to possibly crash into a populated area, he and his radar operator elected to attempt to land at the base.

As they approached the traffic pattern, he reported his controls beginning to give up due to the heat of the fire, but he managed to steer the plane into a field just as he lost all power. The aircraft struck the shoulder of the highway, bounced up through power lines, burst into flames and skidded for nearly half a mile through the plowed field without turning over. Both men were likely incapacitated when they struck the road shoulder and were unable to climb out when the wreckage came to a stop. They burned to death in their seats before help could arrive.

My closest call to a serious incident was caused by anoxia due to a faulty oxygen regulator. I had written up the discrepancy the day before, but the crew chief said the plane checked out OK. No doubt the ground crew's check of the equipment was valid on the ground but the system didn't function at altitude. Midway through an engineering flight that required me to write down instrument readings at different altitudes and power settings, I lost consciousness. A lack of activity apparently lowered my need for oxygen enough to let me awaken, and a gradual descent while I was asleep helped as the oxygen content of the air increased.

As my vision returned, I could see a hazy outline of the Great Lakes area, and it made me wonder what I was doing out there. I'd been flying instinctively with my left hand and was holding a pencil in my right hand, resting it on my kneepad. My last entry on the pad was the time, so it seemed reasonable to write in the new time. Nine minutes had passed, but the significance of that time interval didn't register until hours later.

Somehow, I turned back east and revived enough to realize what had happened and that I should lose more altitude. Although my senses returned slowly, my mind was so foggy I flew on past Vermont into New Hampshire, where it dawned on me to return to Burlington. I asked the tower to monitor my check-list with me so I wouldn't forget my landing gear and told them I would call off my airspeed to prevent a stall or an approach to the landing runway with too much speed to set down. The effect of the anoxia was obvious as I drove home and failed to turn off the main highway to take Route 22 toward home. It was very dif-ficult to focus my attention on anything the rest of the day.

A few nights later, a friend of mine, father of a large family, took off in the same plane and upon returning to the field was attempting to land at Plattsburg Air Force Base in New York. That base was near a city beside Lake Champlain, with another city, Burlington, visible to the east.

From the air, at night, the two airport scenes were nearly identical but in reverse. The pilot was so confused from lack of oxygen that he made several passes at Plattsburg, thinking it was Burlington. The Strategic Air Command (SAC) base he was try-ing to land at was frantic, as he was in contact with Burlington tower, confusing everyone. When the tower at Burlington con-vinced him he was disoriented and guided him to home base, he was low on fuel and his first two attempts to land were made at too high a speed, necessitating two go-arounds.

On his third and last try he was still too fast, so thinking of all those kids at home, he pulled up the landing gear and bellied in on the runway. The metal sliding along the concrete sent out a shower of sparks, but no fire resulted. The next day, technicians drained his fuel tanks and found there was insufficient fuel to have made another go-around. The lesson learned was: Don't depend on oxygen tests on the ground; many mechanical devices sometimes function differently in the thin, cold air.

Active Duty Tours

One of the side benefits of belonging to the Guard was the opportunity to go on short tours of active duty for training. Sur-rounded, as I was, by rank on all sides, my chances of a promo-tion were slim, so I applied for a course in Air Intelligence at Sheppard field in Wichita Falls, Texas. A vacancy for this existed in our fighter squadron and called for the rank of captain. As often happens, politics played its part, and while I was at the school someone else filled that slot.

It was an intensive course, with top-secret information available to us opening my eyes and ears to the astounding intelligence gathered concerning Russia and its technological advances. We studied the methods of gathering intelligence by both sides and worked on many projects and studies to prepare us to perform our duties as Air Intelligence officers. The photos and nomenclature of Russian planes was interesting but a bit startling after comparing it all with ours. Many of our scientific advances were put to use by the communists before our work on the projects were completed. The top secrets of our nuclear successes were literally handed to the Soviets by a few of our own scientists. Our State Department, research centers and universities were infiltrated during World War II with dedicated communists as a result of our alliance with them during hostilities. No one was watching the store.

After completing the course at Sheppard Field, I took the family (Madeleine, John, Michael and Phillip) to Florida while I attended the Jet Qualification course at Selma, Alabama. This was before the civil rights effort had gained much ground so we, as a family, witnessed the terrible hatred directed toward non-white people. In my six subsequent tours in the South, we saw the painful process of moving toward equality underway. One place we lived in was a large development where all non-whites were excluded to the degree that "trespassers" faced arrest, as did anyone who had non-whites as guests. We ignored these appalling laws several times by inviting non-white officers from other countries to our quarters.

Craig Field at Selma, Alabama was well run and maintained its T-33 jets in quite good order. My instructor was a 22-year-old exceptionally well trained pilot who was remarkably skilled in flying the T-33s. He was somewhat impulsive and was positive no one else could fly as well as he could and anyone over 30 years old was over the hill as far as driving airplanes. He was five years old when I first flew an airplane, but I might as well have been a grey-haired old geezer from another planet. One or two maneuvers were his favorites, and he made me fly them over and over and was not only impatient with me but impatient to break off the training to buzz his girlfriend's dormitory at a local college.

Under the Hood

One afternoon, he had me in the back seat under the hood to fly some intricate approach patterns on instruments. I was unfamiliar with the exercises and wasn't doing too well when he yanked the stick out of my hands and said we were wasting time. "Take us back to Selma," he told me. "Sorry, but when someone yanks the controls out of my hands they do the rest of the flying," was my response. We then went for one of the roughest rides I'd ever been on, and I was surprised the wings didn't come off before he settled down to dust off his girlfriend's place.

After he had used up our time and fuel and was on final approach for landing, I decided to tie a knot in his tail. As a superb pilot, he made good landings but went through his checklist by memory. Just before touchdown, I asked him if he should put his landing gear down. Of course, the gear was down, but my remark caught him off-guard to the extent he jammed on power and his landing looked like a student's first day. After the first bounce, he cut the power and tried to regain a landing conformation, but we bounced some more and zigzagged down the runway with tires squealing. He never said a word, but I had made my point. His attitude for the rest of the course was more respectful.

A few students had been sent out one night, although the weather was threatening with considerable lightning to the west. One student had been assigned a route to Memphis, Vicksburg, New Orleans and back, with instructions to navigate using the facilities along the way, tuning to each radio aid to maintain his course. With the weather as it was, this was the only method to use, as lights and check points on the ground were hidden by clouds. Somewhere over Vicksburg, the student flew into a thunderhead and was tossed about until he was completely disoriented.

As he fell out of the storm, he decided to bail out rather than crash. The canopy refused to jettison when he pulled the lever, so he attempted to eject through the canopy as a last resort. The seat failed to eject, but then he saw lights and managed to re-cover control of the plane just above the surface of the river be-low the city. Observers reported he was lower then the bridges that span the river at Vicksburg.

After finding his way back and landing safely, he had the presence of mind to remember he had activated the ejection sys-tem and if he or anyone else opened the canopy he could be blown 200 feet into the air. When the pilot gets settled in the cockpit, he pulls the safety pins that prevent activating the ejec-tion charge. He then hands the pins to the crew chief to keep until his return. To prevent this accident from happening to the badly shaken young man, it was necessary to cut a hole through the side of the plane to hand the pins in to secure the ejection seat. When the student came into the operations room, he threw his helmet across the floor and declared he would never set foot in an airplane again.

All told, I managed to complete seven tours while in the Guard, and these were productive but most importantly for me, they were an escape from cold winters that caused me great dis-comfort. My pay for a six-month tour exceeded the income from the farms, but another side benefit was the chance for my family to live and study in different parts of the country. Our travels took us through many states and to famous geographical points such as history-rich Lookout Mountain near Chattanooga, the beaches of Florida and the diverse landscapes of the West.

The most interesting course was the Army Aviation Tactical course at Ft. Rucker, Alabama where I joined young pilots fresh out of primary flying school attempting to master the L-19, one of the three favorite planes I ever flew. The young pilots damaged a number of planes each day as they practiced intricate landings on side hills or down through a hole in the forest to set down on a winding sand road through the big woods. We landed over barriers, along river banks and places that challenged us all—even me, with my much greater experience.

My instructor was, by that time, a pudgy veteran RAF night fighter pilot from the early days of the Battle of Britain. He had played the deadly cat and mouse game many nights in the dark skies over Europe. His role was to find and shoot down the German night fighters as they probed with their primitive radar for the big British bombers.

Flying was in his blood, he was methodical, precise and had the skills to fly any aircraft he could get his hands on. He had various flying experience after the war and settled into his instructor's profession with 20 years of aeronautical knowledge to impart to his students. Camouflaged under his gruff exterior he had a sly, quiet humor but was all business in the cockpit. His name was Horne and toward the end of my course I got up nerve to ask him if the "e" in his name was silent. "At times," he replied with the faintest trace of a smile. My only tribute to a man of his stature was to work diligently to show that some of his skill rubbed off on me.

Knowing my background, the old pro gave me a hard time, always pushing the envelope, trying to uncover any weak points in my flying abilities. On our last flight, the night before my graduation, he told me to climb to 9,000 feet, quite a climb for the L-19 at night under instrument conditions. It was extremely hazy and although there was a moon high above the overcast, the murky condition necessitated flying entirely on instruments as there was no horizon or any other reference point. The old "Tiger" lolled in the back seat, smoking a cigar and chewing tobacco. On the floor was a tin can half full of water and tobacco juice, obviously meant to be used to quench the cigar before he had his fun with me. Finally, with the cigar floating safely in the tin can, he drawled, "All right, give me my roll." He had often taken the controls and, after tumbling the plane around the sky, had left it in an unusual attitude and told me to recover. Recovering was not difficult, but the technique to accomplish it was what he watched for. This time, keeping in mind the nasty tin can, he didn't touch the controls but expected me to do a perfect barrel roll—perfect because it required just the right centrifugal force to keep the tin can pinned to the floor.

I made a clearing turn to check for the lights of any other plane whose pilot was dumb enough to be up in the murk late at night. I checked my instruments carefully and cinched up my seat belt, then called on Father God, Jesus, Mary and Joseph to keep that can from spattering its contents all over us, the windshield and side windows. Opening the throttle to pick up the necessary speed, I put us into the roll. The can never moved, and the old tiger said, "Let's go home, Captain." Back at the base, when he climbed out of his seat, he knocked over the tin can. "Some people are just plain clumsy," I muttered. He slapped me on the shoulder, shook hands and as both of us felt so much emotion we found it difficult to speak, he just walked away. A hero in his own right and a giant hero to me. Sadly, I was never to see him again.

The Air Guard took over the mission of the Air Force in 1958—the same year Vermont sent the first Democrat to congress in over 100 years. He worked to cut the military budget (in the middle of the Cold War), so they closed the Air Force base in Burlington—in his home state! Our sector of responsibility was between Hudson Bay and Labrador, to hunt for and find Russian planes with our radar. Fortunately for the world, the enemy planes always turned back when we came within visual range.

The high altitude, extreme cold and "G" forces of flying what were, in the 1950's, almost primitive types of jets tested my endurance. So one day I walked across the field to the Army Guard Aviation Company. They welcomed me aboard, and flying their fixed-wing and rotary-wing (helicopters) aircraft was easier for me to tolerate. I ran my farms most of the year but escaped the winters by going on active duty, flying in the warm South and Southwest for a few months. After several years, I accumulated more thousands of hours of flying time, served as instructor pilot, adjutant and very senior member of the company. Two promotions made my pasture years more rewarding as well.

1961, Incident at Sheephole Mountain

As instructor pilot, it was up to me to provide realistic training to the other pilots. I requested permission to make a low-level "nap of the earth" type flight around the United States, to see how well our reconnaissance planes could avoid radar detection by flying very low—under 1,000 feet above the terrain.

I asked to use my favorite plane, our instrument trainer with much updated equipment and the ability to fly as slowly as 35 miles an hour or as fast as 140 miles an hour. It had a fixed landing gear and was painted a bright orange-red color, easier to find if lost but easier to spot if I blundered across an airport at low altitude. This was one of my greatest concerns because it is so

Major Basil Abbott and Captain Angier with L-20 Beaver,
Army Guard Aviation Company, Burlington, Vermont

easy to fly through the traffic pattern of an airfield while navigating at low altitude. The penalties for crossing an airfield unannounced are high and, of course, very dangerous to all concerned.

My route took me just inside the perimeter of the continental United States, out past the Great Lakes and across the Great Plains to the Rocky Mountains. It was late February 1961, and sudden snow squalls were quite common as I proceeded further west. Very often, they rolled down the slopes into the valleys from both sides, reducing visibility to near zero for short periods. To adhere to my self-imposed 1,000-foot altitude limit meant sacrificing any short cuts. It was necessary, at times, to go around these storms by flying over very remote and unfamiliar areas.

In the Blue Mountains of Idaho, I started up a steep winding valley to Deadman's Pass, between LaGrande and Pendleton, Oregon, a section of the old Oregon Trail used by the pioneers. Suddenly, two snow squalls started swirling down the mountain slopes and filled the pass ahead of me while very rapidly overspreading the whole area. Gusty winds and the dark clouds told me this was a major storm developing and because of the mountain peaks in the vicinity it would be hazardous to attempt to climb up through it. I turned around as quickly as possible in the narrow canyon to outrun the storm by heading back to La-Grande, but the overcast was lowering rapidly and visibility was soon down to a few hundred feet as I tried to keep the winding road in sight.

By the time I reached the city, it was so dark the street lights were on although it was noon. I started a search for the airstrip I had noticed on my way past the city earlier, but visibility was limited to directly beneath the aircraft so I was thankful to have a machine with the ability to fly slowly. Looking for the black macadam strip, I passed over it twice before realizing it was already covered with snow. After I landed, the field was closed for 24 hours while over a foot of snow fell, necessitating sweeping off the plane occasionally.

The next day required a climb up through 13,000 feet of weather to cross the mountains, the only time I exceeded my 1,000-foot limitation. Except for being fogged in at Olympia, Washington for two days, the trip was fairly uneventful until I reached southern California.

Leaving Palmdale for Blythe, California on the seventh day of my flight, I threaded my way around Edwards Air Force Base and the marine gunnery range in the desert. I hadn't slept well the night before, as there were no facilities at the new airport in Palmdale. Flying into the morning sun, tired and hungry, I began to plan my breakfast in Blythe: coffee, hotcakes with syrup and sausage, at least two eggs, hash browns and perhaps a doughnut to dunk in my last cup of coffee. They could change the oil and fill my plane with fuel while some pretty waitress took care of me.

My course was to a point on the southwest corner of a topographical feature called Sheephole Mountain, a rounded grassy mound shaped like an elephant lying on its side. At that point, my course would change to the southeast for a straight run to Blythe—and breakfast. I could see an escarpment of black rock on the slope of the mountain precisely where I would make my turn—a good checkpoint, it seemed.

The escarpment was about six or seven hundred feet high and several hundred yards wide, directly on course about five miles ahead and precisely at the point on my map where I would make my turn toward Blythe. My altitude above the desert was 450 feet. It looked as if in about two minutes it would be time to turn to the right and skim up over the left leg of the sleeping elephant called Sheephole Mountain.

Then, for the first time in over 30 years of flying, I fell sound asleep!

There was a loud bang and the aircraft shuddered as I came instantly awake and knew I had fallen asleep. Rough black rock seemed to fill the windshield, and it looked as if the next revolution of the propeller would bite into the face of the cliff. Racking the plane into a violent turn to the left, I noticed the left wheel spinning backwards and a long dark shape falling to the desert floor. Missing the rocks by a few feet, I followed the object down and came back over it a second time very low and slow to identify it as a very large buzzard or condor.

Observing blood on the underside of the left wing, I concluded the bird had struck the top of my tire, causing the wheel to spin backwards and the remains of the large bird to be thrown up against the wing. Except for being elongated—strung out to about10 feet long—the body of the bird pretty much remained intact but left most of its blood on the plane. The men who serviced my plane in Blythe wanted to know what I'd hit. "Probably a sheep at Sheephole Mountain" was the quickest response I could think of.

Over the years, my most profound reflections of events in my life have included these questions: Why was that bird hunting along the rock cliff that morning? Why was he at exactly the height of my rubber tire rather than the windshield or some other vital part of my plane? Why was he just far enough away from the wall to give me time to react? Was it a miracle, luck, coincidence or divine intervention? Perhaps this was one of many indications we have had that there are more unseen hands protecting and supporting us than we realize.

Whirly-birds

Camp Wolters was a helicopter training school out on the plains west of Ft. Worth. My family and I met many fine young men and their families, had picnics out in the rough canyons west of the field and great social times at the officers' club. Phillip, our middle son, was in first grade and bravely hiked up over a big hill to his school everyday. I took him to the Fat Stock show in Ft. Worth, where we met and talked with Dan Blocker, the actor who played "Hoss Cartwright" on the TV show "Bonanza."

Phil was dressed in western gear, chaps, vest, two guns, cowboy boots and a big western hat. Blocker treated him like one of the Cartwrights.

That year, to avoid interrupting Michael and John's school for just three months, we left them in Vermont with family and friends. Mike had it fairly easy, but John stayed on a dairy farm where he worked extremely hard. He toughed it through and had even greater appreciation for his family and life on our non-dairy farm. We missed them both so much we never left them again during their school years.

Our helicopters were Bell H-13s of Korean War vintage, on the primitive side and sensitive to fly. It took both hands and feet to control one of them, so if your nose itched you couldn't scratch it. A friend of mine in the Air Guard, an older man who worked in supply, keeping watch over our flight gear, always downplayed the "Whirl-i-birds." Invented by the devil, he claimed.

Checking the "Jesus Nut."

I saw him occasionally after I joined the Army Aviation company, and he would tease me in his quiet way about those "contraptions." One weekend, I persuaded him to take a ride with me—over his strong objections. I finally challenged him enough to go but had to agree to fly no higher than 50 feet. I had a surprise for him. We had had a wet snow followed by a freeze, and I had seen a fence south of the airport with caps of snow on each post that looked like ice cream cones. I drove up to the fence and carefully scraped the snow cap off the post with one skid of the copter. After two more performances, my passenger said he was finally a believer. He was a very quiet individual but a troubled man. It was sad to hear one day of his suicide.

The Billy Goat at Camp Wolters

For our last test before graduation from helicopter school, we were required to take off and locate specific locations around the countryside using only coordinates on a map. The first stop, for example, could be a sign identifying a military unit, such as 104th Infantry. After recording this information, we found a packet on the back of the sign directing us to the next place to find and so on until I came to a sign located on top of a Mesa with very steep sides.

As the wind had started blowing I found it impossible to land the chopper near the sign and the whole area behind it was wooded leaving only a small clearing on the edge of the steep sides of the Mesa to land. If I could have landed with the wind blowing as it was, it would have been unsafe to leave my machine to read the sign. The wind could easily topple it over the cliff wrecking it and leaving me stranded. I reported back at the air-field to a young second lieutenant that I was unable to read the red sign because it was guarded by a vicious billy goat. He accepted my report without comment and marked my report completed. Sometimes a little ingenuity helps.

My last tour was at the Command and Staff School at Ft. Benning, Georgia. The course was strictly military, and for me—a most un-military person—it presented my greatest challenge. Of the 300 officers attending, most were career people and were told by their commanding officers to complete the course in the top ten percent or it would be the end of their career. I was under no such pressure, nor was my good friend John Barr. John and his family attended Ft. Benning with us twice, and as John had set

his goal to be a general like his grandfather, he was determined
to be in the top five percent. He was full time in the Guard from
high school, studied all the regulations and organized and super-
vised an officer's training center in Vermont. He was also a disci-
ple of Ethan Allen—one subject we disagreed on.

The aggressive career men were, or pretended to be, very
knowledgeable about all things military, sometimes to an irritating degree. One captain was particularly obnoxious and never
spoke without ridiculing the second lieutenants who were sent to
him to train—or to be retrained, as he put it. In the large classroom, seating over 200 officers, if a man wanted to speak out or
answer a question about the problem under discussion, an
enlisted man would run to him with a microphone on a long
cord. The mouthy captain would hold forth in lengthy discourse,
never failing to remind us of how incompetent these "shave-tails"
were.

The first and only time I spoke in front of these professionals
was after one of the captain's tirades. I requested a moment of
silence to respect his mother and to meditate on what she went
through when he was born with those captain's bars on his
shoulders. My remarks, no doubt, made me some points with the
rest of the class and brought a little levity into the room.

All winter, we studied situations using stacks of maps and
documents, always with our adversary (Russia) in the East while
we attacked or defended ourselves in the West. After weeks of
study and planning, we were ordered to carry out our war plans.
In between our desk and chart work, we went into the field to
use the weapons of combat: tanks, artillery, heavily armed troops
and air support. At times, we would assault a fortified hill with
helicopters, landing our infantry and equipment in staging areas.
Our role was to organize and give the orders to all the forces al-
lotted to us. Artillery and mortar fire, along with flame throwers
and phosphorus bombs to drop on the "enemy" fortifications,
added realism to the exercise.

John came to our place many times to coach me, as he realized I lacked interest in ground warfare, but the course was important, he thought, to my progress in the Guard.

"RTP! Read the problem," John emphasized over and over to me while he studied every word of each exercise until the midnight hours. The work and planning culminated in a final exam that carried much weight toward our final score and standing in the group. I spent the first hour of the test studying the situation to determine the best command decisions to accomplish our goal—to drive the enemy back, inflicting as much damage and casualties as possible.

Whoa! What's this? I have always loved maps, and as I perused my stack of charts I discovered the enemy forces were now entrenched in the *western* mountains of the Balkans while ours were in the *eastern* areas. One little sentence gave it away, so every move we made had to be in reverse of what we had worked on all winter. Every decision we made could be an error and subsequent moves completely wrong. For those who missed that vital bit of intelligence, there would be more errors compounded as the exercise progressed.

The instructors had made the problem tricky. In our winter's study, the enemy forces were marked in red while ours were in blue. The little colored blocks had the units identity written beside them such as: 23rd Infantry, 14th Tank Corps, 117th Artillery and so on. For the exam, the colors were changed to green and black, an indication to me to be painstakingly careful given my lack of interest in and knowledge about ground warfare. The only reason for my being in the infantry was that I had to choose a branch—infantry, artillery or some other branch—of the Army when I switched from the Air Guard. Later on, an Army aviation branch was created.

Ironically, I had started out in the infantry and many years later, ended up in it.

Not surprisingly, most of the would-be generals missed the vital guideline. They confidently strode out of the classroom, but when they read the solutions to the problem posted on a bulletin board outside, there was much groaning. Poor John didn't RTP. The only salvation for the professional soldiers was a token award for using accepted methods of solving an operation of such magnitude. The fact that I *did* RTP is what saved me from failing the course. Thanks, John Barr!

Another problem— covering a war theater extending from the entire Mediterranean area to the Black sea, Turkey, eastern Russia and other nations—called for an air strike at oil refineries and transportation centers. We were given the location of our bomber and fighter bases and aircraft carriers as well as the corresponding enemy units. Our heavy bombers based in Saudi Arabia would fly several hundred miles over enemy territory to penetrate deep into Russia. Along the way were missile sites with ground-to-air missiles, anti-aircraft batteries and several groups of jet fighters. All of this defensive hardware between the bombers and the targets made the mission seem impossible without huge losses. I was the only person in the class with combat experience involving airpower, and I relished planning the raid.

The key was to utilize all of our resources, but most of the infantry officers lacked the know-how for coordinating and integrating the tools provided to us in the order for the mission. I decided to send our fighter bombers in from Turkey to neutralize the missile bases and strike airfields around the targets; our fighter escorts, also based in Turkey, would provide cover on the way in, while Navy jets from the carriers in the eastern Mediterranean Sea would cover our withdrawal. The operation was much more detailed and complicated than this, but the game plan was relatively simple. The staff gave me the highest score I had received for the entire course, but I still ended up in the bottom ten percent.

Still Learning

During each tour, I kept up my flying proficiency in my spare time, even to putting in the required night and instrument hours. This gave me opportunities to fly different aircraft and to take some interesting cross-country flights. My skeleton flight records, sent along with me to Shepard Field with my active-duty orders, indicated what aircraft I was qualified in, but an error gave me a little jolt. In order to keep proficient in multi-engined planes, my records should have read C-45, but someone had inserted B-45. I wondered why they told me at Sheppard Field it would be necessary for me to go to Carswell Air Force Base to get my flight time as they didn't have the type I was qualified in. At Fort Worth, I was briefed and issued equipment really not necessary for the small, twin-engine Beech C-45. As I was led out to the flight line, we stopped under a good-sized four-engine jet bomber—the top of the line B-45. It was a magnificent aircraft, and I had seen pictures of it but had never been near one before. As there was only one pilot's seat, I had to decline flying one of our newest type bombers, much to everyone's chagrin. I could not have started it up even if I'd dared to. This promising aircraft was dropped from the Air Force inventory in favor of the Boeing B-47, a six-engine bomber with only three crewmen that carried out the Cold War missions along with the gigantic B-52.

While at Camp Wolters, students had the opportunity to visit the big Carswell Air Force base at Fort Worth to see demonstrations of experimental aircraft. Small, one-man hovercraft with a platform with just barely room enough for a man to stand on, skittered about. A novel aircraft with four ducted fans that looked to me like a good replacement for the helicopters could push its way through treetops and brush without damage. The long rotor blades of helicopters were always vulnerable in the vicinity of obstacles like trees and power lines. Other "ground effect" craft that hovered just above the ground, needing no runways or prepared surface to operate from, were interesting. Ultra-modern helicopters with all types of armament and night vision devices put on good shows.

We saw many flying machines of the future and many models that were later discarded as impractical or unsafe. One scary Buck Rogers type consisted of a backpack with two rockets strapped to the back of a very brave man, who was shot into the air to twist and turn before coming back to solid ground with a gentle touchdown. I wondered what would happen if the rocket malfunctioned or ran out of fuel. A prudent decision led to the elimination of this unsafe development. The man we saw operating it was, no doubt, the only person who could be persuaded to strap it on. The late fifties and sixties were a time of great strides in aircraft development.

The intricate SR-71 "Blackbird" spy plane was used for 40 years, and no technology has produced anything close to it. It could reach altitudes of over 100,000 feet and speeds of over 2,000 miles an hour—three times the speed of sound. It required two kinds of fuel: jet fuel to climb to a certain height, then a switch to an exotic brand that was used in very high altitudes. One of these planes flew from over New York City to a point over London in just an hour and a half. These were times of great engineering and remarkably skilled pilots.

The late fifties and sixties were the time my interest and skills in aviation reached a peak. The disappointing years of not flying and being denied my flight certificate because of the injuries reported on my records had come to an end. I had waived my Veterans Administration pension to get into the Guard and demonstrated my ability to fly many types of aircraft, but the Air Force still would not give me my medical clearance to fly. I had to admit, my physical condition took some of the fun out of it all, but at no time did it cause dangerous situations to arise. The Air Force said it wouldn't know me if I had an accident, but they paid me to ferry some of their planes. My flying in the post-war period was on a temporary waiver and precluded getting retirement pay, but fortunately, when it came time, eight years after I left the National Guard, the VA reinstated my disability status. By that time, I had locked in my pilot's license, along with my single- and multi-engine ratings, instrument certificate, helicopter and jet ratings.

Airline flying never appealed to me, although I was offered at one time an opportunity to fly for the Taiwan Chinese Air Force and at another time for the Saudis in their fledging airline. A man from Middlebury, Vermont took the Saudi position and provided better service than I could have. The pay for either one of these offers was a temptation but not worth leaving my family. Northern Airways in Burlington was struggling to get started, so I was their only qualified pilot for a time. They had a contract to fly General Electric people to Philadelphia three times a week but were unable to find a copilot for me, so I had a different one each trip.

On one of these trips, we had gone about 40 miles when I had to keep adding trim to keep the nose down until there was no trim left and I was holding the control wheel all the way forward. The plane continued to climb. My good friend and fellow Guardsman Everett Stebbins was in the right seat, so I told him to go back and see what was going on back there. My passengers were all big football types and had gathered at the rear of the passenger area to have coffee together!

We usually left about six in the morning to get the passengers there for business at eight and often didn't return until late evening. On checking the weather at about four o'clock one below-zero morning, I noted that icing conditions would prevail along the route until mid-forenoon. GE was in a panic; people just had to be there for an important meeting. It was too cold for ice to form at Burlington, but as the sun rose and we flew farther south, severe icing was bound to occur. I would not leave with those conditions forecast, so Northern Airways called a newly retired colonel who had a plane that held three or four passengers. He was eager for business and could be ready to leave in an hour. They called from Poughkeepsie, New York an hour after takeoff; the plane had barely made it to the runway after picking up a heavy load of ice. I carried the others down when conditions improved.

It was either a lack of confidence on my part or my overly cautious nature, but I refused to fly under questionable conditions. Northern Airways offered charter service and welcomed each one as a windfall. Its finances were such it was unable to pay me regularly. I tried to accommodate the airline but lost the biggest chunk of its charter pie when I turned down a flight to Aspen,

Colorado with a group of wealthy people. The weather was not the best, just within limits, but the project came to a halt when the party arrived with several hundred pounds of baggage, liquor, skis and snobbishness. We would have been very much overweight and they refused to leave anything behind, so I suggested they use the regular airlines. They probably already had tried and been turned down.

A snowplow truck backed into the propeller spinner of the Twin Beech, doing no harm except to the spinner, but the authorities demanded an inspection and the owners decided to remove a gas tank in the nose and replace it with navigation equipment while the plane was in the shop. When I performed the required test flight after the work was done, our son John accompanied me.

It was getting dark as we took off. As I was checking the fuel flow from the modified tanks, both engines stopped and the windshield instantly frosted in the sub-zero temperature. Unable to see out, I glided toward Lake Champlain, hoping the ice would hold up if we had to set down. Luckily, after several tries the engines caught and we headed back. "Is there anything I can do to help?" asked John. I said no as I wiped the sweat off the palms of my hands.

The airline was harassed by other airlines, the FAA and everyone else who didn't want a small airline breaking into the business. While giving the president of the company some instruction that included making a number of landings, we shot a half dozen landings at Lake Placid. There had been no other traffic in the area and they had given us permission to use the airport, but when we left they asked us to come to the office and pay for our landing fees. They had given no hint we would be charged for each landing.

For our next lesson, we used the Rutland airport and on one landing, the tail wheel partially collapsed. It still supported the rear of the plane and rolled OK, but it couldn't swivel to allow us to turn off the runway. I taxied to the end of the runway, out of the way, and called for a mechanic to come with a jack, but the tower sent several vehicles and called Burlington to report Northern Airways had crashed on the runway. A cable that lifted and lowered the wheel had come off the pulley. To replace the cable over the pulley, we merely had to jack the weight off of it. This was the type of harassment that gave the small airline a slow start.

One other discovery that concerned me was finding that a section of the log for the Twin Beech was missing. Investigation revealed that the plane had crashed, killing six people, and had been reconstructed by the former owner and sold—with no record of the accident or the subsequent rebuilding. Finally, John Teal (who was noted for introducing some Alaskan musk oxen to his farm near Camel's Hump), came on board Northern Airways and helped immensely. His wife's first action as office manager was to write me a check for back pay. Shortly after that, my farming operation took up all of my time. Military and commercial flying was now in the past, but the memories would linger on.

Reflections

Over the years, I've pondered many times my good fortune to survive so many close encounters. For what purpose was I spared? Was there some reason, some accomplishment assigned to me that was beyond my comprehension to understand? Perhaps because I took a wrong road and worked so hard at farming I failed to do more important things with my life.

An honest assessment of my contribution to the world has left me with a feeling of failure, but then I think of my family and realize they have much more potential than was my lot to possess and that has to be my legacy. My thankfulness to have survived the savage air battles with not much more than scratches and achy joints has been ongoing. Thanks to divine guidance, prayers from friends and relatives as well as from people who didn't know me, the influence of my role models and others who provided me with good examples—and an extraordinary amount of good fortune, I survived to live and enjoy my life.

I still feel astonishment more than relief to have come through the violent episodes in the air as well as challenges on the ground. There is a small sense of pride that I'm sure other veterans of that air war over Europe feel as time goes by and the significance of what we did becomes more clear to us. Each of us did his small part, most did the best they could and helped change the course of history.

The End.

Appendix

Memories of the last days of WWII in Europe, an article written for the newspapers May 8, 1995, the fiftieth anniversary of VE Day.

In the last months of World War II, Hitler three times ordered the execution of Allied airmen held in various camps throughout Germany and Poland. The generals of the German High Command twice argued against the order and some were shot or hung for opposing him. After the bombing of Dresden the second order went out signed by Heinrich Himmler, and again general officers who had fought for their country in two wars protested on the grounds that the aviators were needed for bargaining with the Allies because of the unconditional surrender terms. Hitler, hoping to the last days that a nuclear weapon would be ready in time for him to win the war, had more of Germany's heroes hung with signs reading TRAITOR attached to their bodies. After the third order went out a few days before Hitler's suicide, there were rumors that Eva Braun prevailed to delay the execution of the POWs. Actually, Hitler's die-hard Nazi followers were planning to use POWs as human shields to defend a planned "Redoubt" in the Alps surrounding Berchesgarden.

In our prison camp a few miles from Dachau, one of our staff officers found and brought out of the SS headquarters the telegram ordering the "destruction of all Allied airmen before recapture". Our senior officers sent two men through the fence with orders to get the information to Switzerland for transmittal to Washington. The mission was carried out successfully; however, as the Americans approached to within a few miles we were in imminent danger of extermination by the SS.

On the morning we were liberated by the 14th armored division on April 29th 1945, a Luftwaffe unit from a nearby base forcibly took control of the camp from the SS. This action without doubt saved our lives. The next day Hitler committed suicide and Americans entered Dachau. We knew what was going on there but never guessed the scope and cruelty of the Nazi "final solution".

The euphoria of freedom for over 100,000 of us was tempered by the news brought to us by soldiers passing through from Dachau and other concentration camps. On the way out of Germany by truck and plane we saw the terrible destruction of nearly every city. We saw tens of thousands of orphaned children walking along the road sides—some going East and some headed West. They survived only because of the concern and generosity of the American troops.

My thoughts were mostly about how all of these people, many of them crippled, would be cared for in all the ruined countries of Europe and how could all those cities be rebuilt. I wondered how the war had progressed against Japan and would there be jobs for our millions of servicemen going home to rebuild their lives.

On VE Day I was within sight of the buildings in Rheims, France where the final surrender was being worked out. After waiting 17 hours for a shower that removed most of the lice, I weighed just under 100 pounds. A partial pay of 4,000 francs allowed me to buy clean clothes, bury my old ones and go to the beautiful cathedral nearby to give thanks for our last-minute deliverance. I meditated on my good fortune to be alive in the springtime with hopefully many years stretching ahead and how sad that so many died in the last few days after enduring so much.

Five weeks of recuperation on the coast of France put me in shape to make the trip home on a new ship commanded by a Vermonter, Captain Dunton. He made a record run to New York for his class of vessel and we passed the Statue of Liberty the morning of my 22nd birthday, June 11, 1945. I was 22 years old and my waistline was 22 inches.

—John Francis Angier

Shot down 25 October 1944 north of Bremerhaven. Held in Stalag Luft III, liberated 29 April 1945 at Stalag 7-A Mooseberg, Germany. Returned to Allied control VE day 8 May 1945.

Opportunity

This I beheld or dreamed it in a dream,
There spread a cloud of dust along the plain
And underneath the cloud or in it raged
A furious battle, and men yelled; and swords
Shocked upon swords and shields.
A princes' banner wavered, then staggered backward,
Hemmed in by foes.
A craven hung along the battle's edge and thought,
"Had I a sword of keener steel—
That blue blade that the King's son bears—
Not this blunt thing."
He snapped it and flung it from his hand.
And lowering crept away and left the field.
Then came the king's son wounded sore,
And weaponless, and saw the broken sword,
Hilt buried in the dry and trodden sand,
And ran and snatched it—and with a battle shout
Lifted afresh, he hewed the enemy down;
And saved a great cause that heroic day.

—Edward Rowland Sill
(1841-1887)

Untitled Poem

Let no man believe that
There is a stigma
Attached to having been
Honorably taken captive in battle.
Only the fighting man ever gets
Close enough to the enemy
For that to happen. That he
Is not listed among the slain
Is due to the infinite care of
The Providence.
Be proud that you carried
Yourselves as men in battle
And adversity. You will be
Enriched thereby.

—Col. T. D. Drake

Glossary

8th AF	Eighth Air Force, larger than all air forces combined. Based in England.
Ball Turret	The most maneuverable gun position located on the underside of the plane.
BG	Bomb Group made up of four squadrons.
CBW	Combat wing. Three Bomb Groups make up a combat wing.
Division	Three or more Combat Wings make up a division.
Escape and Evasion	The art of escaping and evading capture. Usually impossible without aid from the Underground in France and other countries.
ETO	European Theater of Operations
FW 190	German fighter plane. Modified and modernized many times.
Gander	Air base in Newfoundland. One of the starting points for overseas flights.
Glatton	The home of the 457th Bomb Group. Actually located in the hamlet of Conington.
IP	Initial Point. A geographic location used as the starting point of a bomb run.
Lancaster	British heavy bomber capable of carrying extremely heavy loads ~ 11 tons.
ME 109	An older but deadly, heavily armored German fighter. Fought in Spanish Civil War in 1937 and on all fronts in WWII.
P-38	U.S. twin-engine fighter, good fire power but vulnerable if one engine failed.

P-47	A very heavy U.S. fighter. Able to dive at great speed, had exceptional fire power.
P-51	Best U.S. fighter plane of WWII.
Radar Dome	A retractable fiberglass dome placed in the ball turret location, the eye of the radar system. The ball turret had to be left out during construction.
RAF	Royal Air Force (British)
Spitfire	Superb British fighter. Second only to the P-51-D.
Top Turret	The maneuverable gun position located just behind the pilots' seats.
Turbos	Supercharger devices on each engine to increase air supply to engines at high altitude.

To order additional copies of this and future books
by J. Francis Angier, visit
www.JFrancisAngier.com
Or
Francis@AngierMail.net

Printed in the United States
84486LV00005B/1-96/A

9 780970 417510